Eva Pau's
Asian Cookbook

Eva Pau's *Asian Cookbook*

80 authentic recipes for every day

murdoch books
London | Sydney

Contents

Introduction 7

Rice 34

Noodles 56

Asian Herbs & Vegetables 78

Light Bites & Snacks 98

Soups & Salads 122

Curries & Stews 140

Chinese Takeaway Classics 160

Sweet Treats 178

Acknowledgements 201

Index 203

Introduction

Where it all began

You know, people always ask me how I fell in love with Asian cooking. Honestly? It wasn't some dramatic moment or life-changing meal; it was just ... life. My life. Growing up between two worlds, with parents who somehow made that feel completely natural.

My parents opened Asia Market in the early eighties. It wasn't just any other shop. It was our whole world. It was this compact little space in the centre of Dublin, packed floor to ceiling with Asian ingredients that most Irish people at the time had never heard of. Heavy sacks of jasmine rice stacked in the corner, shelves filled with countless condiments and sauces, and a whole section of just noodles. It was our world. My mum and dad worked seven days a week, tirelessly growing this small business.

If I wasn't at school, I was at the shop. Every weekend, every school holiday, every summer break, I was to be found in the shop. I have very fond memories of playing in a fort that my mum made for me under the till. I remember jumping out and scaring customers, hiding in cardboard boxes in the middle of the shop floor and playing hopscotch on the pavement outside. In those early years, it was the best playground any kid could wish for. It was my base. It was my second home.

By the time I was old enough to see over the till, I was already stacking the shelves, weighing out vegetables, working the checkout and - my favourite part - helping customers to find ingredients. As the years went by, my knowledge of the products grew and grew. I learned where each item came from, how it was made, and what range of products was available from particular brands. I didn't realise it or appreciate it at the time, but now I can see that the amount I learned by osmosis in those years has completely shaped my life in food.

My parents sacrificed a lot to get the business up and running. My dad often reminds me that they didn't take a holiday for the first ten years. But they never complained. Alongside all the work and the challenges that came with it, they somehow made space for family, for the little things and lovely memories that have stayed with me ever since.

I was probably six or seven the first time I tagged along with my dad to Meath Street, a historical market street in Dublin with bustling open-air stalls selling fruits, vegetables and household essentials. I loved those Saturday morning trips. We'd walk through the bustling markets, Dad chatting away to stall holders in that easy way of his, while I tried to keep up with his long strides, my small hands clutching whatever bags he'd trusted me to carry.

My parents are both originally from Southern China. My mum was born and raised in Hong Kong, the eldest of four siblings, while my dad was born in Guangzhou and raised in Hong Kong, the eldest of three. He moved to the UK as a teenager to study and work, and it was during a trip back to Hong Kong that he was introduced to my mum. They kept in touch, and it wasn't long before my mum moved to the UK to join my dad in Grimsby. It was here that they got married and started their life together in Europe, later coming to Ireland. It meant our family palate became a true mix of East meets West. Mum might be busy preparing her incredible stir-fries and soups - proper traditional Chinese cooking that she'd learned from feeding her three younger siblings - and then Dad would come home from Meath Street with ingredients for something completely different. It could be anything from a chicken roast dinner or seafood chowder to pork pies, ham hocks or spaghetti bolognese. I grew up thinking everyone's dinner table was like ours. One night we'd be sharing a whole steamed fish with chopsticks, and the next we'd be cutting into Yorkshire puddings with knives and forks.

Mum has been cooking since she was a child. She has this intuitive way with food that I have always been completely mesmerised by. No measuring cups, no timers. Just a pinch of this, a splash of that, and somehow it always comes together perfectly. Her wok is like an extension of her arm, and I used to marvel at the way she'd toss vegetables and noodles with such ease. And I'll never forget her skills with a cleaver, or the way the blade looked so big in the hands of a lady who is only five feet tall. On busy days at our little Asian supermarket in Dublin,

I'd wander over to the noodle section at lunchtime and pick out whatever caught my eye - usually instant noodles, which we'd cook in the microwave in the back room. But Mum would always pimp them up, throwing in some pak choi from the fresh section, cracking an egg on top, maybe adding some pickled vegetables. Even our simple lunches were lessons in how to make something basic into something special.

The weekends were when the real food adventures happened. Dad was incredibly social, and since we were supplying all the Chinese restaurants in Ireland back then, he knew every chef and eatery owner in Dublin. We'd spend Saturday evenings making the rounds, visiting his friends at their restaurants, and I'd get to sit at the big tables while the adults caught up. I don't remember anyone ever looking at a menu or ordering food. It just seemed to arrive at the table, and I'd get to try everything. My dad would always disappear during the meal for a visit to the chefs in the kitchen. Those dinners taught me that food is the language of hospitality, generosity and community. It's about connection, about sharing, about showing love through the act of feeding people. Every celebration, every important conversation, every moment that mattered seemed to happen around a table full of food.

'Food is the language of hospitality, generosity and community. It's about connection, about sharing, about showing love through the act of feeding people.'

My earliest food memories, though, are not from Dublin. They're from my trips to Hong Kong, China, when I was tiny, maybe four or five. Meeting my grandmother and aunties was like stepping into a completely different world - one in which every single gathering revolved around food. We'd sit around those big round tables at dim sum restaurants, and the grown-ups would order dish after dish until the table was completely covered. Har gow, siu mai, char siu bao ... I remember that they were delicious and that everyone was happy, laughing and sharing.

My dear Uncle Hoi, who is like a second father to me, came to Ireland from Hong Kong in the 1980s in order to help my parents run Asia Market. He was a trained dim sum master from China, and he'd make fresh bao buns and dumplings at home, which we would sell in the shop. Sometimes we'd have his char siu bao buns for lunch. I can still smell them now: that sweet, porky filling wrapped in freshly steamed pillowy soft dough. My main memory of my Uncle Hoi at that time is of a very tall, very strong man with huge hands! I have an image in my mind of him carrying a huge 25kg bag of rice on each shoulder. As time went on, Uncle Hoi's wife, Aunt Fong, and their son Kevin moved to Dublin to join us all. Uncle Hoi has the accolade of having bought me my very first cookbook. I honestly remember it like it was yesterday. He collected me from my violin lesson and, as a treat, brought me and Kevin to a nearby bookshop and told us to pick anything we wanted. He steered us towards the children's book section, and I remember seeing a book called *The Children's Step-by-Step Cookbook*. I grabbed it with both hands and held it like it was treasure.

While my parents were working incredibly hard to build the business, I'd sometimes spend afternoons at my mum's friends' houses for playdates. While the other kids were playing, I'd somehow always end up in the sitting room, flipping through their cookbooks. There was this one Chinese cookbook published by *Women's Weekly* that absolutely fascinated me: *American-style Chinese Cooking*. It was packed with glossy photos that made everything look impossibly delicious. I'd sit there for hours and try to memorise the recipes.

I was about twelve when Auntie Beatrice came to visit from Australia and stayed with us for a few months. She was an amazing cook, and one day she announced that she was going to teach me how to make sushi. I remember being so proud that she thought I was old enough to learn something so 'advanced'. We spent an afternoon in our kitchen, and she showed me how to cook the rice properly, how to season it, and how to roll the nori just tightly enough. I've been making sushi the same way ever since.

While my mum and dad were preparing dinner on a Sunday, I would now be right beside them with my step-by-step cookbook, usually baking something or other. I was obsessed with cakes - not even eating them, really, just the pure joy of mixing ingredients and watching them bake in the oven. I started with those box mixes from the supermarket - you know, just add milk and an egg - but even those felt like proper chemistry experiments to me. Dad was always hovering nervously in the background when I cooked, probably worried I'd burn the house down or something. Later, he used to joke that his expanding waistline was entirely my fault because of all my baking experiments.

It wasn't until much later, after I'd lived in Hong Kong and then returned to Dublin and bought my own house, that I really started cooking properly. Having my own kitchen felt like such freedom. I'd invite friends over and attempt recipes from all the cookbooks I'd been collecting for years. Not everything turned out perfectly - there were some real disasters, if I'm being honest - but I loved the whole process.

The real turning point came about thirteen years ago, when I started getting more involved with our family business, Asia Market. I began creating recipes, appearing on morning TV shows, and really thinking about how to showcase the incredible ingredients we had in our store. It was so inspiring to take something like Japanese miso paste or Korean gochujang, ingredients that might intimidate people who weren't familiar with them, and show how approachable they could be in everyday cooking once people understood the flavours.

I started doing tours around the Asia Market store, bringing people on culinary adventures through our aisles. We'd stop at different sections, I'd explain the ingredients, and everyone would get to taste dumplings, fish balls and sweet treats like mochi - often things that were completely new to them. Watching someone's face light up when they try something delicious and different for the first time never gets old. When talking to the customers in person and through the launch of our online store, I could see what people were curious about, what they were buying, what questions they had. There were so many enquiries about sushi-making, about how to use certain sauces, about which noodles to choose, and when to use light or dark soy sauce. All of this fed my passion for recipe development and teaching Asian cooking.

I really am so lucky to get to travel to Asia for work. Every time I visit, I'm like a sponge, soaking up new flavours and techniques, from street food in Thailand and Malaysia to night markets in Singapore and Korea and tiny neighbourhood restaurants in China and Japan. At the other end of the scale, I love experiencing how upscale restaurants in the Far East manage to elevate traditional flavours and ingredients using modern techniques with wonderful presentation. They all inspire dishes that I recreate in my own kitchen.

It is particularly beautiful to see this journey of food come full circle with my own children. Their palates are developing with the same East-meets-West fusion that my dad experienced 60 years ago: the same palate he passed on to me, and that I'm now passing on to them. They're getting to try new flavours and experience different cuisines at an even younger age than I did. Seeing their excitement and curiosity reminds me of why food has always been about so much more than just eating.

When I think back to my ten-year-old self all those years ago, picking up that children's cookbook and muddling my way through the recipes, and reflect on the fact that I am now writing my own cookbook and sharing my food journey and experiences with you, it is nothing short of a dream come true.

So, what's *my* cookbook all about?

Well, it isn't a single-cuisine cookbook. It's a collection of recipes and dishes that I've gathered from all across Asia: Chinese comfort food that reminds me of childhood dinners, Japanese dishes that feel both elegant and approachable, Korean flavours that pack a punch, Thai curries that warm you from the inside out and Malaysian street-food favourites that never fail to make me happy. These are dishes I turn to when I'm cooking for my family, when friends are coming over or when I just need something quick and delicious after a long day.

Coming from a family that's been in the Asian food business for decades, I've seen how intimidated people can get by unfamiliar ingredients. Walking through our store, I'd watch customers pick up a bottle of fish sauce or a packet of miso paste, read the label, then put it back because they had no idea what to do with it. That's exactly what this book aims to fix.

If you are new to Asian cooking and you have never been into an Asian supermarket before, my aim is to provide you with a list of key pantry staples that you can buy with confidence. These will be the foundations of your Asian pantry. From here, you will be able to branch out and explore other ingredients, textures and flavours that you find on the shelves. It won't take long for the alien landscape of an Asian supermarket to feel familiar and fun, and I guarantee that you'll start to feel like an expert in no time.

I've deliberately focused on key ingredients: the ones that will genuinely transform your cooking and appear in multiple recipes throughout the book. Once you've got a bottle of good soy sauce, some sesame oil, rice wine and a few other staples in your pantry, you'll be amazed by how many different dishes you can create.

I'm a home cook, not a professionally trained chef (although I do have an HACCP Level 3 certificate for work!). Every recipe in this cookbook is achievable in a home kitchen with simple utensils and easy-to-find ingredients that you can source either from your local supermarket, an Asian supermarket or online.

Whether you're an Asian foodie or newbie, I hope this collection of recipes inspires you to cook new and exciting dishes, because that's exactly what good food should do: bring joy, comfort, excitement and a little adventure to your everyday life.

My Asian Pantry

Rice

Rice is a staple in Asian cuisine. We eat it almost every night. Growing up in an Asian home, we always used a rice cooker to cook perfect rice. It would 'click' to let you know when the rice was ready. That clicking sound and the plume of mildly scented steam are so familiar to me. It always meant dinner was ready.

What I love most about rice is its versatility. You can turn it into a congee for breakfast, grind it into rice flour for delicate rice cakes, and stir-fry yesterday's leftovers to make fried rice. It adapts to whatever you need. Here are the rice varieties that I always have in my pantry.

Jasmine rice

This is my go-to rice at home. It's a long-grain rice with a sweet, floral aroma. When cooked, it's soft and fluffy, and the grains have just enough stickiness to be picked up with chopsticks without falling apart. It's the kind of rice I grew up eating. I have used it for my Classic Fried Rice (page 37), where it soaks up all the soy sauce and sesame oil. It also makes the perfect accompaniment to my Satay Chicken (page 172) or Black Bean Beef (page 167). I love it with my Malaysian Beef Rendang (page 148) and Thai Green Prawn Curry (page 143), too, because its fragrance complements them beautifully. And when I make Chicken Congee (page 49), I'll simmer jasmine rice slowly until it becomes luxuriously soft.

I like to mix in brown, red, or black jasmine varieties for when I want a nuttier flavour and a bit more texture. What I love most about jasmine is that it isn't fussy. It cooks quickly, it pairs with almost any dish, and it has a warm, gentle fragrance.

Short-grain rice (including sushi rice)

This variety is short and plump, with a stickier texture than medium- and long-grain rice. There are many types of short-grain rice, including Japanese short-grain rice, commonly referred to as sushi rice. It is exactly the type of rice you want when you're rolling sushi, as the grains cling together just enough to hold their shape without turning mushy. I have used sushi rice for my Onigiri (page 42), where you'll learn how it moulds beautifully into rice balls, and for my Salmon Sushi Bake (page 38). It's also perfect for my Miso Cod Ochazuke (page 53), as the short grains soak up the dashi broth while keeping their shape. In Korean cuisine, they use a short-grain rice that is a little softer in texture. Try it in my Bibimbap (page 46) or Korean Kimchi Tofu Stew (page 144). In northern China, short-grain rice is eaten daily with stir-fries and vegetables, and they refer to it as 'dong bei' rice.

Glutinous rice

Glutinous rice, also called sticky rice or sweet rice, is a short-grain rice that becomes really sticky and chewy when cooked. Don't be fooled by the name; it doesn't contain any gluten. It's called 'glutinous' because of its glue-like texture. I have used glutinous rice for my Cantonese Sticky Rice with Chinese Sausage (page 54), where the rice soaks up all the flavours from the lap cheong (Chinese sausage), shiitake mushrooms and dried shrimp. It's also a key ingredient for the classic Thai Mango Sticky Rice (page 197), where the coconut milk clings to the grains and pairs beautifully with ripe mango. It's also used in Chinese zongzi – traditional sticky rice parcels wrapped in bamboo leaves, which are eaten during the Dragon Boat Festival. What I love about glutinous rice is how it transforms a dish. That chewy texture is so irresistible (though I've always been told not to eat too much because it can be hard to digest). It reminds me of special occasions and family gatherings, where sticky rice dishes would appear on the table and everyone would dig in together.

Basmati rice

Basmati rice is a long-grain rice with slender grains that stay separate and fluffy when cooked. It has a subtle nutty aroma and a delicate texture that doesn't clump together. The grains actually elongate as they cook, almost doubling in length, which gives you these beautiful strands on your plate. I serve basmati rice with my Chicken Tikka Masala (page 158), because it's perfect for rich Indian curries, pilafs and biryanis. The light, fluffy texture soaks up sauce without becoming heavy, and that slight nuttiness complements the warm spices. It's the traditional choice for Indian dishes, and once you taste it alongside a good curry, you'll understand why. It's fragrant, it looks elegant on the plate, and it turns a simple curry night into something that feels like you've ordered from your favourite restaurant.

Noodles

I often tell the guests on my shop tours that you need to choose the noodles based on what dish you want to cook. That seems pretty straightforward, I know, but noodles can be quite cuisine specific. In our supermarket, we have a whole aisle dedicated to noodles, which can be quite daunting for the uninitiated. Noodles can generally be divided into two main categories: instant noodles and cooking noodles. We have them further organised by regionality, which helps our customers to find the exact noodle they want.

Unlike cooking noodles, all packets of instant noodles come with a seasoning sachet, so you don't need to make your own noodle soup. I always keep my pantry well stocked with instant noodles, but like my mum, I can never resist pimping them up with anything I happen to find in my pantry - enoki mushrooms, pak choi, a hard-boiled egg, frozen dumplings, even frankfurters on occasion.

There are so many different noodle types. Here are my favourites.

Rice vermicelli

Rice vermicelli are thin, delicate noodles made from rice flour. They come in different thicknesses; some are as fine as angel hair pasta, while others are slightly thicker and sturdier. The key is choosing the right thickness for your dish.

I use the thinner rice vermicelli for my **Vietnamese Summer Rolls** (page 85), where you want delicate noodles that soak up the dipping sauce. I also use them in my **Thai Beef Salad** (page 130), where they add texture without overpowering the other ingredients. For **Singapore Noodles** (page 61) and **Filipino Pancit Bihon** (page 67), I go for slightly thicker vermicelli, because they hold up better in a hot wok and don't break apart or turn mushy when you toss them with the curry paste or vegetables.

I love how quickly rice vermicelli can be cooked. Most just need to soak in hot water for a few minutes, and they're ready to go. They're also naturally gluten-free, which makes them perfect for anyone avoiding wheat. You'll find them labelled as rice sticks, rice noodles, or sometimes bún, bihon or sen mee, depending on where you're shopping. Just remember: thin for soups and salads, thicker for stir-fries.

Beanthread noodles

Beanthread noodles, also called glass noodles or cellophane noodles, are made from mung bean starch. They're thin and become almost see-through when cooked, which is why they're called glass noodles. Unlike rice noodles, they have a slightly springy, slippery texture that's really satisfying to eat. They don't have much flavour on their own, but they soak up whatever sauce or broth you cook them in.

I use beanthread noodles in my **Steamed Beanthread Noodles with Scallops** (page 72), where they absorb all the garlic, soy and sesame oil beautifully. They're also perfect in my **Crispy Vietnamese Spring Rolls** (page 104), because they add texture without making the filling too heavy. When I make my **Spicy Sichuan Boiled Fish Stew** (page 151), I'll toss in some beanthread noodles to soak up that fiery, numbing broth. What I love most about these noodles is how light they are. They don't fill you up the way other noodles do, so they're perfect when you want something delicate. They also cook quickly, and they keep forever in the pantry, so I always have a packet on hand.

Ramen noodles

Ramen noodles are wheat-based noodles with a springy, chewy texture. They're usually curly or wavy, which helps them hold on to broth and sauce. You can find them fresh, frozen or dried, and each has a slightly different texture.

I use dried ramen noodles for my **Cold Ramen Sesame Noodle Salad** (page 139), where that chewy texture works well with the creamy sesame dressing. Fresh ramen noodles are my preference when I can get them, though; they have a springiness that dried noodles can't quite match. You'll also find instant ramen packets everywhere. What I love about ramen is that satisfying bounce when you bite into the noodles. They're versatile enough for hot soups, cold salads or even stir-fries. Just don't overcook them, or you'll lose that springy texture.

Udon noodles

Udon noodles are thick, chewy Japanese wheat noodles with a soft texture. They're much thicker than ramen. They're almost like fat, slippery tubes, and they have a real bounce when you bite into them. You can find them fresh, frozen or dried, though I find frozen udon noodles are often the best option if you can't get fresh ones. They're already cooked, so they just need a quick rinse and heat through.

I use udon for my **Sausage Gochujang Udon** (page 62), where those thick, chewy noodles soak up the spicy Korean gochujang (red pepper paste). The thickness of udon means they can handle bold flavours without getting lost in the dish. They're also great for stir-fries, because they don't break apart easily when you toss them in a hot wok. They are so satisfying and versatile. You can pair them with anything from a dashi broth to a spicy sauce.

Dried egg noodles

Dried egg noodles are wheat noodles traditionally made with egg. Most brands now don't actually contain any egg, although they still have an appealing golden colour and a tender texture. They come in various thicknesses; thin/fine ones for soups, medium for stir-fries, and thick ones for heartier dishes. Some are flat like ribbons, while others are round like spaghetti.

I use thin dried egg noodles in my **Black Pepper Beef with Crispy Egg Noodle Pancake** (page 75). They're also great in wonton noodle soups or tossed with simple sauces, like you'd find in most Chinese takeaways. Really, they work in almost any Asian noodle dish, and have a comforting, homey flavour that reminds me of the meals my mum used to make.

Flat rice noodles

Flat rice noodles, also known as rice sticks, hor fun, bánh phở and kway teow are flat noodles made from rice flour. They come in different widths, typically thin (3mm/⅛in), medium (5mm/¼in) and thick (1cm/½in). You can buy them fresh or dried. Fresh ones are soft, silky and delicate, while dried ones need soaking before cooking. I always keep the dried ones in my pantry, but I prefer to use fresh ones when I can because they have a nicer texture.

I use fresh medium flat rice noodles in my **Vietnamese Phở Bò** (page 65), where they soften in the hot broth and soak up all those aromatic flavours from the star anise and cinnamon. For my **Pad Thai with Prawns** (page 76), I use thin flat rice noodles, which become chewy and slightly sticky when stir-fried with tamarind and fish sauce. I love how well sauces cling to these noodles, meaning every bite is packed with flavour. Just be gentle when cooking them - they can break easily if you're too rough.

Sweet potato glass noodles (Korean vermicelli)

Sweet potato glass noodles, known as dangmyeon in Korea or hongshufen in China, are noodles made from sweet potato starch. They're thick and translucent with a slightly grey colour. I use sweet potato glass noodles for my **Korean Japchae** (page 71), where they're stir-fried with vegetables and beef in a sweet-and-savoury sesame soy sauce. The noodles soak up the sauce really well, but what I love most about dangmyeon is that unique texture; they are unlike any other noodle. They're slippery and glossy, and have this addictive chew that keeps you going back for more.

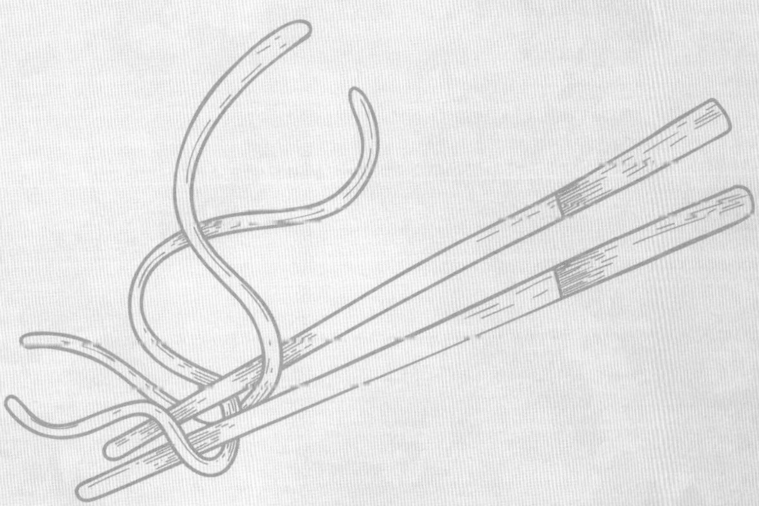

Asian vegetables and herbs

Walk into any Asian kitchen, and you'll be hit with the aroma of ginger and garlic sizzling in hot oil. That is the foundation of Asian cooking: the aromatic base that makes every dish so flavourful. Fresh herbs and aromatics aren't just garnishes in Asian cuisine; they're key to bringing flavour. I keep ginger, garlic and spring onions (scallions) in my pantry at all times. They're my holy trinity; the rest depends on what I'm cooking that week.

Ginger and garlic

This duo forms the backbone of Asian cooking. I love to use them in almost everything I cook, be it stir-fries, soups, marinades or curries. Fresh ginger has a warm and spicy kick, and fresh garlic is pungent and aromatic - not to mention all their health benefits. I always keep a few big chunks of ginger and a bunch of garlic bulbs in my kitchen. You'll find them in my Sesame Prawn Toast (page 101), my Korean Fried Chicken (page 107), my Classic Chinese Dumplings (page 108), and pretty much every dish in this cookbook. I couldn't imagine my life without them.

Spring onions (scallions)

I love how spring onions add a lovely green crunch to all my dishes. I use them to garnish almost everything, from Japanese Oyakudon with Chicken (page 44) to my Biang Biang Chilli Oil Noodles (page 59). The bottom white parts are more onion-like, while the green top parts are delicate and slightly sweet. I usually use the white parts for cooking and the green tops for garnish. They make every dish feel so vibrant and fresh.

Pak choi/bok choy

You say bok choy, I say pak choi. The names are interchangeable. Some say they describe two different varieties; others that they are regionalised names for the same thing. Either way, this vegetable has white or green stems with dark leaves. It is mild and slightly sweet in flavour (baby pak choi is smaller, sweeter and more tender). I love how quickly pak choi cooks, making it perfect for stir-fries and soups. I've used it in my Pak Choi with Garlic Oil (page 81) and Classic Fried Rice (page 37). When cooked, the stems stay crunchy and juicy while the leaves wilt down, which gives you two different textures in one vegetable.

Coriander (cilantro)

For me, this is a must-have herb. It's so fresh and citrusy, and it brightens up every dish, from curries to salads. I add it fresh at the end of cooking or as a garnish for soups, salads and noodles. It's great for stocks and stir-fry bases too. I have used it in my Vietnamese Summer Rolls (page 85) and my Curry Prawn Laksa (page 68) - and it features in practically every South East Asian dish I make at home. I would never throw the stems away, because they're just as flavourful as the leaves; finely chop them and stir them in. If you are not a big coriander fan, I would suggest you simply leave it out, especially when it's used as a garnish.

Thai basil

This is a must-have for your Thai pantry. The leaves are darker than Italian basil and slightly purple, and the flavour is stronger and more aromatic, almost aniseed like. I've used it in my Thai Basil Pork Stir-Fry (page 97), Thai Green Prawn Curry (page 143) and Vietnamese Beef Bò Kho (page 153). I always add it near the end of cooking for maximum aroma and to preserve its structure. I love this herb; it's really unique and helps to transform everything from curries to stir-fries.

Morning glory

Morning glory, or tung choi, has long, hollow stems with tender leaves. It has a mild and grassy taste, and is quite popular in South East Asian dishes. I've used it in my Stir-Fried Morning Glory (page 81), where it's quickly tossed with garlic, chillies and oyster sauce. Cook it over a high heat to maintain a crisp texture and vibrant colour. Use all the stem, not just the leaves. Cut them into bite-sized pieces before stir-frying.

Storing fresh herbs

Fresh herbs wilt quickly, but here's my simple trick to keep them fresh for over a week. I always trim the stems, wrap the herbs loosely in a slightly damp paper towel, then store them in a paper bag in the fridge. The moisture keeps them from drying out, but it's not so wet that they rot. For herbs like coriander and Thai basil, you can also treat them like flowers. Trim the stems and stand them upright in a glass of water in the fridge, loosely covered with a paper bag. If you have leftover herbs, chop them and then freeze in an ice-cube tray to make little cubes, which you can add to stir-fries.

Chinese leaf

Chinese leaf, also known as Chinese cabbage, has pale green, crinkly leaves with thick, crisp white stalks. It's one of my favourite vegetables, as it tends to keep for longer in the fridge, lasting for 2-3 weeks, while other Asian vegetables perish within a few days. It's often used in kimchi, Chinese hotpots and stir-fries. I've used it in my **Simple Kimchi** (page 92) and my **Spicy Sichuan Boiled Fish Stew** (page 151). What keeps me coming back is the gentle crunch that holds up well even after cooking. It soaks up whatever you cook it with, without becoming mushy.

Beansprouts

These are always nice to have in your fridge. They work well in stir-fries, soups, noodles and salads. I love adding them to noodle dishes raw and letting the hot broth slightly cook them, as in my **Vietnamese Phở Bò** (page 65): this gives you a fresh, crunchy texture without overpowering the flavour of the dish. I've also used them in my **Pad Thai with Prawns** (page 76) and my **Curry Prawn Laksa** (page 68). Always rinse well before using, and add at the last moment to retain their crunch. They don't take long to cook, and are one of those ingredients that makes every dish feel light and fresh.

Enoki mushrooms

Enoki mushrooms typically grow in clusters, and have delicate, long white stems with tiny caps. I often think they look like an elegant bouquet of flowers. They have a mild and slightly earthy flavour, and a distinctive crunchy texture when you cook them lightly. Try using them to make **Japanese Beef and Enoki Mushroom Rolls** (page 82) or my **One-Pot Thai Red Curry Dumplings** (page 156). I always trim the root base and separate them before cooking. They cook in a few seconds, and are great for last-minute additions to soups and stir-fries.

Shiitake mushrooms (fresh or dried)

Shiitake mushrooms have a deep, earthy and umami-rich flavour that I just adore. As you cook them, these flavours become more intense. Fresh ones are meaty and have a chewy texture, while the dried ones have a concentrated flavour. They're commonly used in soups, stir-fries and steamed dishes. I've used fresh shiitake mushrooms in my **Korean Japchae** (page 71), and dried shiitake in my **Cantonese Sticky Rice with Chinese Sausage** (page 54) and my **Hot-and-Sour Soup** (page 126). You just soak them in warm water first, and they'll plump up. I never dump the soaking liquid; it's gold. Use it in your cooking to add some extra depth.

Lotus root

Lotus root is a crunchy and slightly sweet but mild root vegetable. It has these beautiful holes running through it that look like lace when you slice it. I love how it stays crisp even after cooking, making it perfect for adding crunch to my stir-fries and braises. I've used it in my **Chinese Crispy Stuffed Lotus Root with Pork and Prawn** (page 90). Peel it and soak it in vinegar water to prevent browning if you are not using it straight away.

Daikon

Daikon is a large white radish with a mild, slightly peppery flavour and a wonderfully crunchy texture. It's perfect for braising, as it soaks up all the cooking liquid, transforming it into a flavour-packed tender vegetable. It's also great as a pickle. I've used it to make my **Pickled Daikon** (page 96), which works perfectly as a side dish for steamed rice and grilled meats. It's also great in soups, giving a lovely, delicate flavour.

Banana shallots

Banana shallots are milder and sweeter than your regular white or brown onions. I like to use them for their flavour and colour. I find them perfect for stir-fries and curries where I don't want the sharpness of onions overpowering every other flavour. I've used them in my **Bacon and Kimchi Fried Rice** (page 55) and **Tom Yum Soup** (page 125). They cook down beautifully and add a subtle sweetness to every dish.

Lemongrass

Lemongrass has a bright, citrusy, almost floral flavour. I always use the lower and thicker part of the stalk, and usually bruise or finely chop it to release the aroma. You can also crush or slice it to infuse into soups, curries or tea. I use lemongrass in my **Vietnamese Phở Bò** (page 65), **Thai Beef Salad** (page 130) and **Vietnamese Lemongrass Pork Chop Bánh Mì** (page 114). I'd recommend you remove it before serving, unless it's very finely minced.

Galangal

Galangal is from the ginger family, but it tastes completely different. It's sharper, more citrusy and floral, with a slightly peppery flavour. It has a pine-like smell that reminds me of walking through the woods. It's usually sliced or pounded and removed from a dish before serving, as it's quite tough to eat.

I have used it in my **Tom Yum Soup** (page 125), **Curry Prawn Laksa** (page 68), and **Thai Green Prawn Curry** (page 143). It's essential to achieving authentic Thai flavours. The skin can be easily removed by gently scraping it off with a teaspoon.

Makrut lime leaves

In Asian cooking we use fresh makrut lime leaves. These are sometimes quite difficult to find outside of Asia, but you can use frozen lime leaves instead. These are quite different to dried lime leaves. Fresh (or frozen) lime leaves have an incredible fragrance. The leaves are dark green and look super glossy. Their aroma is hard to describe; it is bright and citrusy, almost like lime zest but more floral. I use them in my **Tom Yum Soup** (page 125), **Thai Green Prawn Curry** (page 143) and **Malaysian Beef Rendang** (page 148). I usually tear them or thinly slice them to release their beautiful aroma. Best added early on in cooking to allow their aroma to infuse broths and sauces.

Edamame

I always have a bag of these young soybeans in my freezer. You can get them either in their pods or shelled. They have a sweet, slightly nutty flavour with a lovely firm bite. They're great for healthy light snacks. You'll usually find them frozen, already blanched and ready to use. They're bright green and wholesome, and add a pop of colour and protein to salads, rice bowls and noodle dishes. I use them in my **Classic Fried Rice** (page 37), where they bring a fresh, sweet contrast to the savoury rice. I love the way they make a dish feel more balanced and nutritious without any extra effort. Just toss them in at the end of cooking; they only need a minute to heat through.

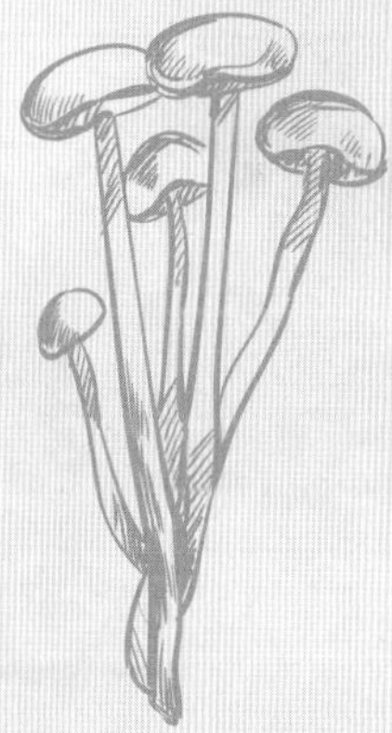

Pandan leaves

Pandan is a tropical plant from South East Asia that is used a lot in both sweet and savoury dishes. In Malaysia, Singapore, Thailand and the Philippines, you will find curries, rice dishes and many desserts flavoured with pandan. It has a lovely aroma that smells like a blend of freshly steamed rice, coconut and vanilla. I use pandan leaves and pandan extract in my **Onde Onde Cake** (page 188) and **Halo-Halo Ice-Cream Sundae** (page 194). I just love how pandan gives desserts this beautiful green colour and an aromatic fragrance that makes everything smell and taste exotic.

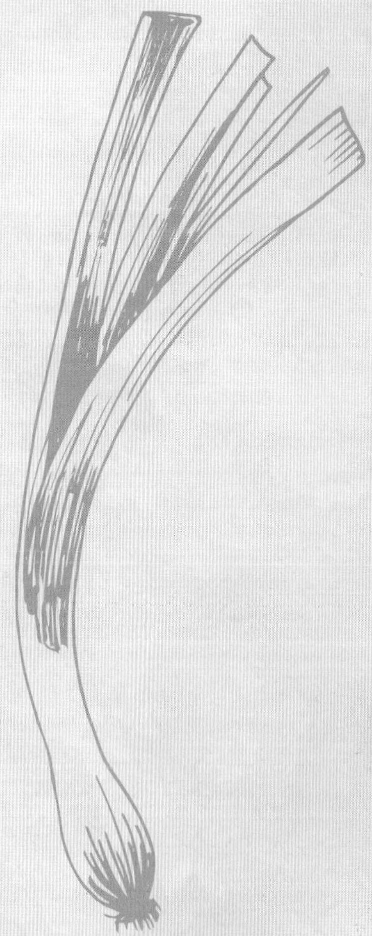

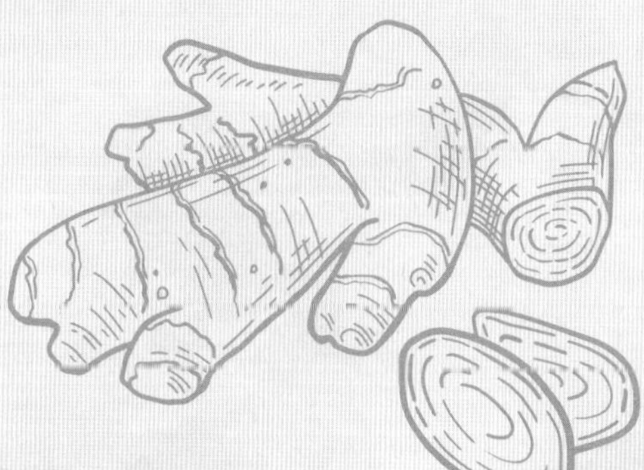

Spices and seasonings

If you open my spice drawer, you'll find loads of little jars that smell of different countries. Every spice reminds me of a favourite Asian dish. They are bold and aromatic, and they transform your dishes in ways that salt and pepper never could. A few toasted black sesame seeds, a few pieces of star anise or a pinch of Chinese five-spice can be the difference between, 'This tastes good' and 'What's your secret recipe?' I always toast my whole spices before using them, because it helps to wake them up and release their beautiful aromas. I keep my most-used spices in jars near the stove because I reach for them constantly. Some, like white pepper and five-spice, are everyday staples. Others, like shichimi togarashi or gochugaru, are more specific but absolutely essential for certain dishes. Once you start building your spice collection, you'll find yourself easily creating those deep, complex flavours that make Asian food so addictive.

White pepper (whole and ground)

Both white and black pepper come from the same peppercorn - the only difference is that white pepper has had its dark outer layer removed, revealing a milder, more delicate core. I love it for its subtle heat and flavour, especially in dishes where I don't want the dark flecks of black pepper to stand out. I've used it in my **Chicken Congee** (page 49), **Classic Fried Rice** (page 37) and **Hot-and-Sour Soup** (page 126). I love its warming heat, which builds slowly rather than hitting you immediately. Once you start using this, you'll notice it everywhere in Asian cooking. It's subtle but essential.

Black pepper (whole and ground)

There is nothing better than the smell of freshly ground black peppercorns being added to a dish or marinade. They have such a lovely, slightly spicy aroma. They're commonly used in braised dishes and marinades where you want that peppery warmth to infuse slowly into the dish. I've used them in my **Chicken Adobo** (page 155), where they simmer with vinegar and soy sauce, releasing their spicy, woody flavour.

Star anise

This beautiful star-shaped spice is my favourite among all whole spices. It has a strong liquorice-like flavour. It's one of those spices that truly defines Chinese braised dishes. I've used it in my **Vietnamese Beef Bò Kho** (page 153), **Aromatic Duck Pancakes** (page 164) and **Spicy Sichuan Boiled Fish Stew** (page 151). Just one or two stars are enough; too much and it can overpower all other flavours. I add star anise whole to simmering sauces and remove them before serving.

Cinnamon (sticks and ground)

Cinnamon isn't just for desserts. In Asian cooking, it's one of those background spices that adds a depth that you can feel but can't quite describe. It adds warmth and a subtle sweetness to savoury dishes. It's used in my **Duck in Plum Sauce** (page 175), **Five-Spiced Pork Belly with Steamed Bao Buns** (page 116) and **Malaysian Beef Rendang** (page 148). I prefer using whole cinnamon sticks rather than ground cinnamon, because they infuse their flavour slowly without becoming too overpowering.

Cloves

I remember biting into a whole clove by accident when I was a kid. My mouth started burning and I ran to my mum. She told me that cloves are a medicinal spice and are very potent. They are intensely aromatic, with a warm and bitter flavour. They're very powerful, so you only need a few. Cloves feature in my **Vietnamese Phở Bò** (page 65), where they add a distinctive spiced warmth. I also use whole cloves to infuse meats, stews, soups and drinks with their warming flavour.

Bay leaves

I have a bay tree in my garden, and it's so handy. I love how bay leaves add a subtle herbal and slightly floral note to dishes that cook for a long time. I use them in soups and stews, stocks and sauces, roasts and braises, and even in marinades. In this book, I've used them in my **Aromatic Duck Pancakes** (page 164), **Duck in Plum Sauce** (page 175) and **Chicken Adobo** (page 155). I don't find them as bold as other spices, but they tend to round out flavours. I always remove them before serving, as they're tough and not meant to be eaten. Thankfully, they're big and easy to scoop out.

Cumin (ground and seeds)

Cumin has an earthy, slightly smoky flavour that's essential in Indian and Central Asian dishes. I like the convenience of ground cumin, but whole cumin seeds have more aroma, especially when you toast them first. In this book, I've used ground cumin in my **Chinese Cumin Lamb Skewers** (page 121) and **Chicken Tikka Masala** (page 158). It's one of those spices that smells incredible when it hits hot oil.

Turmeric (fresh and ground)

Turmeric isn't just for colour; it adds a warm, slightly peppery flavour that's hard to replicate. It's earthy and slightly bitter, and is said to have many health benefits. And, yes, it gives dishes a gorgeous golden hue. I like the vibrancy and aroma of fresh turmeric root more than the ground version, but both work well. Ground turmeric is more convenient and is easily available. I've used it in my **Curry Prawn Laksa** (page 68), **Malaysian Beef Rendang** (page 148) and **Chinese Chicken Curry** (page 159). Turmeric can stain very easily, so be careful - and use rubber gloves when preparing fresh turmeric.

Ground coriander

Ground coriander is much gentler than the fresh herb and adds warmth to any dish. It tastes slightly floral and citrusy, with a nutty, earthy aroma. I use it in my **Curry Prawn Laksa** (page 68) and **Chicken Tikka Masala** (page 158). It's one of those spices that works in the background, rounding out other flavours without shouting for attention.

Sichuan pepper (whole and ground)

Sichuan peppercorns aren't actually that spicy; rather, they're numbing, creating a tingling sensation on your tongue that's completely unique. They smell quite floral and have a citrusy, slightly earthy taste. They're in my **Spicy Sichuan Boiled Fish Stew** (page 151) and **Kung Pao Chicken** (page 171). I always toast them lightly first to bring out their aroma, then grind them if needed. They're one of those ingredients that make you realise there's more to 'spicy' than just heat.

Chinese five-spice

Chinese five-spice is a blend of star anise, cloves, cinnamon, Sichuan peppercorns and fennel seeds. It's sweet, warm and aromatic. You'll find it used in my **Chinese Crispy Stuffed Lotus Root with Pork and Prawn** (page 90), as well as my **Chinese Chicken Curry** (page 159) and **Salt-and-Chilli King Prawns** (page 163). A little goes a long way. It's potent and can easily overpower a dish, so use sparingly. When used correctly, it adds that unmistakable Chinese flavour that's both complex and savoury.

Shichimi togarashi

Shichimi togarashi is a Japanese seven-spice seasoning blend featuring chilli, sesame seeds, seaweed and citrus peel. It's spicy, nutty and slightly tangy in flavour. It's great for adding some colour and flavour to a dish. I use it as a finishing spice for my **Japanese Oyakodon with Chicken** (page 44). Once you try it, you'll want to put it on everything!

Mushroom powder

Mushroom powder is made from dried mushrooms ground into a fine powder, and it adds instant savoury depth to literally any dish. I use it in my **Classic Fried Rice** (page 37) when I want that extra layer of flavour without adding more soy sauce. I love using this as a brilliant little cheat for boosting umami flavour in vegetarian dishes, too. Once you try it, you'll find a million other dishes where it can work its magic. You can even sprinkle it on chips to add a special umami flavour.

Gochugaru (Korean red pepper flakes)

Gochugaru are Korean chilli flakes, famous for their fruity, smoky and slightly sweet heat. They're not as fiery as other chilli flakes. I love how they bring that signature Korean sweet-and-spicy heat, along with a gorgeous deep red colour. I use gochugaru in my **Simple Kimchi** (page 92), **Bacon and Kimchi Fried Rice** (page 55) and **Korean Kimchi Tofu Stew** (page 144). Gochugaru has a unique taste that defines Korean cooking, so substituting regular chilli flakes won't have the same effect.

Toasted sesame seeds

These aren't like regular sesame seeds - they have been pre-toasted, which makes all the difference! Their aroma is just stunning. I always keep both white and black sesame seeds in my pantry. They are the perfect garnish, and you'll see that I have used them in this way throughout this book. I've also used them to make a beautiful Japanese goma salad dressing (see page 139). Have a look out for other flavours, including wasabi-flavoured toasted sesame seeds, which are green, and soy-sauce flavoured ones, which are brown.

KIKKOMAN
NATURALLY BREWED
Soy Sauce
1 LITRE e
OVER 300 YEARS OF EXCELLENCE
Tung Chun
KEWPIE
MAYONNAISE
355ml
Peringatan
SWEET
SOYA BEAN SAUCE
FORTUNE
BRAND
好運牌
Net Wt.: 454 g
LEE KUM KEE
510g
GO-CHU-JANG
HOT PEPPER PASTE
비비고
紹興
SHAO XING
LAOGANMA
Crispy Chilli in Oil
Net Weight: 210 g
ゆであずき
味噌

Sauces, pastes and condiments

If you were to peek inside my pantry, you'd find dozens of bottles and jars, containing all my favourite essentials. My husband jokes that I have a sauce-hoarding problem, but I call it being prepared for whatever I need to cook. These sauces, pastes and condiments are the flavour-builders of every Asian dish: the secret weapons that transform a simple stir-fry into something that makes people ask for the recipe. Some, like light soy sauce and sesame oil, I use every single day. Others, like chu hou paste or tamarind concentrate, are more specialised but irreplaceable in certain recipes. Building up your collection takes time, but these are the ingredients that will sit in your cupboard for months, ready whenever you need them. And trust me: once you start cooking with them, you'll wonder how you ever managed without them.

Soy sauce

Chinese light soy sauce

Light soy sauce is the hero ingredient of Asian cooking. It's called 'light' because of its lighter colour and thinner consistency compared to dark soy sauce. It's salty and savoury, and adds an essential umami depth. Any time I mention light soy sauce in my recipes, this is what I'm referring to. I use it in my **Classic Fried Rice** (page 37), **Hot-and-Sour Soup** (page 126), **Black Pepper Beef with Crispy Noodle Pancake** (page 75) and pretty much every stir-fry I make (I go through almost a bottle a month!). My preferred brands are Lee Kum Kee, Pearl River Bridge and Haitian.

Chinese dark soy sauce

Dark soy sauce is thicker, darker and slightly sweeter than light soy sauce. It's aged for longer and often has molasses or caramel added, which gives it that deep, almost black colour. It's used for colour and richness rather than saltiness. It's essential in my **Cantonese Sticky Rice with Chinese Sausage** (page 54), **Kung Pao Chicken** (page 171) and **Singapore Noodles** (page 61). I would never use it as a substitute for light soy sauce. Just a splash adds a rich, glossy sheen to stir-fries and braises. My preferred brands are Lee Kum Kee, Pearl River Bridge and Haitian.

Japanese soy sauce (shoyu)

This is smoother, darker in colour and slightly sweeter than Chinese soy sauce. It's what you'll usually find on the table at sushi restaurants. I use it in my **Salmon Sushi Bake** (page 38), **Miso Cod Ochazuke** (page 53) and **Japanese Chicken Gyoza** (page 112). It's perfect for teriyaki glazes, drizzling over rice bowls, and of course for dipping sushi and sashimi. I like the Kikkoman and Yamasa brands.

Korean soy sauce (ganjang)

This is lighter and less salty than Chinese light soy sauce. I use it when I want a clean and savoury flavour that isn't overpowering. I use it in my **Korean Beef Bibimbap** (page 46), **Korean Japchae** (page 71) and **Korean Kimchi Tofu Stew** (page 144). Japanese soy sauce is a closer substitute than Chinese. I like the Sempio brand.

Filipino soy sauce (toyo)

This ingredient really defines Filipino cooking; if you substitute it for regular soy sauce, the dish won't taste quite right. Filipino soy sauce is darker in colour and saltier than Chinese soy sauce, with a little sweetness. I've used it in my **Chicken Adobo** (page 155), where it balances the sharp acidity of the vinegar beautifully, and in my **Filipino Pancit Bihon** (page 67), where it adds colour, saltiness and sweetness to the noodles. My preferred brands are Silver Swan, Datu Puti and Marca Pina.

Vietnamese soy sauce (nước tương)

This is lighter than Chinese soy sauce, with a cleaner, less assertive flavour. It works well alongside fish sauce, the star of Vietnamese cooking, so it's more subtle. I use it in my **Vietnamese Shaking Beef with Red Rice** (page 50) and **Vietnamese Lemongrass Pork Chop Bánh Mì** (page 114). It's great for light seasoning when you don't want anything too strong. I like the Chin-su brand. If you can't find Vietnamese soy sauce, use Chinese light soy sauce.

Thai light soy sauce (aka thin soy sauce)

This is slightly sweeter and less intense than Chinese light soy sauce. I use it in my **Stir-Fried Morning Glory** (page 81) and **Pad Thai with Prawns** (page 76). It's used alongside fish sauce, which is the dominant salty element in Thai cooking, so it plays more of a supporting role. I use the Dek Som Boon brand.

Thai sweet soy sauce

Thai sweet soy sauce is thick, dark, and sweet – similar to kecap manis. I've used it in my **Thai Basil Pork Stir-Fry** (page 97), where it adds a glossy sweetness that balances the heat from the chillies. I use the Dek Som Boon brand.

Kecap manis

Pronounced 'ketchup manis', this is an Indonesian sweet soy sauce: thick, sticky and intensely sweet, with a molasses-like richness. I use it in my **Satay Chicken** (page 172), where it adds gloss and sweetness. It's very different from regular soy sauce. You can make a substitute by simmering soy sauce with brown sugar, but the real thing tastes better. My preferred brands are ABC or Habhal.

Sesame oil

The smell of sesame oil reminds me of my mum and dad's kitchen, where they always add a little drizzle to lend a beautiful nuttiness to their dishes. Dad always says you don't need a lot of sesame oil, as it can easily overpower your dish. I use it in my **Kung Pao Chicken** (page 171), **Cold Ramen Sesame Noodle Salad** (page 139) and **Black Bean Beef** (page 167). Look out for pure sesame oil rather than blended - it has an amazing flavour and aroma.

Neutral oil

Throughout the book, when I call for the use of a neutral oil, I typically use peanut oil, but sunflower, grapeseed or vegetable oil would work too. Just don't use olive oil, as it will affect the flavour.

Oyster sauce

Don't let the name put you off - oyster sauce doesn't taste particularly fishy. This sauce is a cornerstone ingredient in Asian cooking, with many regional variations. It is thick, dark and deeply savoury, with a slight sweetness. It's made from oyster extract, soy sauce and sugar, and it adds a rich umami depth to stir-fries, marinades and stews. You'll find it in my **Classic Fried Rice** (page 37), **Beef with Broccoli in Oyster Sauce** (page 176) and **Stir-Fried Morning Glory** (page 81). I always use Lee Kum Kee premium oyster sauce; it has a richer and more intense flavour, and is my secret for making vegetables and noodles taste restaurant-quality.

Shaoxing wine

Shaoxing wine is a Chinese rice wine used in the same way you might use white wine in Western cooking. It adds depth and flavour to stir-fries and marinades, and also helps to tenderise meat. I have used it in my **Singapore Noodles** (page 61), **Classic Chinese Dumplings** (page 108), and **Sichuan Dry-Fried Green Beans with Pork** (page 89). Don't skip it; it adds a layer of flavour that's hard to replicate. If adding Shaoxing wine to a stir-fry, pour it around the hot edges of the wok, which allows the alcohol to evaporate, leaving behind the delicious flavour.

Hoisin sauce

Hoisin sauce is thick and sweet, with a deep, spiced, fermented soybean flavour. Think of it as Chinese barbecue sauce. I use it in my **Vietnamese Summer Rolls** (page 85), **Aromatic Duck Pancakes** (page 164), and **Vietnamese Beef Bò Kho** (page 153). I also use it in marinades and as a dipping sauce, and I brush it on grilled meats. It's one of those sauces that makes people lick their fingers. It's fabulous!

Soybean paste/soybean sauce

An essential component in Asian cooking, soybean pastes and sauces are made from fermented cooked soybeans and salt. They can be fermented for a few months or up to a few years. There are many types of soybean pastes. The most well known is probably **Japanese miso paste,** which is fermented with koji (a Japanese fermentation starter). There are three main types of miso: white miso (shiro miso), which has a mild savoury and slightly sweet flavour and is usually fermented for a short time; red miso (miso), which has a rich, savoury and more intense flavour, and is usually fermented for a longer time; and awase miso (a mix of red and white). I use white miso in my **Salmon Miso Soup** (page 138), **Miso Cod Ochazuke** (page 53) and **Miso Caramel Banoffee Pie** (page 182). In Korean cooking, a slightly stronger soybean paste known as **doenjang** is used. I use it to flavour Korean soups and stews, and always have a tub in my fridge. Another type I love is Chinese soybean paste or sauce, also known as **yellow soybean paste** or sauce. This is fermented with wheat flour. It's great in stir-fries, marinades and soups. I use it to marinade the pork char siu for my **Singapore Noodles** (page 61), where it adds a complex, savoury flavour. Thailand also has its own soybean paste, known as **taochiao**. This is not as thick as other soybean pastes. It contains whole beans, and it's lighter in colour and more pourable. I use it in my **Thai Basil Pork Stir-Fry** (page 97).

Chilli bean paste

Also known as doubanjiang or toban sauce in Chinese, this paste is deeply savoury, with a complex heat that builds slowly. I've used it in my **Hot-and-Sour Soup** (page 126) and **Spicy Sichuan Boiled Fish Stew** (page 151). It's at the very soul of Sichuan cooking and Chinese cuisine in general: earthy, spicy, and full of umami. It adds layers of flavour that develop as the dish cooks.

Chu hou paste

Chu hou paste, also known as five-spice paste, is a thick, savoury Chinese paste made from fermented soybeans, garlic and spices. It has a deep, slightly sweet, complex flavour. I use it in my **Five-Spiced Pork Belly with Steamed Bao Buns** (page 116). It's not as common as some of the other pastes I've mentioned here, but it's worth seeking out if you want an authentic Cantonese flavour.

Fermented black beans

Fermented black beans are salted fermented soybeans with an intense, umami-rich flavour. In my **Black Bean Beef** (page 167), they create a deep and savoury sauce that clings to everything. You can buy them whole and mash them yourself, or buy a ready-made black bean sauce. They are like tiny flavour bombs: a little goes a long way.

Chilli oil

Chilli oil is vegetable oil infused with chilli flakes, often with garlic, ginger and Sichuan peppercorns, but there are loads of other varieties too. It's spicy and fragrant, adding heat, flavour and texture all at the same time. I use it in my **Biang Biang Chilli Oil Noodles** (page 59) and **One-Pot Thai Red Curry Dumplings** (page 156). Different regions have their own versions, like peanut rayu from Japan or crispy chilli oil from China. One of my favourites is crispy prawn chilli oil. Once you have a jar of good chilli oil in your pantry, you'll want to drizzle it on everything!

Worcestershire sauce

This is not traditionally Asian, but it's become a staple in Japanese, Filipino and Chinese cooking, where it adds a tangy and savoury depth. I use it in my **Japanese Pork Katsu Curry** (page 147), where it adds a layer of tanginess that rounds out the curry sauce beautifully.

Gochujang (Korean chilli paste)

Gochujang is a staple in Korean cuisine. It is a thick, sticky chilli paste made from fermented soybeans, glutinous rice, and gochugaru (see page 19). I love how it's spicy, sweet and savoury all at the same time. You'll find it in my **Sausage Gochujang Udon** (page 62), **Korean Fried Chicken** (page 107) and **Bacon and Kimchi Fried Rice** (page 55). It's completely unique; you can't substitute it with anything else. Once you start cooking with gochujang, you'll find yourself adding it to everything!

Fish sauce

Fish sauce is central to South East Asian cooking, and every country has its own version. It's made from fermented anchovies and salt - and yes, it smells intense in the bottle, but in dishes it adds an incredible savoury depth. Vietnamese fish sauce tends to be lighter and clearer, while Thai fish sauce is slightly more pungent. I use it in my **Vietnamese Phở Bò** (page 65), **Pad Thai with Prawns** (page 76), **Curry Prawn Laksa** (page 68) and **Tom Yum Soup** (page 125). Don't be put off by the smell; it transforms dishes in a way nothing else can. Just try not to spill it - you'll be smelling it for days!

Thai chilli paste (nam prik pao)

Nam prik pao is a Thai chilli paste made with roasted chillies, garlic, shallots and shrimp paste. It's smoky, sweet, spicy and deeply savoury all at once. I use it in my **Tom Yum Soup** (page 125), where it adds that essential Thai depth and complexity. It also works well in a quick vegetable stir-fry.

Red/green Thai curry pastes

Thai curry pastes are concentrated blends of chillies, lemongrass, galangal, garlic, shallots and spices. Red curry paste, made with red chillies, is medium-hot and slightly sweet, while green curry paste, made with green chillies, is spicier and hotter. I use red curry paste in my **One-Pot Thai Red Curry Dumplings** (page 156) and green curry paste in my **Thai Green Prawn Curry** (page 143). Homemade is always best, but good-quality store-bought pastes are almost as good and so convenient. They pack so much flavour that making curry becomes effortless.

Tamarind paste/tamarind concentrate

Tamarind is a fresh, date-like fruit with a very hard stone in the middle. The flavour is sour and fruity, with a complex tanginess that's hard to replicate. It's essential in South East Asian cooking, especially for dishes like pad thai and curries. I use it in my **Pad Thai with Prawns** (page 76) and **Malaysian Beef Rendang** (page 148). In general, you can buy tamarind as a paste that comes in a block - definitely choose the seedless option - but what I find even better is tamarind concentrate. This is already diluted with water, and you can easily add a tablespoon into your cooking.

Sriracha

Sriracha is versatile and accessible, and adds a bright, spicy kick to everything. It's a tangy, garlicky chilli sauce with a medium heat. I use it in my **Salmon Sushi Bake** (page 38) and **Asian-Style Coleslaw** (page 133). It's not traditional in every Asian cuisine, but it's become quite a pantry staple. As its popularity has grown, so too have the number of varieties available, with flavours like turmeric, lemongrass, makrut lime, garlic, super-hot, mustard, wasabi ... the list goes on. Explore your local Asian supermarket to see what varieties of sriracha they have on offer.

Sweet chilli sauce

Sweet chilli sauce is sticky, sweet, garlicky and mildly spicy. It's brilliant as a dipping sauce, drizzled over crispy nibbles and added to stir-fries. I love dipping pizza crusts in it! I've used it in my **Chinese Crispy Stuffed Lotus Root with Pork and Prawn** (page 90), **Vietnamese Summer Rolls** (page 85) and **Sesame Prawn Toast** (page 101). It's one of those sauces that makes everything taste more interesting without being too complicated.

Vinegar

Black rice vinegar/Chinese black vinegar

Chinese black vinegar is dark, slightly sweet and malty, with a complex, aged flavour. It's less sharp than white vinegar and adds depth rather than just acidity. I use it in my **Biang Biang Chilli Oil Noodles** (page 59), **Sichuan**

Dry-Fried Green Beans with Pork (page 89), Asian Cucumber Salad (page 132) and Classic Chinese Dumplings (page 108). It's great in dipping sauces, salad dressings and stir-fries - I always think of it as China's answer to balsamic vinegar.

Rice vinegar/white rice vinegar/rice wine vinegar
Rice vinegar is mild, slightly sweet, and much gentler than Western spirit vinegars. It's used in dressings, pickles and sushi rice. I use it in my Pickled Daikon (page 96), Sweet-and-Sour Pork (page 168) and Asian-Style Coleslaw (page 133). It adds acidity without being harsh, which makes it perfect for delicate dishes.

Chinese red vinegar
Chinese red vinegar is less common, but has a distinctive tangy and slightly sweet flavour. I normally use it as a garnish or dipping sauce. It has a unique taste that's hard to describe, but instantly recognisable once you know it. I use it as a garnish in my Hot-and-Sour Soup (page 126), where it adds that essential sour note to balance the flavours.

Korean apple vinegar
Korean apple vinegar is fruity, mild and slightly sweet. It's less acidic than rice vinegar and adds a gentle tang. I use it in my Korean Beef Bibimbap (page 46) and Korean Fried Chicken (page 107) to help balance the flavour. If you can't find it, you can use white rice vinegar.

Filipino white cane vinegar
Filipino white cane vinegar is sharper and more acidic than rice vinegar, with a clean, bright flavour. It's essential in Filipino cooking, especially for my Chicken Adobo (page 155), where it cuts through the richness of the soy sauce and creates that perfect balance.

Japanese rice vinegar
Sushi vinegar is rice vinegar seasoned with sugar and salt. It's what gives sushi rice that glossy, slightly sweet, tangy flavour. I use it in my Onigiri (page 42) and Salmon Sushi Bake (page 38) to season the rice. It's convenient if you're making sushi regularly, though I often make my own by mixing Japanese rice vinegar with sugar and salt.

Dashi stock/dashi powder

Dashi is the foundation of lots of Japanese dishes: a clear, umami-rich stock made from kombu (dried kelp) and bonito flakes (dried, fermented smoked tuna). You can use dried shiitake mushrooms instead of bonito flakes to make it vegetarian friendly. It has a beautiful smokiness that is quite complex and sophisticated. You can make it fresh, which is relatively simple (see opposite) or use dashi powder for convenience. I use it in my Japanese Oyakodon with Chicken (page 44), Miso Cod Ochazuke (page 53) and Salmon Miso Soup (page 138). It's lighter and more delicate than chicken or beef stock, and it has a clean, ocean-like umami that's completely unique. Once you taste it, you'll understand why it's so essential.

Fresh dashi stock (makes about 1 litre/4 cups)

1 piece of kombu (about 10g/⅓oz)
20g (¾oz) bonito flakes

Combine the kombu with 1 litre (4 cups) cold water in a large saucepan and leave to soak for a minimum of 30 minutes. Now place the pan over a medium heat and bring to a simmer. You should be able to see some bubbles forming, but you do not want to boil the liquid. Once simmering, take out the kombu and discard, then add the bonito flakes and bring back to a steady simmer for 2 minutes.

Turn off the heat and let the bonito flakes rest in the stock for 10 minutes, or until the flakes settle to the bottom. Strain the dashi stock into a separate clean pan or container. It will keep for 3-5 days in the fridge.

Mirin

Mirin, a sweet Japanese rice wine, is a staple in Japanese cooking. It adds a gentle sweetness and helps balance salty flavours. I use it in my Wakame Seaweed Salad (page 132), Japanese Beef and Enoki Mushroom Rolls (page 82) and Teriyaki Chicken (page 173). It's not just about sweetness; it adds depth and a gentle gloss to sauces. If you can't find it, a mix of sake and sugar is the closest substitute.

Sake

Sake is Japanese rice wine. Like Shaoxing wine, it's used to add depth and help tenderise meat. I use it in my Japanese Oyakodon with Chicken (page 44), Miso Cod Ochazuke (page 53) and Teriyaki Chicken (page 173). It's lighter and cleaner than Shaoxing wine, with a more delicate flavour. I just use normal drinking sake, but you can use cooking sake, which has a higher salt content.

Japanese mayonnaise

Japanese mayonnaise has really taken Europe by storm - and for good reason. It is richer, tangier, creamier and more flavourful than regular mayo. It's made with rice vinegar and egg yolks, which gives it that distinctive flavour. I use it in my Onigiri (page 42), Salmon Sushi Bake (page 38), Cold Ramen Sesame Noodle Salad (page 139), and K-Toast (page 120). Once you try it, you won't want to go back. If you are making sushi, you really need to have this. The most common brand is Kewpie.

Dried products

Dried wood ear/black fungus mushrooms

These are usually added to dishes more for texture than for taste. Wood ear mushrooms are smaller, thinner and lighter in colour than black fungus mushrooms, which are bigger, darker and crunchier. Choose either depending on what is available. I use them in my **Crispy Vietnamese Spring Rolls** (page 104) and also my **Hot-and-Sour Soup** (page 126). The lovely crunchy texture they bring is hard to replicate.

Dried shrimp

These are a staple in East and South East Asian cuisine. I usually keep a jar in my fridge and a larger packet frozen. Rehydrate them before adding to stir-fries, soups and pastes to lend a wonderful umami flavour. On a recent visit to Hong Kong, I visited Tai O, a small fishing village. They had about 20 different varieties of dried shrimp air-drying in the sun! I use them in my **Cantonese Sticky Rice with Chinese Sausage** (page 54) and **Chinese Crispy Stuffed Lotus Root with Pork and Prawn** (page 90).

Dried shiitake mushrooms

There are many different grades and sizes available. The more expensive ones are larger and thicker. One of my favourite dishes when I was younger was braised shiitake mushrooms in oyster sauce. My granny would bring over extra-large ones from Hong Kong, and I remember being so excited! Try them out in my **Cantonese Sticky Rice with Chinese Sausage** (page 54) and also my **Hot-and-Sour Soup** (page 126).

Dried anchovies

You will usually find these in the chilled section of an Asian supermarket in small, medium and large sizes up to 10cm (4in) in length. I've seen small anchovies deep-fried and served with peanuts as a snack, used as a topping in meals like nasi lemak, or stir-fried in soy sauce as a Korean banchan (side dish). The larger anchovies are usually used to add flavour to stocks, as I have done for my **Korean Tteokbokki Rice Cakes** (page 102).

Kombu

Used in Japanese cuisine to make a flavoursome dashi soup stock, kombu is a type of dried, thick, dark green, edible kelp. Don't wash it before use; just wipe it gently. The white chalky powder that you see on kombu is made of natural glutamates, which add depth and umami flavour. I use it to make my **Dashi Stock** (page 25), **Korean Tteokbokki Rice Cakes** (page 102) and **Salmon Miso Soup** (page 138).

Wakame

A dark green seaweed that's usually sold dried. When you rehydrate the tiny shrivelled pieces in water, they expand and become much larger. Wakame has a soft, springy, silky texture, and is mild and subtly sweet in flavour. It's a key ingredient in making miso soup (such as my **Salmon Miso Soup**, see page 138) and it's lovely used in salads (see my **Wakame Seaweed Salad**, page 132).

Bonito flakes (katsuobushi)

These are wafer-thin shavings of dried, smoked and fermented bonito fish (also known as skipjack tuna). They are a key ingredient in Japanese cuisine when making dashi stock (see page 25). You can eat bonito flakes straight out of the packet, and may have seen them used as a delicate topping on sushi or takoyaki, a popular Japanese street food.

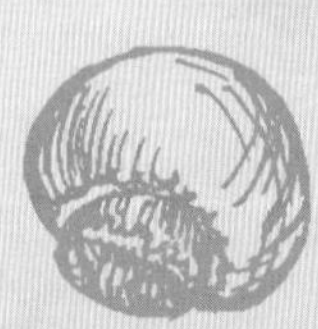

Sugar and sweets

Matcha powder

Matcha is finely ground green tea powder with an earthy, slightly bitter and grassy flavour. I love its vibrant green colour and incredible aroma. I use it in my **Matcha Basque Cheesecake** (page 191), where it adds a beautiful colour and distinctive tea flavour that balances the richness of the cream cheese. Quality matters with matcha; culinary grade is fine for baking, but ceremonial grade (which is a lot more expensive) has a smoother and more refined flavour. Matcha has become really trendy in recent years. It can divide opinion, but I'm a big fan.

Ube macapuno/ube extract

An ube is a purple yam with a sweet, mildly nutty flavour and a gorgeous violet colour. Ube macapuno is ube mixed with soft, jelly-like young coconut, and I find it absolutely delicious. Ube extract is a concentrated form used in baking and desserts. I use it in my **Halo-Halo Ice-Cream Sundae** (page 194), where it adds that signature Filipino flavour and colour.

Palm sugar/gula melaka

Palm sugar (jaggery) is made from the sap of palm trees and has a deep, caramel-like sweetness with a slight smokiness. It's a lot less refined than white sugar and adds a rich, complex flavour. Gula melaka is Malaysian palm sugar, often sold in solid blocks that you need to grate or chop. I use it in my **Thai Green Prawn Curry** (page 143), **Curry Prawn Laksa** (page 68) and **Onde Onde Cake** (page 188). It's not as sweet as white sugar, and it has a gorgeous, molasses-like depth. Coconut sugar, which is made from coconut palm sap, is similar but slightly lighter. It works great as a substitute.

Chinese rock sugar

Also called bing tang, this is an unrefined cane sugar formed into irregular crystal-like chunks. It retains a lovely, natural caramelised sweetness when added to dishes, and adds a gorgeous glossy sheen. I use it in my **Five-Spiced Pork Belly with Steamed Bao Buns** (page 116) and my **Duck in Plum Sauce** (page 175).

Sweetened red-bean paste

Sweetened red-bean paste is hugely popular in Asia. It's used in steamed buns, drinks, pastries and desserts. It is made from red beans (aka adzuki beans) that have been cooked down with sugar until thick and smooth. It's earthy and slightly sweet, and has a texture somewhere between jam and mashed potato. I use it in my **Korean Red-Bean Doughnuts** (page 198), where it's the main filling. It's not as sweet as many Western dessert fillings, which makes it feel more balanced. You can buy it ready-made in tins or packets, or you can make your own if you have the time.

Coconut whipping cream

Coconut whipping cream is thick coconut cream that can be whipped like dairy cream. It's rich and slightly sweet, with that distinctive coconut flavour. It's so good. I use it in my **Onde Onde Cake** (page 188), where it adds a luscious tropical creaminess. It's a brilliant dairy-free alternative, though it behaves slightly differently from regular cream; it needs to be very cold before whipping, and it won't hold its shape for as long.

Freshly grated coconut

Freshly grated coconut is sweet, crunchy and fragrant in a way that dried coconut can never match. I use it in my **Onde Onde Cake** (page 188). If you can't find fresh coconut, frozen grated coconut is the next best thing. Dried desiccated coconut also works, but it's drier and less flavourful.

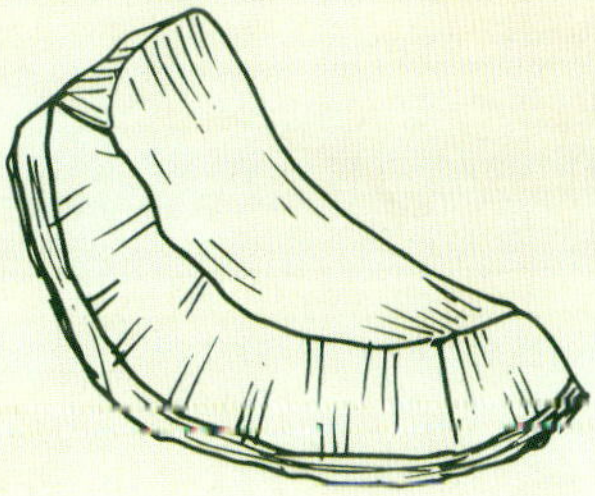

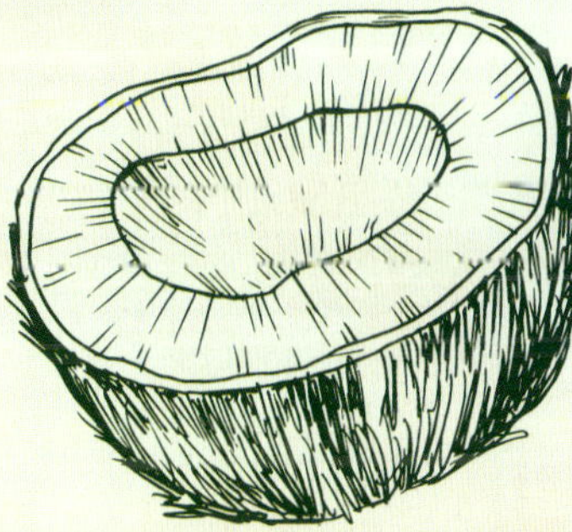

My favourite Asian snacks and drinks

If you know me well, one thing you will surely notice is my love of snacks! Here are some of my favourite Asian snacks and drinks. Definitely try them out next time you see them.

1. Pocky sticks

Thin biscuit sticks dipped in chocolate. They're so addictive. When I was young, there were only strawberry and chocolate flavours. Now? The selection is vast, with almond, hazelnut, white chocolate, dark chocolate and even matcha. I love using them as cake decorations.

2. Hawthorn flakes

These tangy, disc-shaped wafers are made from hawthorn fruit, which is popular in China. They're almost chalky in texture, but in a good way. When I was a kid, I'd get through an entire roll in one sitting.

3. Prawn crackers

Not the puffy white chips you get from a Chinese takeaway - these are crunchy corn strips with a prawn flavour. We call them 'har tieu' in Chinese, which translates to prawn strips. I used to bring these to school and watch my friends devour them. They're light and crunchy, with that savoury-sweet taste that's impossible to resist.

4. Sunflower seeds

These aren't plain sunflower seeds; they have a flavoured coating on the shell, so you get a burst of taste before you even crack them open. In China, these are everywhere. People munch on them at the cinema, during long train rides, or while watching TV at home. They come in dozens of flavours: caramel, hickory nut, green tea and more.

5. White Rabbit Creamy Candy

This is the iconic milk candy of my childhood. These chewy sweets come wrapped in edible rice paper, although a lot of people don't realise this and try to peel it off. White Rabbit was one of my absolute favourite treats as a kid. The original milky flavour is still the best, but now there are more than twenty different flavours: pineapple, red bean, Coca-Cola - you name it.

6. Crispy Hong Kong-style egg rolls

Also called 'dan guen', these crispy egg wafer rolls are the ultimate afternoon snack. My grandmother always had a tin of these at home. The plain ones remind me of my childhood, but there are various flavours, including black sesame, seaweed and coffee.

7. Sichuan peanuts

These are so addictive: crisp and crunchy with a spicy kick. They are the perfect accompaniment to drinks, and I sometimes like to sprinkle them on to salads too.

8. Vita Lemon Tea

Vita is a Chinese brand, and their lemon tea is one of my favourite drinks. It's perfectly balanced: not too sweet and not too tart. Vita also makes Vita Soy, a malted soy drink that was a childhood favourite of mine. Eventually, we were able to import them, so we started stocking them in the store and now I can enjoy them all the time!

9. SkyFlakes

SkyFlakes are thin crackers from the Philippines. I usually get the plain salted ones, which are great for nibbling on when you feel a bit peckish. They come in many flavours, including garlic, onion and chives, sweet Mantikilya (sweet butter cream), Condensalda (sweet milk) and chocolate. I love serving the savoury crackers on a cheeseboard.

10. Wong Lo Kat (Chinese herbal tea)

This is like the Chinese version of Coca-Cola. Its red can with yellow Chinese writing is iconic and can be found throughout China. It's a sweetened herbal tea with a unique, slightly sweet flavour that's a bit herbal and medicinal - but in a pleasant way.

11. Seaweed snacks

I love these! They are crispy, slightly chewy and full of flavour. They come in many different flavours: wasabi, salted, barbecue, teriyaki ... the world is your oyster! I keep a bag in my purse for when I get a craving.

12. Want Want rice crackers

These rice crackers come in dozens of flavours and styles, and all are delicious and so satisfying to eat. The Senbei cracker (pictured here) is my favourite, as it's sweet and savoury. These crackers definitely hit the spot when you want something crispy to munch on.

13. Hi-Chew candy

I remember buying a packet of these candies when I visited Japan as a kid. They're sweet and very chewy, with an intense fruity flavour. Be careful, you can easily go through a whole packet in one sitting!

14. Wasabi broad beans

You can also get wasabi peanuts, but I think the broad beans are better. They're bigger and crunchier, and you get more of a wasabi hit. That sharp, nose-tingling heat mixed with the crunchy bean is absolutely addictive.

HATA
冰红茶
LOTTE
コアラのマーチ
王老吉
10
3
2
黄飞红
7
Vitasoy
維他奶
12
Khao Shong
Wasabi
Broad Beans
14
A+ HoSan
SEAWEED SNACK
11
绿茶
Pocky
1
PEPE
Yakult
洽洽
瓜子加WiFi
快乐更自在
香瓜子
4
CUP NOODLES
合味道
6
九製陳皮
HI-CHEW
13
5
椰树牌
8
Ceylon
LEMON TEA DRINK
SkyFlakes
CRACKERS
9

Other pantry staples

Coconut milk

Coconut milk is rich, creamy and slightly sweet. It's the base for curries, laksa and desserts across South East Asia. The higher the fat content, the better. Good-quality coconut milk should have a fat content of 18–20 per cent. I use it in my **Thai Green Prawn Curry** (page 143), **Curry Prawn Laksa** (page 68), **Malaysian Beef Rendang** (page 148) and **Thai Mango Sticky Rice** (page 197). Unless the recipe tells you otherwise, always shake the can before opening, because the cream separates and rises to the top.

Tofu

Tofu, also known as beancurd, is a soybean protein made from coagulated soy milk. You can buy pressed tofu in blocks, which is medium, firm or extra-firm, or unpressed silken tofu, which has retained its high water content, making it very smooth and silky to eat. In Asian cooking, tofu isn't seen as a meat substitute; it is valued in its own right. It is incorporated into many dishes, even meat dishes, like the famous mapo tofu, stir-fried tofu with minced pork in a spicy Sichuan sauce. I have used silken tofu in my **Hot-and-Sour Soup** (page 126) and **Korean Kimchi Tofu Stew** (page 144), while firm tofu is the star of my **Crispy Tofu in Chilli Garlic Sauce** (page 177). You can also get tofu puffs, which are deep-fried, creating a lovely hollow centre. They're perfect for soaking up sauce, which is how I've used them in my **Curry Prawn Laksa** (page 68).

Panko breadcrumbs

Panko are Japanese breadcrumbs made from crustless bread. They're lighter, crispier and flakier than regular breadcrumbs. I use them in my **Japanese Pork Katsu Curry** (page 147) to create that perfect golden crispy coating. Once you start using panko, you won't want to go back to regular breadcrumbs; the texture is just so much crispier.

Rice paper wrappers/Vietnamese rice paper

Rice paper wrappers are thin, translucent sheets made from rice flour. They're brittle when dry but become soft and pliable when briefly dampened in water. I use them in my **Vietnamese Summer Rolls** (page 85) and **Crispy Vietnamese Spring Rolls** (page 104). They're delicate and can tear easily, so handle them gently. They come in various diameters, so make sure you buy the right size for what you're making. They are very versatile; I always keep a packet in my pantry. I've made rice paper noodles from them and I love wrapping them with a prawn filling to make Chinese cheung fun rice rolls.

Gyoza wrappers/wonton wrappers

These are thin sheets of dough used to wrap dumplings. Gyoza wrappers are made with wheat flour, and are round and white. Wonton wrappers are made with wheat flour and egg, and they are square and yellow. I use gyoza wrappers for my **Japanese Chicken Gyoza** (page 112) and wonton wrappers for my **Wonton Soup** (page 129). Making them from scratch is time-consuming, so I always keep a pack or two frozen. You can find them in the freezer section of any Asian supermarket. They thaw quickly and make dumpling-making so much easier, freeing me up to play around with new and delicious fillings.

Flours

Cornflour (cornstarch)

I always have cornflour in a jar sitting next to my salt, pepper and sugar. I mainly use it for two things: in batter mixtures to make a good crispy coating, and to thicken sauces. When I use it for thickening, I mix it with cold water (not hot, or it will make the sauce turn gloopy), then pour it in at the end. Reduce the heat when pouring in the cornflour mixture, and remember to add it slowly, stirring all the while. Potato starch is also hugely popular in Asian cooking, and is often used in place of cornflour to thicken sauces.

Dumpling wheat flour

This is a high-gluten wheat flour (also known as dumpling flour). The higher gluten content creates a more elastic dough, which is easier to work with when wrapping and filling dumplings. The end result will also be slightly chewier in texture. I love how the flour is also super fine and white, which creates a really smooth, white-coloured dough.

Low-gluten wheat flour

This flour is used when a soft and delicate texture is needed, typically for steamed buns and cakes, like my delicate **Bao Buns with Five-Spiced Pork Belly** (page 116). I also use it in my **Chinese Spring Onion Pancakes** (page 95) to create a lovely smooth and light dough.

Batch-cooking

Asian cuisine really lends itself to batch-cooking. Sometimes when I am preparing a curry or a stew, I like to make a larger portion and divide it into smaller containers so they're ready to grab during the week. Freezing homemade dumplings is also a great way to batch-make a quick and tasty snack for when you are feeling a bit peckish – see page 108.

Cooking utensils

You don't need a kitchen full of fancy equipment to cook Asian food, but a few key tools do make life easier. These are the things I use all the time. You'll be grateful to see a nice overlap with Western cooking utensils, too.

Steamer

I use a bamboo steamer for dumplings, bao buns and gyozas. It sits perfectly over a wok or pot of boiling water. Metal steamers work too, but bamboo feels more authentic and looks beautiful on any table.

Rice cooker

A rice cooker takes all the guesswork out of cooking rice. I grew up with a rice cooker and still use one almost daily; it's one of those appliances that definitely earns its place on the counter. They come in different capacities, so choose one based on your family size. They have a useful warming feature once the rice is cooked.

Chinese cleaver

A Chinese cleaver looks intimidating, but it's incredibly versatile. The one I use is a half-sized cleaver, meaning the blade is not as deep. I use it for everything: slicing meat, chopping vegetables, crushing garlic, even scooping ingredients into the wok. The wide blade makes it easy to transfer chopped food, and the weight does most of the work for you. Once you have mastered it, you'll love it.

Sharp knives

Beyond a cleaver, having a good sharp chef's knife and a small paring knife makes prep work so much faster. Asian cooking involves a lot of chopping, so sharp knives aren't just convenient; they're essential.

Wok

A wok is essential for stir-frying. The sloped sides allow you to toss ingredients without them flying everywhere, and the shape concentrates heat for quick, high-temperature cooking. I use mine for stir-fries, deep-frying, steaming and even making fried rice. Carbon steel woks are best; they heat up quickly and develop a natural non-stick surface over time. I recommend choosing a wok with a diameter of at least 33cm (13in). The last thing you want is for the wok to be overcrowded. If that happens, you won't be stir-frying, you will be stewing.

Pestle and mortar

I use a pestle and mortar to grind spices, make curry pastes, and crush garlic and chillies. Doing this releases oils and aromas in a way that a blender just can't. A large, heavy granite one is best; the mortar (the bowl) won't slip around and the pestle will be able to handle tougher ingredients. The technique is to pound in a circular motion, scraping from the sides into the centre as you go. If you're grinding dry spices, toast them lightly in a dry pan first to wake up their flavour. The smell alone is worth it, believe me.

Fine grater (microplane)

A fine grater is perfect for grating ginger and garlic into a paste. It saves so much time. I use mine constantly; it's small but useful, not to mention very satisfying to use.

Mandoline or julienne peeler

A mandoline or julienne peeler makes quick work of shredding vegetables into thin, even strips. I use mine for salads, pickles and garnishes. Just be careful; they're sharp and it's easy to catch your fingers if you aren't paying attention.

Wire sieve (spider strainer)

A wire sieve or spider strainer is essential for scooping dumplings, noodles or fried food out of boiling water or oil. It drains quickly and doesn't hold heat like a slotted spoon. I use mine every time I make noodles or deep-fry anything.

Ladle

A good ladle is essential for serving soups, broths and curries. I prefer one with a deep bowl and a long handle, so I can reach into large pots without burning myself.

Citrus juicer

A simple handheld juicer is perfect for getting every drop of juice from limes and lemons. Asian cooking uses a lot of citrus, and squeezing by hand just doesn't get it all out.

Casserole dish (Dutch oven)

A good casserole dish (Dutch oven) or heavy-bottomed pot is essential for braising, making curries and cooking rice on the stove. It distributes heat evenly and holds temperature well, which prevents burning.

Saibashi (Japanese cooking chopsticks)

Made from wood or bamboo, these are longer than eating chopsticks, and are perfect for stir-frying, turning and fishing things out of hot oil. They give you more control than tongs and won't scratch your wok. Once you get used to them, you'll use them for everything.

Wooden spoons and spatulas

Wooden spoons and spatulas won't scratch your wok or non-stick pans, and they don't conduct heat. I use them for stirring, tossing and scraping up all those bits stuck to the bottom of the pan.

壽
壽

Asian cooking techniques

Asian cooking isn't just about having the right ingredients; it's about understanding the techniques that bring those ingredients to life. Growing up, I learned these methods by watching my mum and dad in the kitchen, and over time, they became second nature. What I love about Asian cooking is that once you master these core techniques, you can apply them to almost any dish. Here are the ones I use most often, along with the tips and tricks that make all the difference.

Cooking rice

Growing up in an Asian household, I have always used a rice cooker to cook rice; it gives me perfect rice every time. I love that once you set it, you can leave it cooking, and when it's done, it keeps the rice warm until you are ready to eat. It is also very versatile - I often add raw chicken and vegetables at the start and let them cook together with the rice. Simple, quick and delicious! If you don't have a rice cooker, though, don't worry - I have included instructions for cooking rice in a saucepan too. However you choose to cook your rice, there are a few essential rules to follow.

First, you need to properly rinse the rice to remove excess starch. Rinse it in cool water, agitating gently with your fingers, then drain the cloudy water and repeat until the water runs mostly clear. This prevents gumminess and ensures fluffy, separated grains.

Second, you need to get the water ratio right when cooking. I always measure the water levels using the finger-tip method, and it never fails. Start by shaking the pot of rice gently to level the rice at the bottom, then place your middle finger so the tip touches the surface of the rice. Add cold water until it reaches halfway to the first knuckle crease of your finger, or to the top of your nail. Give it a go. You will be surprised how effective this method is. (However, if you prefer precise measurements, they're mentioned in the recipes.)

Third, you must control the heat and have patience. Rice cooking has two phases: boiling to gelatinise the starch, then steaming to finish cooking. Never rush or lift the lid until it's ready, or you'll release crucial steam and create uneven cooking. Let it rest for 10 minutes after cooking with the lid on; this final steaming makes all the difference.

Stir-frying

Stir-frying is all about high heat, speed, and constant movement. The key is to have everything prepped and ready before you turn on the stove. Once you start, there's no time to chop or measure. Your wok needs to be smoking hot before you add oil, and then you need to work fast, tossing and stirring constantly so nothing burns. I always cook ingredients in batches rather than crowding the wok, which drops the temperature and causes stewing instead of frying. You want that smoky, slightly charred flavour; it's called wok hei, and it's the hallmark of great stir-frying.

Marinating

In Asian cooking, we almost always marinate meat before stir-frying. A basic marinade includes soy sauce for saltiness, a bit of sugar to help caramelisation, sesame oil to add some nuttiness, and sometimes cornflour (cornstarch) to create a protective coating that locks in moisture. One trick I use for tougher cuts of beef is adding a tiny pinch of bicarbonate of soda (baking soda) to the marinade. It breaks down the proteins and makes the meat tender.

Seasoning the wok

When you first get a carbon steel wok, you need to season it by heating it over a gas flame until it's smoking, then rubbing oil all over the surface. Repeat this a few times, and a dark patina will build up. Never use soap on a seasoned wok; just rinse with hot water and scrub gently with a brush. The more you use it, the better it gets. A well-seasoned wok is naturally non-stick and adds that smoky flavour you can't get from a regular pan.

After cooking, clean the wok while it's still warm, dry it completely over the heat, and rub a thin layer of oil over the surface to prevent rust. A good wok becomes an heirloom. My mum's wok is over 30 years old, and cooks better than any non-stick pan.

Steaming

Steaming is very commonplace in Asian cuisine. It's one of the healthiest and cleanest ways to cook. What I love about steaming is that you can cook multiple things at once. You stack bamboo steamers on top of each other over a single pot of boiling water, and you've got a whole meal going. The key is to make sure the water is boiling before you place the steamer on top, and to keep the lid on tightly so steam doesn't escape. You can make your own steamer at home as well if you can't get your hands on a bamboo steamer. Use an up-turned bowl as a trivet inside a lidded pot. For dumplings, I line the steamer with baking paper or cabbage leaves, so they don't stick.

Rice

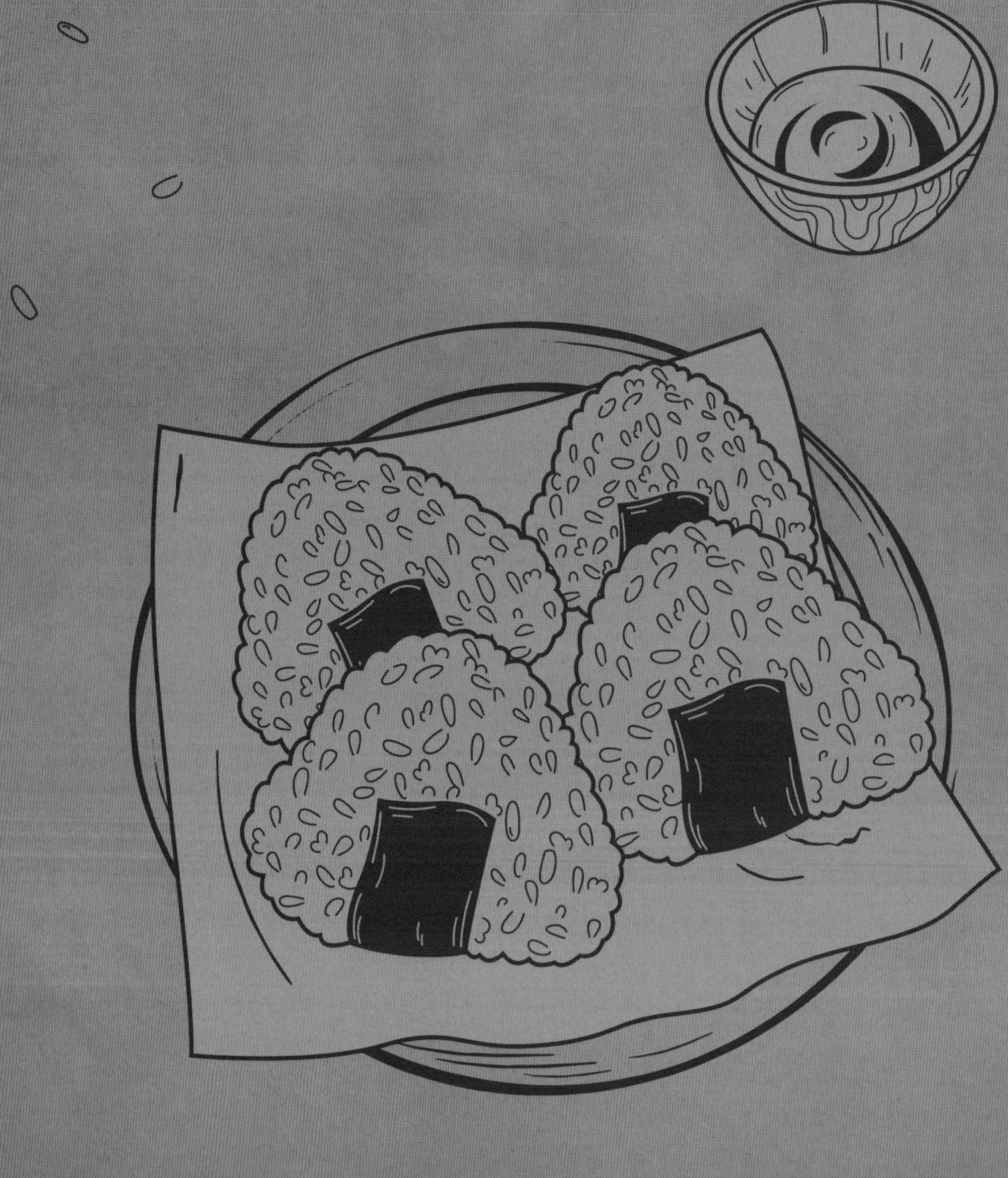

Classic Fried Rice 37

Salmon Sushi Bake 38

Onigiri 42

Japanese Oyakodon with Chicken 44

Korean Beef Bibimbap 46

Chicken Congee 49

Vietnamese Shaking Beef with Red Rice 50

Miso Cod Ochazuke 53

Cantonese Sticky Rice with Chinese Sausage 54

Bacon and Kimchi Fried Rice 55

Classic Fried Rice

Serves: 2 as a main, 4 as a side

Prep time: 15 minutes **Cook time:** 15 minutes

2 tablespoons light soy sauce
1 teaspoon sesame oil
pinch of ground white pepper
1 tablespoon oyster sauce
½ teaspoon mushroom powder (optional)
2 tablespoons neutral oil
1 carrot, peeled and finely diced
2 garlic cloves, finely chopped
2cm (¾in) piece of fresh ginger, finely chopped
2 banana shallots, finely diced
2 eggs, beaten
400g (14oz) cooked jasmine rice
30g (1oz) frozen edamame beans, defrosted
1 pak choi, dark green leaves only, roughly sliced
1 spring onion (scallion), finely chopped
1 red chilli, finely sliced

I make this at least once a week for my kids; they love it, and it is a simple way to get veggies into their diet. Fried rice always brings back the fondest memories of my uncle Hoi. When I was younger, I would visit him every Saturday, and he would whip up fried rice for lunch, using whatever was left from Friday night's dinner. It could be some black bean spare ribs, stir-fried Asian veggies like choi sum, or braised white radish with beef. I would watch him make it, and he taught me a little trick: you know the fried rice is ready when you see the little grains dancing on the bottom of the wok. In this recipe, I have used a special ingredient: mushroom powder (see page 19). This is not essential, but it adds a lovely umami flavour to your fried rice, making it extra delicious.

In a small bowl, mix together the soy sauce, sesame oil, white pepper, oyster sauce and mushroom powder, then set aside.

Heat the neutral oil in a large wok over a medium-high heat. Once hot, add the carrot and stir-fry for 6 minutes until almost fully cooked, then add the garlic, ginger and shallots and stir-fry for 3 minutes more.

Move the vegetables to one side of the wok and pour the beaten egg into the space you've cleared. Let it sit for 30 seconds until it sets slightly, then, while some of the egg is still slightly runny, add the cooked rice and stir everything together.

Pour the sauce into the wok, stirring to combine. Add the edamame and pak choi, and stir-fry for a further 3 minutes until everything is piping hot.

Stir through half the sliced spring onion and red chilli, then spoon the rice into bowls. Garnish with the remaining spring onion and red chilli.

TIPS

- Fried rice is known to be better if you use leftover rice, as the rice grains are drier and firmer and give the fried rice a better texture. Sometimes I cook extra rice the day before, just so that I can prepare fried rice the next day. If you don't have leftover rice, though, you can spread freshly cooked rice on a baking tray to let the moisture evaporate before stir-frying.
- Feel free to use different vegetables, depending on what you have.
- Add small cooked prawns, diced cooked chicken or ham for extra protein and flavour.
- You can make this into a classic cha han by switching the jasmine rice for sushi rice.

Salmon Sushi Bake

Serves: 4

Prep time: 15 minutes **Cook time:** 30 minutes

A sushi bake consists of a layer of sushi rice with a topping, baked in the oven. To eat it, all you do is grab a small piece of nori seaweed, scoop up some of the sushi bake on to it and enjoy. No rolling, no cutting, no hassle - just the lovely flavours of sushi! The first time I tried a sushi bake was when a friend from the Philippines made it for me. She told me they make this dish a lot as it's perfect for gatherings. I've included instructions for a very simple furikake, which you can buy ready-made in many different flavours if you prefer.

300g (10½oz) sushi rice
400g (14oz) skinless salmon fillets
¾ teaspoon salt
2 tablespoons Japanese rice vinegar
1 tablespoon caster (superfine) sugar
100g (3½oz) Japanese mayonnaise (see page 25)
50g (1¾oz) cream cheese
2 tablespoons sriracha
1 tablespoon Japanese soy sauce (see page 21)
1 teaspoon sesame oil
2 spring onions (scallions), finely sliced

FOR THE FURIKAKE
1 nori sheet, cut into 3cm (1¼in) squares
½ tablespoon sesame seeds, toasted

FOR THE SRIRACHA MAYONNAISE
5 tablespoons Japanese mayonnaise
2 tablespoons sriracha

TO SERVE
1 avocado, peeled, stoned and finely sliced
8–10 nori sheets, each cut into 6 squares

TIP

✱ If I'm serving this dish to children, I leave out the sriracha in the bake and serve it without the sriracha mayonnaise, or only drizzle it on half the dish so that adults can enjoy it.

Preheat the oven to 180°C fan (350°F/gas mark 4).

Rinse the sushi rice under cold water until the water runs clear. Tip the rinsed rice into a saucepan and add 375ml (1½ cups) water. Bring to the boil, then reduce the heat to low and cover with a lid. Simmer for 15 minutes, then remove from the heat and leave to sit, still covered, for 10 minutes. Alternatively, use a rice cooker.

Meanwhile, season the salmon with ½ teaspoon of the salt, then air-fry at 180°C (350°F) for 8–10 minutes until cooked through. Once cooked, remove to a plate and leave to cool before flaking into large pieces. Alternatively, cook in an oven preheated to 180°C fan (350°F/gas mark 4) for 10 minutes.

To make the furikake, place a small frying pan over a medium heat. Add the nori and sesame seeds, and dry-fry for 2 minutes until the seaweed pieces are crispy. Tip into a bowl and crush the nori into little pieces, then set aside. If you prefer, you can blitz it in a spice grinder.

In a small bowl, combine the rice vinegar, sugar and remaining ¼ teaspoon salt, and stir until the sugar and salt dissolve. Stir this mixture into the warm rice.

In another bowl, combine the mayonnaise, cream cheese, sriracha, soy sauce and sesame oil. Stir until smooth, then add the cooked, flaked salmon and half the sliced spring onions and stir.

To assemble, tip the seasoned sushi rice into a 20 × 25cm (8 × 10in) baking dish and spread out into an even layer. Sprinkle half of the furikake over the top, then add the salmon mixture and spread it out into an even layer over the rice. Sprinkle the remaining furikake over the top, then bake for 15 minutes, or until the top is slightly golden and bubbling.

Meanwhile, combine the sriracha mayonnaise ingredients and set aside.

Remove the sushi bake from the oven and drizzle with the sriracha mayonnaise, then garnish with the avocado and remaining spring onions. Slice into squares and serve warm, with the nori sheets for scooping.

Salmon Sushi Bake, page 38

Onigiri, page 42

Onigiri

Makes: 8 onigiri

Prep time: 15 minutes **Cook time:** 20–25 minutes

360g (12¾oz) sushi rice
3 tablespoons sushi vinegar (see page 25)
¼ teaspoon salt
½ teaspoon caster (superfine) sugar
1 nori sheet, cut into 8 strips
toasted white sesame seeds, to garnish

FOR THE FILLING
100g (3½oz) tinned tuna
2 tablespoons tinned sweetcorn
3 tablespoons Japanese mayonnaise (see page 25)

I first had these fun, triangular Japanese rice parcels (pictured previous page) in a convenience store in Tokyo when I was about fourteen years old. I remember having to decipher a three-step illustration on the packaging on how to successfully unwrap it - quite the ordeal when all I wanted to do was take a bite! There were lots of fillings to choose from, including pickled plum, tuna mayo, crab mayo and Japanese eel, but the one I chose was salmon mayo. It was so tasty, and the coolest part was that you could easily eat it on the go.

Fast-forward to my life now, and I often make these for my kids' lunchboxes. I tell them that they are fancy Japanese rice sandwiches, and they love them.

Thoroughly rinse the rice in cold running water until the water runs clear. You will have to do this a few times to ensure the rice is properly rinsed.

Combine the rice and 500ml (2 cups) water in a saucepan. Place over a medium heat and bring to the boil, then cover and reduce the heat to low. Leave to simmer for 10-15 minutes until the water has evaporated, then turn off the heat and leave to steam for another 10-15 minutes. Alternatively, use a rice cooker.

Once the rice is ready, season it with the sushi vinegar, salt and sugar while it is still hot. Mix well with a flat rice paddle or plastic spatula to avoid breaking any grains, then transfer to a large tray. Spread it out evenly and leave to cool for 15-20 minutes.

To make the filling, combine the tuna, sweetcorn and mayonnaise in a small bowl. Mix and set aside.

When the rice has cooled, it's time to shape the onigiri. To do this, wet your hands with a little water, then take about 115g (4oz) of the rice and gently roll it to form a ball.

Now, gently shape the ball into a triangle. Flatten the rice triangle slightly, then place 1 teaspoon of the filling in the centre, and cover it with a little more rice. Carefully press the filled rice back into a triangle shape, making sure to not expose the filling. Repeat until all the rice and filling have been used up.

To finish, wrap a strip of nori around the onigiri just before serving, and garnish the top with a sprinkling of sesame seeds.

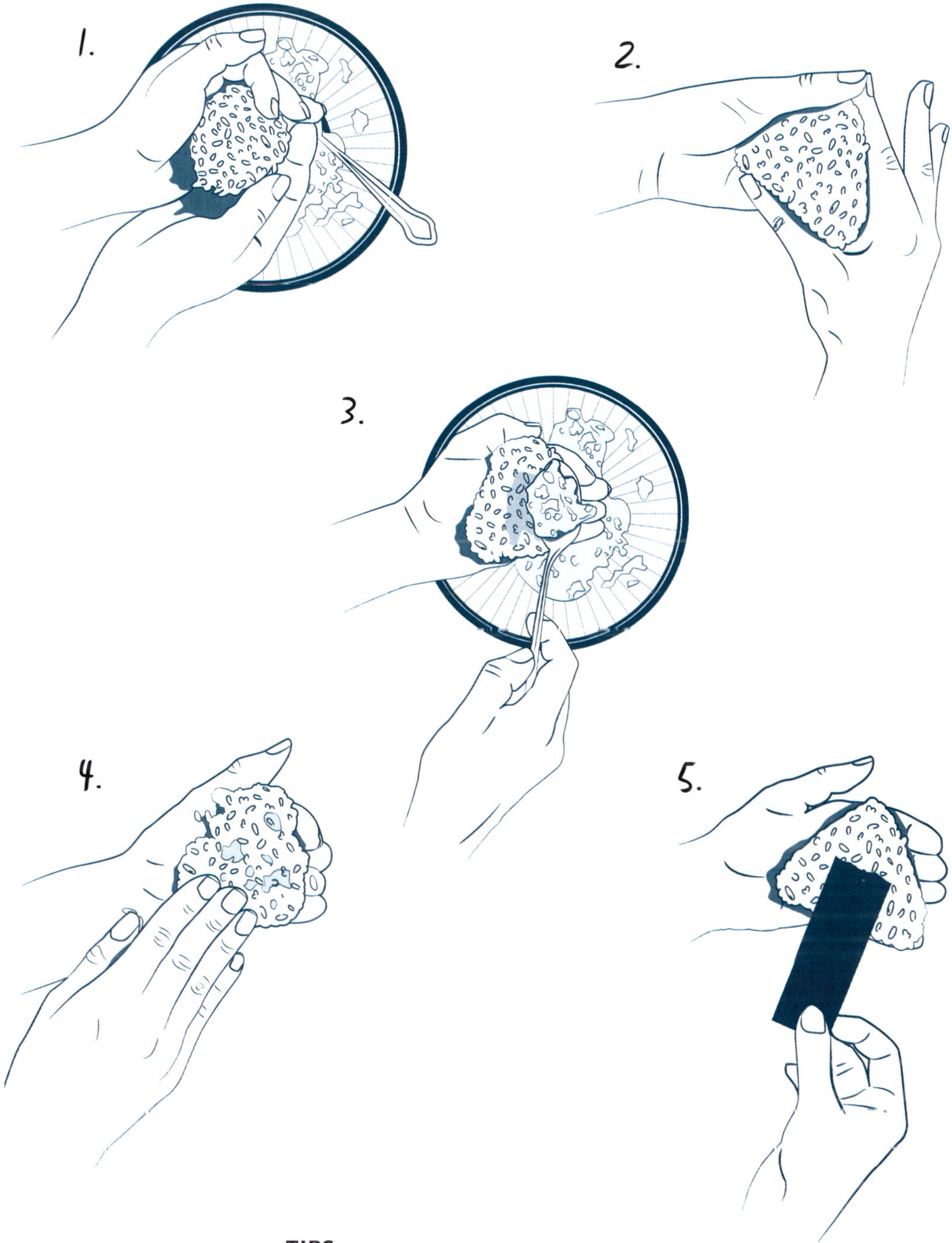

TIPS

- ✱ Keep a small bowl of water nearby to wet your hands as you go - this stops the rice sticking to your hands.
- ✱ If you don't like tuna, you can replace it with the same amount of cooked salmon and omit the sweetcorn.
- ✱ Onigiri can be eaten at room temperature and stored in the fridge for up to 24 hours, although it's best eaten on the same day it's made.

Japanese Oyakodon with Chicken

Serves: 2

Prep time: 10 minutes **Cook time:** 10 minutes

275g (9¾oz) sushi rice
250ml (1 cup) dashi stock (see tip)
2 tablespoons Japanese soy sauce (see page 21)
1 tablespoon mirin (see page 25)
1 tablespoon sake (see page 25)
1 teaspoon caster (superfine) sugar
½ onion, thinly sliced
200g (7oz) boneless chicken thigh or breast, cut into bite-sized pieces
2 large eggs, gently beaten
2 spring onions (scallions), thinly sliced
shichimi togarashi (see page 19), to serve (optional – you could also use lightly crushed chilli flakes)

Oyakodon is a Japanese rice bowl topped with a soft omelette. It is quick to make and perfect for a tasty weekday meal. The secret is in the careful simmering of the egg, which is mixed with a flavoursome dashi broth that adds a lovely flavour and helps to give this dish its slightly runny texture. I remember having this dish at a very traditional Japanese canteen in the heart of the central business district in Hong Kong, where I was working. The menu was in Japanese, and the staff only spoke Japanese, so my only hope of ordering was to point at what someone else was having and order that. It turned out to be oyakodon, and it was so worth it! One of the nicest omelettes I have ever had. In this recipe, I have used chicken, but this can be substituted with pork, Japanese eel, fish cake or salmon.

Rinse the sushi rice under cold water until the water runs clear. Tip the rinsed rice into a saucepan and add 275ml (generous 1 cup) water. Bring to the boil, then reduce the heat to low and cover with a lid. Simmer for 15 minutes, then remove from the heat and leave to sit, still covered, for 10 minutes. Alternatively, use a rice cooker.

Meanwhile, pour the dashi stock into a saucepan, then add the soy sauce, mirin, sake and sugar. Add the onion and bring to a simmer over a medium heat. Cook for 2–3 minutes until the onion has slightly softened and mellowed in flavour, then add the chicken pieces and simmer for a further 5–6 minutes until the chicken is cooked through.

Pour the beaten eggs over the simmering chicken and onion, pouring in a circular motion. Cover the pan with a lid and cook for 2 minutes, or until the egg is just set but still slightly runny.

Spoon the hot rice into deep bowls. Gently slide or scoop the egg-and-chicken mixture over the top of the rice. Garnish with spring onions and a sprinkling of shichimi togarashi or chilli flakes to serve.

TIP

* To make your own fresh dashi stock, see page 25. If you prefer, you can use 6g (⅛oz) dashi powder mixed with 250ml (1 cup) just-boiled water.

Korean Beef Bibimbap

Serves: 2

Prep time: 30 minutes **Cook time:** 30 minutes

200g (7oz) Korean short-grain or sushi rice
neutral oil, for frying the eggs
2 eggs

FOR THE BEEF

200g (7oz) beef sirloin, cut into very thin strips
2 teaspoons Korean soy sauce (see page 21)
1 teaspoon sesame oil
1 teaspoon soft light brown sugar
1 garlic clove, minced
1 tablespoon neutral oil

FOR THE VEGETABLES

4 tablespoons sesame oil
200g (7oz) Chinese spinach, cut into 5cm (2in) pieces
1 garlic clove, finely sliced
4 teaspoons Korean soy sauce
1 teaspoon salt
150g (5½oz) beansprouts
90g (3¼oz) carrot, peeled and julienned
80g (2¾oz) shiitake mushrooms, thinly sliced

FOR THE BIBIMBAP SAUCE

4 tablespoons gochujang (see page 24)
1 tablespoon Korean soy sauce
1 tablespoon Korean apple vinegar (see page 25) or white rice vinegar
1 teaspoon sesame oil
1 garlic clove, minced
1 tablespoon caster (superfine) sugar
1 teaspoon toasted sesame seeds, plus extra to serve

Bibimbap is a classic Korean rice dish. It typically consists of seasoned vegetables, meat and a fried egg, served on top of rice with a side of gochujang sauce. The presentation of this dish is very special. Each of the vegetables is cooked separately and arranged separately on top of the finished dish. I like to make bibimbap in a dolsot, which is a traditional Korean stone bowl, but you can use a regular bowl too.

Rinse the rice under cold water until the water runs clear. Tip the rinsed rice into a saucepan and add 275ml (generous 1 cup) water. Bring to the boil, then reduce the heat to low and cover with a lid. Simmer for 15 minutes, then remove from the heat and leave to sit, still covered, for 10 minutes. Alternatively, use a rice cooker.

Meanwhile, in a small bowl, combine all the ingredients for the bibimbap sauce. Mix well and set aside.

Place the thinly sliced beef in a separate bowl, and add the Korean soy sauce, sesame oil, brown sugar and garlic. Stir to combine, then set aside.

To prepare the vegetables, heat 1 tablespoon of the sesame oil in a non-stick wok over a medium heat. Add the spinach and garlic, and stir-fry for 2-3 minutes until wilted. Season with 1 teaspoon of the soy sauce and ¼ teaspoon salt. Set aside in a bowl.

Add another 1 tablespoon of the sesame oil to the wok, followed by the beansprouts. Stir-fry for 2 minutes, then season with 1 teaspoon of the soy sauce and ¼ teaspoon salt. Set aside in a bowl.

Repeat this stir-frying and seasoning process for the carrot (2–3 minutes) and mushrooms (2–3 minutes), setting each element aside after cooking.

Now heat the 1 tablespoon neutral oil in the wok over a medium-high heat. Add the beef and stir-fry for about 3 minutes until fully cooked. Set aside.

Lastly, heat a small drizzle of oil in a frying pan over a medium-high heat and fry the eggs until done to your liking.

If you're using Korean stone bowls to serve, place each bowl over a gas hob, brush with a thin layer of sesame oil and add half the rice to each, increasing the heat slowly so that the rice crisps up on the bottom. If using regular bowls, simply divide your rice between the bowls.

Arrange the beef, spinach, beansprouts, carrot and mushrooms neatly over the rice in sections, then top each bowl with a fried egg and a sprinkle of toasted sesame seeds. Drizzle with the bibimbap sauce or serve it on the side. Mix everything together before eating. Enjoy!

Chicken Congee

Serves: 4

Prep time: 15 minutes **Cook time:** 1½ hours

1 tablespoon neutral oil
4 bone-in, skin-on chicken legs (marylands), cut into thighs and drumsticks
2.5cm (1in) piece of fresh ginger, peeled and roughly chopped
2 spring onions (scallions), roughly chopped
150g (5½oz) jasmine rice
¼ teaspoon ground white pepper
1½ teaspoons salt

FOR THE TOPPING

2 spring onions, finely sliced
2.5cm (1in) piece of fresh ginger, peeled and cut into thin matchsticks

Congee, or rice porridge, is a popular dish in Asia, with many regional variations and differing names. Although congee is often associated with breakfast, you can enjoy it at any time. It is a deeply comforting dish: when I was growing up, my mum would make plain congee for me anytime I felt poorly, and I would spice it up by crushing a packet of Tayto cheese and onion crisps over the top. Another version I will always remember was the one my confinement lady made for me in the days after I had my first baby, George. It had red dates, yam, goji berries and shredded pork, and was garnished with sesame oil and coriander (cilantro). It was delicious and nutritious, and shows how versatile congee can be.

Heat the oil in a large stockpot over a medium heat. Once hot, add the chicken and lightly brown on all sides for 8–10 minutes, then add the ginger and spring onions and cook for a further minute or so until fragrant. Add the rice and stir to coat in the aromatics, then pour in 1.8 litres (7 cups) water. Bring to the boil, then reduce the heat to a gentle simmer and cook for 1 hour, stirring occasionally.

After an hour, remove the chicken from the pot and set aside on a plate. Add another 300ml (10½fl oz) cold water to the pot, and increase the heat slightly. Cook the rice for a further 30 minutes until the grains are broken down but not gloopy.

Meanwhile, shred the chicken using 2 forks and season with the white pepper and ½ teaspoon of the salt.

Stir the chicken into the congee, keeping a little back for garnish. Season the congee with the remaining 1 teaspoon salt, then ladle it into bowls and garnish with the reserved chicken, sliced spring onions and ginger matchsticks. Serve immediately.

TIPS

✱ I sometimes like to top my congee with something crispy for texture. For a really quick fix, you can follow my childhood method of crumbling over some crisps! Alternatively, pour neutral oil into a saucepan to a depth of 2.5cm (1in) and heat until it reaches 180°C (350°F). Meanwhile, cut some defrosted wonton wrappers into thin strips or triangles. Once the oil is hot enough, fry the sliced wrappers for 1–2 minutes until crispy and puffed up, then remove and drain on paper towels before using as a crispy, crunchy topping.

✱ I sometimes reheat frozen youtiao (fried dough sticks) to enjoy with the congee. You can buy them in most Asian supermarkets. Simply follow the instructions on the packet to prepare.

Serves: 2

Vietnamese Shaking Beef with Red Rice

Prep time: 15 minutes, plus marinating **Cook time:** 30 minutes

- 250g (9oz) beef sirloin or ribeye, cut into 2.5cm (1in) cubes
- 2 tablespoons neutral oil
- 2 red onions, thinly sliced

FOR THE MARINADE

- 1 tablespoon Vietnamese soy sauce (see page 21) or light soy sauce
- 1 tablespoon fish sauce
- 1 tablespoon oyster sauce
- ½ teaspoon freshly ground black pepper
- ½ teaspoon bicarbonate of soda (baking soda)

FOR THE RED RICE

- 1 tablespoon neutral oil
- 2 garlic cloves, minced
- 400g (14oz) cooked jasmine rice, cooled
- 2½ tablespoons tomato paste (concentrated purée)
- 2 teaspoons Vietnamese soy sauce (see page 21)
- ½ teaspoon granulated sugar
- ¼ teaspoon salt

TO SERVE

- ½ head frisée lettuce (curly endive)
- 1 tomato, cut into wedges
- ½ large cucumber, sliced

This dish was described to me by my Vietnamese friends as Vietnam's version of steak and onions. The name 'shaking beef' comes from the technique of shaking small cubes of beef with onion in a hot pan to ensure they're seared on all sides. The red rice is a tomato-and-garlic-flavoured jasmine rice. It's very simple to make, but super tasty - and it goes really well with the beef. My marinade for the beef includes a little bicarbonate of soda, which helps with tenderising. I first tried this dish in a small, bustling restaurant down a side street in Hanoi. The place was hot and noisy, and you could see the chefs tossing the beef in flaming woks, getting the meat perfectly charred and flavoured. It was incredible, all washed down with a refreshing iced lime soda.

In a bowl, mix the beef cubes with the marinade ingredients. Cover and leave to marinate for 30 minutes at room temperature, or overnight in the fridge.

To prepare the rice, heat the 1 tablespoon neutral oil in a medium saucepan over a medium heat. Add the garlic and fry for 20 seconds, taking care not to let it burn, then add the cooked, cooled rice, along with the tomato paste, soy sauce, sugar and salt. Stir-fry for 3-4 minutes until the tomato purée is well distributed and the rice is piping hot. Divide between 2 bowls.

For the beef, heat the 2 tablespoons neutral oil in a large wok or frying pan over a high heat until smoking hot. Add the red onions and cook for 30 seconds, then add just enough of the beef to sear in a single layer in the wok - you will probably need to do this in batches, as if you overcrowd the pan, the beef will start to boil instead of fry. Let the beef cook, undisturbed, for 1-2 minutes to give the outsides a lovely crust, then shake or toss for 3-4 minutes to cook it medium-rare. Remove the cooked onions and beef from the pan and repeat with the remaining beef if needed.

Arrange the lettuce, tomatoes and cucumber on a serving platter, and top with the hot shaking beef and onions. Serve alongside the red rice.

Miso Cod Ochazuke

Serves: 2

Prep time: 20 minutes, plus marinating **Cook time:** 10 minutes

300ml (10½fl oz) dashi stock (see tip)
½ teaspoon Japanese soy sauce (see page 21)
1 teaspoon mirin (see page 25)

FOR THE MISO COD
60ml (¼ cup) sake (see page 25)
60ml (¼ cup) mirin
3 tablespoons white miso paste
2 tablespoons caster (superfine) sugar
2 large skin-on cod fillets, around 150g (5½oz) each
1 tablespoon neutral oil

TO SERVE
200g (7oz) steamed Japanese short-grain rice
1 nori sheet, shredded or cut into thin strips
2 teaspoons toasted white sesame seeds
1 tablespoon pickled ginger or umeboshi, thinly sliced

Ochazuke is a Japanese rice bowl, served with various toppings and soaked in dashi or green tea. In this recipe, I am making miso cod as the main topping, which works really well with a light dashi broth. Usually, I get the cod marinating in the morning before heading to work. That way, when I get home, I just need to bake it in the oven while the rice is cooking. This dish is quite complex and sophisticated in flavour, yet simple to make. I sometimes serve it at dinner parties, pouring the dashi stock into a teapot to serve at the table.

Begin by preparing the cod. Combine the sake and mirin in a small saucepan over a medium-high heat. Bring to the boil and boil for 1 minute, then reduce the heat to low. Add the miso paste and whisk until smooth, then add the sugar and stir until dissolved. Pour the mixture into a lidded container and allow to cool.

Once cool, add the cod, then cover and leave to marinate in the fridge for 8–10 hours or overnight, depending on how much time you have, turning once or twice.

When you're ready to cook, preheat the oven to 210°C fan (450°F/gas mark 6–7). Wipe any excess marinade off the cod, which could cause it to burn. The saltiness in the miso pulls the moisture from the fish, so it should have firmed up and will be quite easy to handle.

Meanwhile, heat the oil in an ovenproof frying pan over a medium heat. Place the fish, flesh-side down, into the hot oil and cook for 3 minutes on each side until slightly blackened and nicely charred. Transfer the whole pan into the oven and cook for 5–6 minutes until the cod is cooked through and the flesh is opaque.

While the cod is cooking, heat the dashi stock in a small saucepan over a medium heat, then add the soy sauce and mirin to season.

To serve, divide the hot rice between 2 bowls and top with the cooked miso cod. Sprinkle over the nori, sesame seeds, pickled ginger or umeboshi, then pour the hot dashi over the rice – just enough to gently soak it, but not drown it. Serve immediately, with any extra dashi on the side.

TIPS

* If you're in a rush, you can skip the long marinating time – your fish will not be as firm, but will still taste delicious!
* To make your own fresh dashi stock, see page 25. If you prefer, you can use 8g (⅓oz) dashi powder mixed with 300ml (10½fl oz) just-boiled water.
* You can replace the nori and sesame seeds with 1 tablespoon furikake.

Cantonese Sticky Rice with Chinese Sausage

Serves: 4

Prep time: 20 minutes **Cook time:** 25 minutes

- 200g (7oz) glutinous rice (see page 11)
- 100g (3½oz) jasmine rice
- 1 teaspoon dark soy sauce
- ½ teaspoon salt
- 6 dried shiitake mushrooms
- 15g (½oz) small dried shrimp (see page 26)
- 2 tablespoons neutral oil
- 2 Chinese sausages (lap cheong), thinly sliced
- 2 spring onions (scallions), finely sliced, to serve
- small handful of coriander (cilantro), finely chopped, to serve

FOR THE SAUCE

- 1½ tablespoons light soy sauce
- 1½ tablespoons dark soy sauce
- 1 tablespoon oyster sauce
- 1 teaspoon Shaoxing wine (see page 22)
- 1 teaspoon granulated sugar
- ½ teaspoon salt
- ½ teaspoon sesame oil

Known as lao mei fan in Chinese, the main ingredient in this recipe is a gloriously sticky glutinous white rice. It can be served sweet, but here I have offered a savoury recipe, with Chinese sausage, shiitake mushrooms, soy sauce and a sprinkling of freshly chopped spring onions and coriander. There are essentially two ways to make this dish. The first is to constantly stir-fry the rice from raw, slowly adding water to get the right texture - this is very time-consuming. The second way (and the way I prefer) is to cook the rice first, and then mix it all together. This method is much quicker - and just as delicious.

Begin by combining the glutinous rice and jasmine rice in a sieve, then rinsing thoroughly in cold water until the water runs clear. You will have to do this a few times to ensure the rice is properly rinsed.

Tip the rinsed rice into a small saucepan and add 400ml (14fl oz) cold water, along with the dark soy and salt. Stir and bring to the boil, then reduce the heat to medium and cover with a lid. Simmer for 20 minutes, then remove from the heat and leave to sit, still covered, for 10 minutes. Alternatively, use a rice cooker.

Meanwhile, put the dried mushrooms in a small bowl and pour over enough just-boiled water to cover. Leave to rehydrate for 10 minutes. In a separate bowl, do the same with the dried shrimp. Once they've finished soaking, finely chop the mushrooms, reserving their soaking liquid. Drain the shrimp and roughly pat dry with paper towels.

To make the sauce, mix 6 tablespoons of the reserved mushroom soaking liquid with the sauce ingredients, then set aside.

Once the rice is cooked, tip it into a large shallow bowl and leave to cool for 15 minutes.

Heat a non-stick wok over a high heat. Once hot, add the oil and give it a swirl to coat the wok. Add the Chinese sausage, shrimp and chopped mushrooms and cook, stirring, for 2-3 minutes until everything is fragrant and lightly golden. Now add the rice to the wok and stir briefly before pouring over the sauce. Stir-fry everything for a few minutes until the rice is piping hot, mixing thoroughly so the rice is evenly coated and takes on a rich, brown colour. Add a splash of water or any extra mushroom soaking liquid if the rice feels too dry.

Divide the rice between bowls and garnish with some sliced spring onions and chopped coriander.

Bacon and Kimchi Fried Rice

Serves: 2

Prep time: 10 minutes **Cook time:** 5 minutes

1 tablespoon neutral oil, plus extra for frying the eggs
80g (2¾oz) smoked streaky bacon, finely chopped
80g (2¾oz) kimchi, roughly chopped
2 banana shallots, finely diced
2 garlic cloves, finely diced
1 spring onion (scallion), white and green parts separated, thinly sliced
300g (10½oz) steamed Korean short-grain rice or sushi rice
2 eggs

FOR THE SAUCE

2 tablespoons Korean soy sauce (see page 21) or light soy sauce
1 tablespoon gochujang (see page 24)
1 teaspoon sesame oil
½ teaspoon gochugaru (Korean red pepper flakes, see page 19)
¼ teaspoon ground white pepper

TO GARNISH

1 tablespoon toasted sesame seeds

This is a super dish to try if you are new to kimchi. When kimchi is stir-fried, it tastes richer and sweeter, and this is a fantastic way to infuse that distinctive kimchi taste into your fried rice. I often store small cans of kimchi in my pantry because they last much longer than fresh kimchi, and it means I can easily make this dish anytime. This is not a traditional Korean dish, but rather a modern variation with the addition of bacon. In this recipe, I've also used gochujang, which adds an exciting twist, and I've opted for a Korean short-grain rice, which adds a lovely texture.

In a small bowl, combine all the sauce ingredients and mix well.

Heat the neutral oil in a large wok over a medium-high heat. Add the diced bacon and cook for 2-3 minutes, or until crispy. Push the bacon to one side of the pan, then add the kimchi, shallots and garlic, along with the spring onion whites. Sauté in the rendered bacon fat for 1-2 minutes, or until fragrant.

Add the cooked rice, followed by the sauce. Increase the heat to high and stir-fry everything together for another 2-3 minutes until well combined and heated through.

Lastly, heat a small drizzle of neutral oil in a frying pan over a medium-high heat and fry the eggs until done to your liking.

Divide the fried rice between bowls and garnish with the sesame seeds and spring onion greens. Serve hot, with a fried egg on top.

Noodles

Biang Biang Chilli Oil Noodles 59

Singapore Noodles with Char Siu Pork 61

Sausage Gochujang Udon 62

Vietnamese Phở Bò 65

Filipino Pancit Bihon 67

Curry Prawn Laksa 68

Korean Japchae 71

Steamed Beanthread Noodles with Scallops 72

Black Pepper Beef with Crispy Noodle Pancake 75

Pad Thai with Prawns 76

Biang Biang Chilli Oil Noodles

Serves: 2

Prep time: 30 minutes, plus resting **Cook time:** 10 minutes

Biang biang noodles are hand-pulled Chinese wheat noodles that are famously wide, thick and deliciously chewy. In this recipe, we make a quick dough that gets proved twice, and then the fun begins as you pull your own noodles. It's a great dish for getting your friends or kids involved, and banging the noodles on the table to elongate them into thin strips is a great stress-reliever! The noodles cook very quickly, then you get to enjoy them with a homemade (and almost instant) chilli oil.

375g (13oz) plain (all-purpose) flour
½ teaspoon fine salt
neutral oil, for greasing
1 head of pak choi, leaves separated
1 spring onion (scallion), finely sliced

FOR THE CHILLI OIL

2–3 tablespoons chilli flakes, depending on how spicy you like it
1 tablespoon toasted sesame seeds
3 garlic cloves, finely diced
2 spring onions, finely sliced
200ml (7fl oz) neutral oil
3 tablespoons light soy sauce
2 tablespoons black rice vinegar (see page 24)

Combine the flour and salt in a large bowl, then add 200ml (7fl oz) water and mix until a tough dough forms. Remove the dough from the bowl and knead until it becomes smooth. Cover the bowl with a clean tea towel and leave to rest for 20 minutes in a warm place.

After the resting time is up, roll the dough into a log. Cut in half, then divide each half into 6, so you have 12 pieces in total (see illustrations on next page on how to roll and cut the noodles).

Oil your work surface with neutral oil, then take the first piece of dough and use a rolling pin to press it into a rectangle measuring about 5 × 10cm (2 × 4in). Repeat with the remaining pieces of dough, then leave to rest for 2 hours to allow the gluten to relax.

To make the chilli oil, combine the chilli flakes, sesame seeds, chopped garlic and spring onions in a heatproof bowl and stir to combine. Pour the oil into a small saucepan set over a medium-high heat. Heat the oil until it reaches about 130°C (250°F), then carefully pour it over the aromatics in the bowl - it will bubble vigorously. Once the oil has settled, mix everything together, then set aside.

After the dough's resting time is up, bring a large pot of water to the boil, then salt it lightly and reduce to a simmer.

Now, cut each rectangle of dough into 3 long strips. From here, you can begin to pull each strip into a long noodle by slapping it on the bench and gradually stretching it until it's about 45-55cm (18-22in) long. This slapping or banging motion is where the name of the noodle comes from. Place the noodle in a bowl of cold water to prevent sticking, then continue with the remaining dough strips.

Bring the pot of water back to the boil and add the pulled noodles. Cook for 3–4 minutes, depending on their size, then remove the noodles from the water with some tongs and divide between 2 bowls. Add the pak choi to the still-boiling water and cook for 1½-2 minutes, then transfer this to the serving bowls too.

continued →

continued →

Season the chilli oil with the soy sauce and black vinegar, stirring to combine, then dress the biang biang noodles with the oil. Garnish with the finely sliced spring onion, and mix everything together before tucking in.

1.

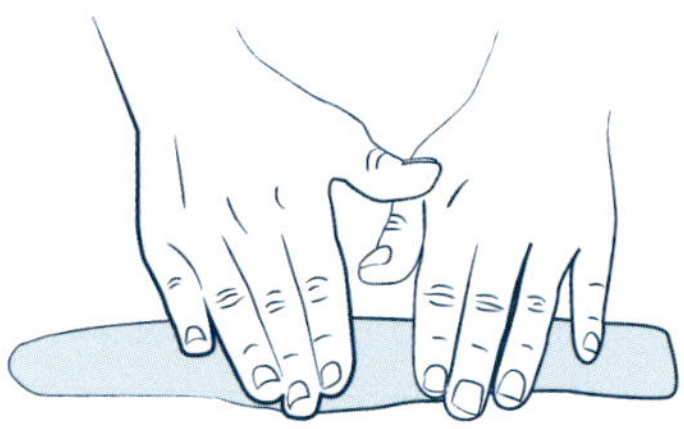

2.

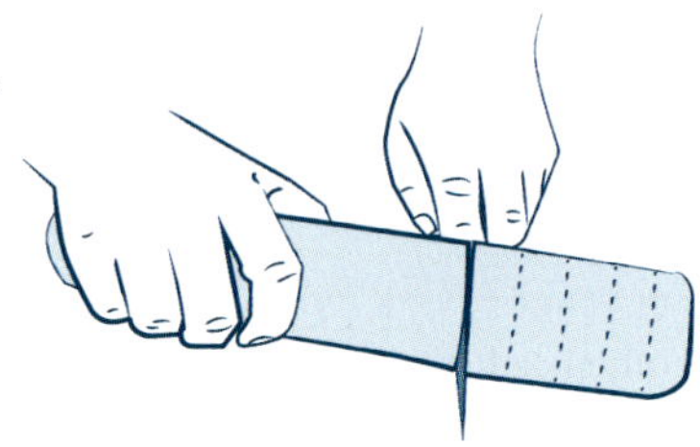

3.

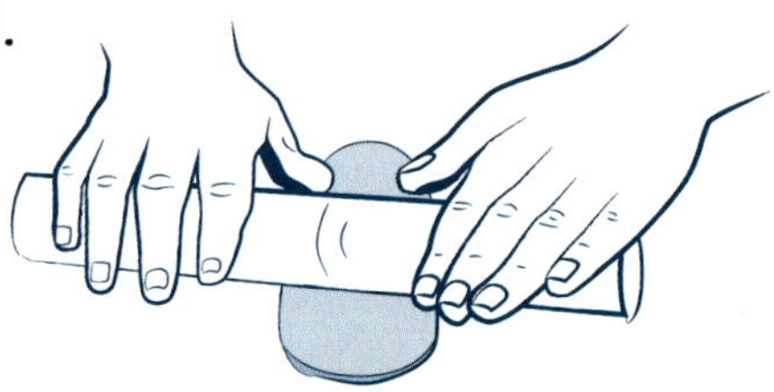

4.

5.

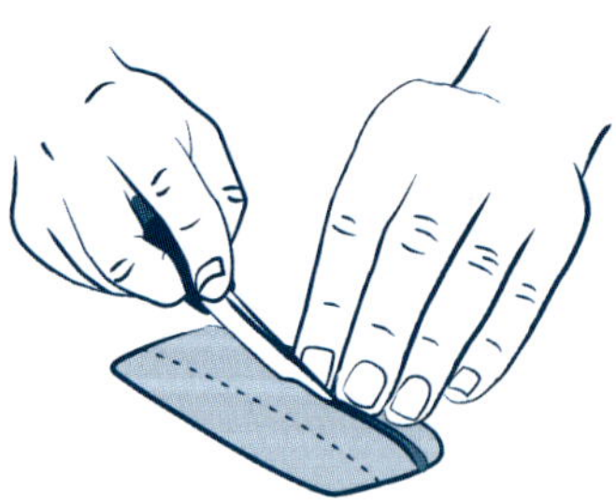

6.

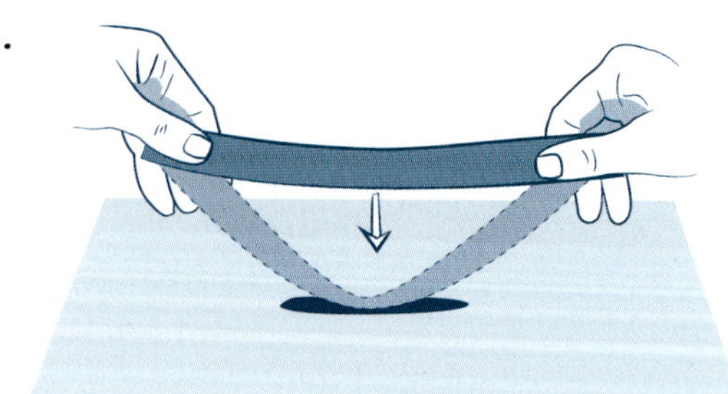

TIP

✱ If you prefer the chilli oil to be less spicy, you can use gochugaru (Korean red pepper flakes, see page 19), which provides that rich red colour without the heat.

Serves: 2

Singapore Noodles with Char Siu Pork

Prep time: 20 minutes, plus marinating **Cook time:** 35 minutes

250g (9oz) rice vermicelli noodles
sesame oil, for drizzling
3 teaspoons neutral oil
1 egg, beaten
80g (2¾oz) raw prawns, peeled and deveined
⅓ green pepper (capsicum), thinly sliced
⅓ red pepper (capsicum), thinly sliced
1 small carrot, julienned
½ red onion, thinly sliced
3 teaspoons mild Indian curry paste
1 tablespoon light soy sauce
pinch of salt
70g (2½oz) Char Siu Pork (see below), thinly sliced
80g (2¾oz) beansprouts
2 spring onions (scallions), cut into 4cm (1½in) pieces, plus extra, finely sliced, to garnish

FOR THE CHAR SIU PORK

200g (7oz) pork neck, collar or fillet
1 tablespoon yellow bean sauce (see page 22)
1 tablespoon hoisin sauce
1 tablespoon oyster sauce
1 tablespoon dark soy sauce
1 tablespoon light soy sauce
2 tablespoons granulated sugar
¼ teaspoon salt
1 tablespoon Shaoxing wine (see page 22)

Singapore noodles is a classic stir-fried noodle dish. Despite the name, it doesn't come from Singapore at all! When I lived there I remember trying to find this dish in restaurants only to discover it didn't really exist. It actually originated in Hong Kong, China, and is an intoxicating mix of Chinese and Indian flavours: a wonderful, moreish noodle dish with a gentle curry hit. I remember having this dish when I was eight years old at a dim sum restaurant, and loving the way it seemed to have a mix of everything in it. The perfect surf-and-turf, Asian style!

The char siu pork makes more than you need for this dish. The rest will keep in the fridge for up to 3 days and is delicious with fried rice.

To make the char siu pork, combine all the ingredients in a large bowl, then mix well to coat the pork. Cover and marinate in the fridge for at least 30 minutes, or ideally overnight.

Preheat the oven to 180°C fan (350°F/gas mark 4), place the marinated pork in a roasting tray and cook for 20 minutes, or until cooked through. Alternatively, air-fry at 180°C (350°F) for 15-20 minutes. Set the pork aside to cool completely. You'll need 70g (2½oz) sliced pork for this recipe.

Bring a saucepan of water to the boil and add the rice vermicelli. Immediately turn off the heat and cover the pan with a lid, then let the noodles soak for 2 minutes before draining. Toss the noodles with a little sesame oil to prevent them sticking, then set aside in the colander, covering it with a wet tea towel.

Heat a non-stick wok over a high heat. Once hot, add 1 teaspoon of the neutral oil and give it a swirl to coat the wok. Pour in the beaten egg and stir gently to scramble. Remove while still slightly soft and set aside on a plate.

Add another 1 teaspoon neutral oil to the wok, then add the prawns and stir-fry for about 1 minute per side until lightly pink. Set aside with the egg.

Add the final 1 teaspoon of neutral oil. Add the peppers, carrot and red onion, and stir-fry for 1-2 minutes, then add the curry paste and stir through for another 1-2 minutes until fragrant.

Now add the cooked noodles, along with the soy sauce and salt. Toss everything together to combine, then return the prawns and scrambled egg to the wok. Add the char siu slices and stir, then finally add the beansprouts and spring onions and cook for a further 1-2 minutes to warm everything through. Serve in bowls, garnished with sliced spring onions.

Sausage Gochujang Udon

Serves: 2

Prep time: 15 minutes **Cook time:** 10 minutes

- 400g (14oz) straight-to-wok udon noodles
- 1 tablespoon neutral oil
- 200g (7oz) pork sausages, casing removed (use a spicy sausage if you like heat)
- 1 tablespoon salted butter
- ½ banana shallot, finely diced
- 2 garlic cloves, minced
- 2 tablespoons gochujang (see page 24)
- 2 tablespoons light soy sauce
- 100ml (3½oz) double (heavy) cream
- 50g (1¾oz) Parmesan cheese, finely grated
- 2 spring onions, finely sliced
- 1 teaspoon toasted white sesame seeds

This is a modern Korean fusion dish using gochujang, soy, cream and cheese to make a really unctuous sauce. I've used udon noodles, which are thick, round wheat noodles that offer a delicious bite and perfectly carry all that beautiful sauce. (If you can't find them, this recipe works equally as well with egg or ramen noodles, or even pasta.) The sausage adds just the right amount of meatiness to the dish. All in all, it's a great (and quick) weekday meal.

Bring a large saucepan of water to the boil. Add the udon noodles and boil for 2 minutes just to loosen them, then drain and set aside.

Heat the neutral oil in a large non-stick frying pan or wok over a medium-high heat. Add the sausage meat and cook, breaking it up with the back of a wooden spoon, for 5-6 minutes until browned and slightly caramelised. Remove from the pan and set aside.

To the same pan, add the butter. Once melted, add the chopped shallot and garlic, and stir-fry for 1-2 minutes until fragrant. Now add the cooked udon noodles to the pan and stir to coat in the buttery mixture, then reduce the heat to medium. Add the gochujang, soy sauce and cream, stirring to combine and evenly coat the noodles. Let it simmer for 1-2 minutes until the cream thickens slightly, then return the browned sausage meat to the pan, along with the grated Parmesan cheese. Cook for a further minute or two until the cheese has melted, then remove from the heat and stir through the sliced spring onions.

Divide the noodles between 2 bowls and sprinkle with the sesame seeds to serve.

Vietnamese Phở Bò

Serves: 4

Prep time: 20 minutes **Cook time:** 4½–7 hours

250g (9oz) beef sirloin
300g (10½oz) dried or 600g (1lb 5oz) fresh medium flat rice noodles

FOR THE BROTH

1 large onion, halved, skin on and root removed
10cm (4in) piece of fresh ginger, halved lengthways
800g (1lb 12oz) oxtail
1 tablespoon salt
15g (½oz) rock sugar (see page 27) or caster (superfine) sugar
1 tablespoon chicken bouillon powder
4 tablespoons Vietnamese fish sauce (or any kind you have)

FOR THE SPICES

1 cinnamon stick
3 star anise
4 cloves
1 tablespoon coriander seeds
1 teaspoon fennel seeds
1 teaspoon cardamom pods, lightly bashed

TO SERVE

200g (7oz) beansprouts
small handful of Thai basil
small handful of coriander (cilantro) leaves
½ red onion, thinly sliced
2 spring onions (scallions), thinly sliced
2 small red bird's-eye chillies, thinly sliced
lime wedges, for squeezing
sriracha, hoisin sauce and chilli oil, for drizzling

Vietnamese phở is a delicious bowl of flat rice noodles, a savoury spiced broth and thin slices of beef or chicken, topped with lots of fresh elements including beansprouts, mint, basil and coriander. In this recipe, I will be making phở bò, which is a beef broth topped with thin slices of raw beef that then cook in the hot broth. Grilling the onion and ginger for the broth is really important and adds so much flavour, so don't skip this step! Phở always makes me think of Paris, strangely enough, because that's where I had my first bowl of authentic Vietnamese phở. My father has many friends who live in the 13th arrondissement there, which is home to a large Asian community - including many from Vietnam who emigrated there in the early 70s. The phở is definitely a highlight of my trips to Paris.

Begin by preparing the broth. First, place the onion and ginger directly over a gas flame or under a grill for 5-10 minutes until lightly blackened, turning occasionally. Alternatively, preheat your oven to the highest possible temperature and place the onion and ginger on a baking tray. Cook for 20 minutes, flipping every now and then. Set aside.

Place the oxtail in a large stockpot and cover with cold water. Bring to a rolling boil for 5 minutes, then drain and rinse the bones to remove any impurities.

Clean the stockpot, then return the oxtail to the pot. Add 3 litres (12 cups) fresh water, along with the charred onion and ginger.

Lightly toast the spices in a dry frying pan over a medium heat for 2-3 minutes until golden and aromatic, then tie in a spice bag or some muslin and add to the stockpot, along with the salt, sugar and chicken bouillon powder. Bring to a gentle simmer, taking care not to boil, and cook, covered, for at least 4 hours - though the longer you can cook the stock, the better the flavour. I recommend 6-7 hours if you have the time! Keep an eye on your stock as it cooks, and skim off any foam or fat occasionally.

When the stock is ready, remove the spice bag, onion, ginger and oxtail, reserving the oxtail but discarding the rest. Shred the meat from the oxtail and set aside in a bowl.

Strain the stock through a fine sieve into a clean saucepan, then taste and season with the fish sauce. You can add more salt and sugar here as needed.

continued →

continued →

When you're ready to serve, slice the sirloin into paper-thin slices, slicing against the grain (see tip). Cook the noodles according to the packet instructions. Drain and rinse briefly under cold water to stop them from overcooking.

Reheat the broth until piping hot, then add the reserved oxtail meat and heat through for a couple of minutes.

Divide the cooked noodles between 4 bowls and top with the raw beef slices, then ladle the hot stock over the top; it will cook the raw beef instantly. Divide the oxtail meat between the bowls, then serve alongside all the garnishes so that everyone can customise their own bowl.

TIPS

* Chilling the beef in the freezer for 15 minutes before slicing helps you achieve really thin slices.
* If you'd like to use a pressure cooker for the stock, follow the instructions given here but instead of simmering the stock for hours, cook it on high in your pressure cooker for 1 hour, then allow the steam to release naturally.

Filipino Pancit Bihon

Serves: 4

Prep time: 25 minutes **Cook time:** 20 minutes

200g (7oz) dried rice vermicelli noodles
300g (10½oz) chicken breast or thigh, thinly sliced
½ teaspoon granulated sugar
¼ teaspoon salt
¼ teaspoon ground white pepper
2 tablespoons neutral oil
4 garlic cloves, minced
1 onion, thinly sliced
1 carrot, peeled and julienned
100g (3½oz) green beans, sliced
100g (3½oz) white cabbage, shredded
4 tablespoons Filipino soy sauce (see page 21 and tip)
1 tablespoon oyster sauce
1 teaspoon fish sauce
a few pinches of freshly ground black pepper

TO SERVE

2 spring onions (scallions), finely sliced
6–8 fresh calamansi (see tip), halved, or 1 lime, cut into wedges

Pancit bihon is a popular Filipino dish traditionally served at family celebrations, as the long vermicelli noodles symbolise long life and good health. I've used chicken here, but you can try other meats, like pork or prawn, or omit it entirely for a vegetarian version. Take care to toss the noodles gently when stir-frying, as they can easily break up into tiny pieces. Many of the ingredients for this dish are pantry staples, making it a go-to recipe for when you want something quick and delicious that the whole family will love.

Soak the rice vermicelli noodles in a large bowl of warm water for 10-15 minutes until softened but still firm. Drain and set aside.

Place the sliced chicken in a bowl and add the sugar, salt and white pepper. Stir to combine.

Heat the oil in a large wok or deep-sided frying pan over a medium heat. Add the chicken and cook for 4-5 minutes until lightly browned and cooked through, then add the garlic and onion and fry for a further 1-2 minutes until fragrant. Add the carrot, green beans and cabbage to the pan and cook for 2-3 minutes until the cabbage has just wilted.

Now add the Filipino soy sauce, oyster sauce, fish sauce and black pepper, along with 3 tablespoons water. Bring to a gentle simmer for 8-10 minutes until the vegetables are tender.

Add the softened noodles to the pan and gently toss everything together for 4-5 minutes until the noodles absorb the liquid and are fully cooked. Taste and adjust the seasoning if needed, adding more soy sauce, pepper, or a splash of fish sauce to taste.

Transfer the noodles to a serving platter and serve garnished with sliced spring onions, along with calamansi or lime wedges for squeezing.

TIPS

* Rice vermicelli has a tendency to get mushy if overworked, so be gentle when tossing the noodles in the sauce. I like to do this with chopsticks in one hand and a spatula in the other, as I find it is the most gentle way to work with them.
* If you can't find Filipino soy sauce, use 3 tablespoons light soy sauce mixed with 1 tablespoon dark soy sauce.
* Calamansi (also known as Philippine lime or lemon) is a type of citrus found in parts of South East Asia.

Curry Prawn Laksa

Serves: 4

Prep time: 15 minutes **Cook time:** 30 minutes

1 tablespoon neutral oil
400ml (14fl oz) coconut milk
750ml (3 cups) chicken stock
2 tablespoons fish sauce
1 teaspoon palm sugar (jaggery) or soft light brown sugar
250g (9oz) raw prawns, tails on, peeled and deveined
100g (3½oz) tofu puffs, halved or quartered depending on size
120g (4¼oz) dried rice vermicelli noodles
165g (5¾oz) dried thick egg noodles
150g (5½oz) beansprouts

FOR THE LAKSA PASTE
3 dried red chillies
2 fresh red chillies, roughly chopped
4 garlic cloves, peeled
2 shallots, roughly chopped
30g (1oz) galangal (see page 16), peeled and roughly chopped
10g (⅓oz) fresh ginger, peeled and roughly chopped
3 lemongrass stalks, white parts only, roughly chopped
1 teaspoon ground turmeric
1 teaspoon ground coriander
1 tablespoon fish sauce, or 1 teaspoon shrimp paste
2 tablespoons neutral oil

TO SERVE
2 hard-boiled eggs, halved
small handful of coriander (cilantro) leaves
1 red chilli, sliced
2 tablespoons crispy shallots
1 lime, cut into wedges

Laksa is a spicy Malaysian noodle dish, most commonly made with a coconut and curry soup base, fresh veggies and noodles - it's truly addictive and incredibly comforting, especially during the chilly winter months. On my visits to Malaysia I have been lucky enough to sample many regional laksa varieties, some without any curry at all, but I believe the curry version is a great introduction to the world of laksa, so that's what I've gone with here. The laksa paste here makes more than you need, but it freezes brilliantly so it makes sense to whip up a larger batch.

Begin by preparing the laksa paste. Soak the dried chillies in a bowl of warm water for 10 minutes, then drain and transfer to a food processor. Add the rest of the paste ingredients and blend until smooth, adding a splash of water if needed to help it blend.

Heat the neutral oil in a large saucepan or wok over a medium heat. Add the paste and fry for 3-4 minutes, stirring often, until aromatic. Pour in the coconut milk and stock and bring to a gentle simmer. Cook for 3-4 minutes, then add the fish sauce and sugar. Taste and adjust - it should be slightly spicy, a little salty and a bit sweet.

Add the prawns and tofu puffs and cook for 3-4 minutes more until the prawns are just pink and cooked through.

Meanwhile, cook the two types of noodles in separate saucepans according to the packet instructions, then drain and divide between 4 serving bowls. Divide the beansprouts between the bowls too, then ladle the hot laksa broth, prawns, and tofu puffs over the top.

Top each bowl with half a boiled egg, along with some fresh coriander, chilli slices and crispy shallots. Serve with lime wedges for squeezing.

TIPS

✱ If you prefer, you can use store-bought laksa paste - you'll need 4-5 tablespoons.

✱ If you don't have both rice vermicelli and egg noodles, you can of course use just one type or the other. Laksa typically has both for texture, but don't worry if you don't have them.

✱ Shrimp paste is used a lot in South East Asian cooking to add an umami savoury depth to curries, soups and stir-fries. It is made from fermented small shrimp (krill) mixed with salt and ground into a thick paste.

Korean Japchae

Serves: 2

Prep time: 20 minutes **Cook time:** 20 minutes

100g (3½oz) Korean-style sweet potato glass noodles (see page 13)
100g (3½oz) beef sirloin, sliced into thin strips
2 tablespoons neutral oil
½ small onion, finely sliced
½ carrot, julienned
½ red pepper (capsicum), thinly sliced
2 garlic cloves, finely chopped
60g (2¼oz) Chinese spinach, cut into 5cm (2in) pieces, or baby spinach, finely sliced
2 spring onions (scallions), whites cut into 5cm (2in) pieces and greens finely sliced
50g (1¾oz) fresh shiitake mushrooms, finely sliced
salt

FOR THE MARINADE

1 teaspoon light soy sauce
2 teaspoons finely grated Korean pear or regular pear
¼ teaspoon salt
½ teaspoon granulated sugar
¼ teaspoon ground black pepper
½ teaspoon sesame oil

FOR THE DRESSING

3 tablespoons Korean soy sauce (see page 21) or light soy sauce
½ tablespoon sesame oil
1 tablespoon granulated sugar
½ teaspoon ground black pepper
1 garlic clove, finely chopped
½ tablespoon toasted sesame seeds, plus extra to serve

Japchae is a Korean stir-fried noodle dish, featuring sweet potato glass noodles, vegetables and beef. To tenderise the beef, the recipe traditionally includes sweet Korean pear. If you can't find a Korean pear, a regular pear will do, but the Korean variety adds extra sweetness, and its acids help break down and tenderise the meat. In secondary school, I studied with a friend from Korea who is now a TV reporter living back in Seoul. She often posts pictures of her family making japchae together at home. This recipe is a classic household dish in Korea, and definitely one to add to your repertoire.

Bring a saucepan of water to the boil, then cook the sweet potato glass noodles for 7-8 minutes until soft.

Meanwhile, in a bowl, combine all the marinade ingredients. Add the beef and stir to combine, then set aside.

In a large bowl, combine the ingredients for the dressing, stirring well to dissolve the sugar. When the noodles are ready, drain them through a sieve, then pour them into the bowl of dressing and toss to coat.

Heat 1 tablespoon of the neutral oil in a frying pan or wok over a medium heat. Add the onion, carrot and red pepper and sauté for 2 minutes, then add the garlic, spinach and spring onion whites and stir-fry for 2 minutes more until they are soft but still have a bite. Season with a little salt before transferring the contents of the pan into the bowl with the noodles.

Return the pan to the heat and add the remaining neutral oil, followed by the beef and mushrooms. Stir-fry for 2-3 minutes until the beef is cooked through and the mushrooms are soft. Add to the bowl with the noodles. Mix well and serve sprinkled with the sesame seeds and finely sliced spring onion greens.

TIPS

- In a traditional japchae, all the vegetables are cooked separately, allowing the cook to control the texture of each vegetable. For convenience and to save time, I have grouped some together to cook in batches - the results are still delicious.
- Although beef is traditionally used, you can substitute with pork, chicken or tofu.

Serves: 4 as a starter

Steamed Beanthread Noodles with Scallops

Prep time: 15 minutes **Cook time:** 20 minutes

50g (1¾oz) dried beanthread noodles (see page 12)
1 tablespoon neutral oil
3 garlic cloves, finely minced
3 spring onions (scallions), finely sliced
8 fresh scallops, without roe (ask your fishmonger for the shells for serving for extra wow factor)
1 red chilli, finely sliced (optional)

FOR THE SAUCE

1 tablespoon light soy sauce
1 tablespoon oyster sauce
1 teaspoon Shaoxing wine (see page 22)
1 teaspoon sesame oil
½ teaspoon granulated sugar

This is a true Chinese classic, and definitely one for any garlic lovers! Delicate beanthread noodles, also known as mung bean vermicelli, become lovely and translucent when cooked, and here they are steamed with fresh scallops and a delicious sauce. It is certainly an impressive dish to serve as a starter for dinner parties, or you could add rice and vegetables to make it a main course.

Place the noodles in a large bowl and cover with warm water. Let them soak for 10-15 minutes until softened but still slightly firm. Drain well and cut into shorter lengths if desired.

Heat the oil in a small saucepan over a medium heat. Add the garlic and two-thirds of the sliced spring onions, and cook for 30-45 seconds until fragrant and just golden. Remove from the heat immediately, being careful not to burn the garlic, and set aside.

In a small bowl, combine the sauce ingredients with 1 tablespoon water and mix well.

If you're using scallop shells to serve, place a small nest of noodles on each shell, then top with a scallop. Drizzle a little of the garlic and spring onion oil on top of each one, then drizzle a little of the sauce over each shell, using about two-thirds and saving the rest for garnish. If you're not using the shells, spread out the noodles in a shallow heatproof dish and arrange the scallops on top, then drizzle the garlic and spring onion oil over the scallops. Pour two-thirds of the sauce over everything, reserving the rest for garnish.

Place the shells or heatproof dish into a steamer set over a pan of boiling water. Steam for 6-8 minutes, depending on the size of your scallops, or until they are just cooked through and opaque.

Serve topped with the reserved sauce, the remaining spring onion and some freshly sliced red chilli if you'd like some spice!

TIP

✱ If using a heatproof dish for steaming, make sure to use a thin dish so that everything steams faster, and choose one with sides so that none of the lovely sauce gets lost.

Serves: 2

Black Pepper Beef with Crispy Noodle Pancake

Prep time: 15 minutes **Cook time:** 15 minutes

220g (8oz) sirloin steak, thinly sliced
95g (3½oz) dried thin egg noodles
2 tablespoons neutral oil
1 red onion, thinly sliced
2 garlic cloves, thinly sliced
½ red pepper (capsicum), thinly sliced
½ green pepper (capsicum), thinly sliced
2 spring onions (scallions), cut in 2cm (¾in) lengths and julienned, plus extra, finely sliced, to garnish

FOR THE MARINADE
1 tablespoon light soy sauce
½ tablespoon Shaoxing wine (see page 22)
1 teaspoon granulated sugar
1 tablespoon cornflour (cornstarch)
½ teaspoon bicarbonate of soda (baking soda)
¼ teaspoon ground white pepper

FOR THE SAUCE
1 tablespoon light soy sauce
1 tablespoon oyster sauce
1 tablespoon Shaoxing wine
1 tablespoon dark soy sauce
½ tablespoon white rice vinegar
2 teaspoons granulated sugar
1 teaspoon coarsely ground black pepper

Black pepper beef is a go-to Chinese restaurant dish: tender strips of beef stir-fried in a light sauce with a fiery black pepper punch. Coarsely ground black pepper is the key ingredient here, but for me the real star of the dish is the crispy golden noodle pancake served under the beef stir-fry. What I love most is how the noodles stay so crispy on the outside while softening slightly underneath where the sauce hits. This pancake looks impressive, but it's actually pretty simple to make at home.

Combine all the marinade ingredients in a bowl. Add the sliced beef and stir to coat. Set aside.

In a separate bowl, mix together all the sauce ingredients and set aside.

Place the egg noodles in a large bowl and pour over enough just-boiled water to submerge. Cover the bowl with a plate and leave for 2 minutes, then drain. Place the noodles on a tray lined with paper towels or a dry tea towel so that they can dry out slightly.

Heat 1 tablespoon of the oil in a 20cm (8in) frying pan over a medium heat. Add the noodles to the pan and spread them out to fill the pan like a thin pancake. Fry for 3–4 minutes on each side or until golden brown. Place on a plate and set aside.

Place a non-stick wok over a medium-high heat. Add the remaining 1 tablespoon oil and heat until shimmering. Add the red onion and stir-fry for 20 seconds, then add the garlic and the marinated beef and stir-fry for a further 3 minutes.

Add the red and green peppers and stir-fry for a further 3–4 minutes, then add the spring onions and sauce mix. Stir-fry for a couple of minutes until slightly thickened, then spoon the black pepper beef over the middle of the crispy noodle pancake and garnish with finely sliced spring onions to serve.

TIPS

- Another way I love to enjoy this crispy noodle pancake is to make it thinner, cut it into squares and dip it in some granulated sugar and Chinese black vinegar – this is a classic way to serve it in Chinese Chiu Chow cuisine.
- If you don't have time to make the pancake, toss the cooked noodles in the wok with the stir-fry for a quick and tasty meal.

Pad Thai with Prawns

Serves: 2

Prep time: 15 minutes, plus soaking **Cook time:** 15 minutes

- 200g (7oz) dried thin flat rice noodles
- 2 tablespoons neutral oil
- 200g (7oz) raw prawns, peeled and deveined
- 2 garlic cloves, minced
- 1 small shallot, finely chopped
- 2 eggs
- 100g (3½oz) beansprouts
- 2 spring onions (scallions), cut into 3cm (1¼in) pieces

FOR THE SAUCE

- 2 tablespoons tamarind concentrate (see page 24)
- 3 tablespoons fish sauce
- 1 tablespoon dark soy sauce
- 1 teaspoon Thai light soy sauce (see page 21) or any other soy sauce
- 1½ tablespoons palm sugar (jaggery) or soft light brown sugar
- 1 teaspoon sriracha

TO SERVE

- 2 tablespoons roasted peanuts, crushed in a pestle and mortar
- small handful of coriander (cilantro) leaves
- pinch of chilli flakes
- 1 lime, cut into wedges

Pad thai is probably one of Thailand's most famous noodle dishes. The combination of rice noodles, egg, prawns, beansprouts and peanuts - not forgetting the tamarind, which brings a complex blend of sweet and sour - makes pad thai totally addictive. I love ordering this dish whenever I'm eating out at a Thai restaurant, but creating it at home is so simple and fast. Once you have all your prep done, putting it all together only takes a few minutes. Soaking the noodles is a key step to making this dish successful and giving them the right amount of bite.

Soak the rice noodles in a bowl of boiling water for 15 minutes until soft but still slightly firm, then drain and set aside.

In a small bowl, mix the sauce ingredients with 2 tablespoons warm water. Stir until the sugar is fully dissolved, then set aside.

Heat 1 tablespoon of the neutral oil in a non-stick wok or large frying pan over a medium-high heat. Add the prawns and cook for 3 minutes until they are just cooked through. Remove from the pan and set aside.

To the same pan, add the remaining 1 tablespoon neutral oil, then add the garlic and chopped shallot. Sauté for about 30 seconds until fragrant, then push the aromatics to one side of the pan and crack in the 2 eggs. Scramble lightly and cook until just set, then mix together with the aromatics.

Reduce the heat to medium and add the drained noodles to the pan, then pour over the sauce and toss everything together using tongs or a spatula for 2 minutes until the noodles are glossy and evenly coated. Return the cooked prawns to the pan, along with the beansprouts and spring onions, and toss for another 30-60 seconds until everything is heated through.

Serve on plates and garnish with the crushed peanuts, coriander leaves and chilli flakes, with lime wedges for squeezing.

Asian Herbs & Vegetables

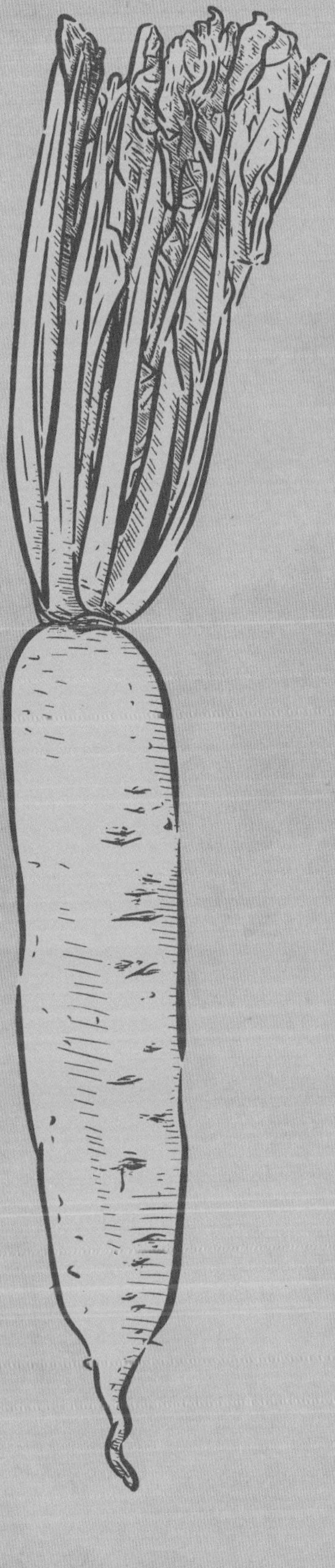

Stir-Fried Morning Glory 81

Pak Choi with Garlic Oil 81

Japanese Beef and Enoki Mushroom Rolls 82

Vietnamese Summer Rolls 85

Sichuan Dry-Fried Green Beans with Pork 89

Chinese Crispy Stuffed Lotus Root with Pork and Prawn 90

Simple Kimchi 92

Chinese Spring Onion Pancakes 95

Pickled Daikon 96

Thai Basil Pork Stir-Fry 97

Stir-Fried Morning Glory

Serves: 2

Prep time: 5 minutes **Cook time:** 5 minutes

1 tablespoon oyster sauce
1 teaspoon light soy sauce
1 teaspoon fish sauce
½ teaspoon caster (superfine) sugar
1 tablespoon neutral oil
3 garlic cloves, finely sliced
1–2 red bird's-eye chillies, smashed (use more or less, depending on how spicy you like it), plus sliced chillies to serve
200g (7oz) morning glory, washed and cut into 8–10 cm (3¼–4in) lengths

Morning glory, which I usually call by its Chinese name, tung choi, is a popular leafy Asian vegetable. The technique in this recipe can be used for stir-frying other leafy greens, if you like. Preparing the morning glory is really easy - just wash the leaves, then cut across the leaf and stalk into strips. I often make this as a side dish to accompany a meat stir-fry, but it's also lovely served simply with some steamed rice. In Thailand, fermented soybean paste is often added; in Malaysia and the Philippines, shrimp paste is used; and in China, cooks may add fermented bean curd.

In a small bowl, combine the oyster sauce, soy sauce, fish sauce and sugar. Add 1 tablespoon water, stir well and set aside.

Heat the oil in a wok or large frying pan over a high heat. Add the sliced garlic and smashed chilli(es), and stir-fry for a few seconds until fragrant but not browned. Then immediately toss in the morning glory and pour in the sauce. Stir-fry quickly and continuously for 1-2 minutes until just wilted but still bright green. Serve immediately, topped with sliced chillies.

Pak Choi with Garlic Oil

Serves: 2–3

Prep time: 5 minutes **Cook time:** 6 minutes

3 tablespoons neutral oil
4 garlic cloves, thinly sliced
300g (10½oz) green pak choi (baby or regular), halved or quartered lengthways
pinch of salt
1 teaspoon light soy sauce
sesame oil, for drizzling

A quick and easy vegetable dish, this is like Chinese veg cooking 101. Growing up, this was an absolute staple at all family meals. Regardless of the meat or fish dishes on offer, this simple and delicious pak choi always featured. You can use regular pak choi, but I prefer to use baby pak choi, because you can cut them in half to create bite-sized pieces while still retaining their lovely shape. A little trick to keep your veggies vibrant green is to cover them with a lid while they cook in the wok.

Heat the neutral oil in a small frying pan over a medium heat. Once hot, add the sliced garlic and gently fry, stirring often, for 2-3 minutes until the garlic is golden brown and crisp. Immediately remove from the heat and strain the oil through a sieve into a small bowl to prevent the garlic from burning. Set aside the crispy garlic and reserved garlic oil.

Heat half the garlic oil in a wok or large frying pan over a medium-high heat. Add the pak choi, salt and 1 tablespoon water. Cover with a lid and let the pak choi cook for 2 minutes.

Transfer the pak choi to a serving plate, then drizzle with the remaining garlic oil and sprinkle with the crispy garlic chips. To finish, drizzle with the light soy sauce and a few drops of sesame oil.

Japanese Beef and Enoki Mushroom Rolls

Makes: about 20 rolls

Prep time: 30 minutes **Cook time:** 10 minutes

200g (7oz) enoki mushrooms
250g (9oz) beef sirloin, very thinly sliced
1 tablespoon neutral oil
1 small onion, sliced

FOR THE SAUCE

3 tablespoons Japanese soy sauce (see page 21)
1 tablespoon mirin (see page 25)
1 tablespoon sake (see page 25)
2 teaspoons granulated sugar
1 garlic clove, minced

TO SERVE

1 spring onion (scallion), cut into 5cm (2in) pieces and julienned
1 tablespoon toasted white sesame seeds
steamed jasmine rice

I always keep a couple of packets of enoki mushrooms in my fridge because they're just so versatile. From soups and stews to noodle recipes, enoki mushrooms always bring their distinctive bite to any dish. This dish is popular in izakayas (casual pubs) in Japan, where it is called enoki no gyuniku maki. It is also common in Chinese cuisine, usually cooked in broth, while in Korea it is served as a banchan (side dish). The combination of the enoki bite with tender beef in that unctuous sauce is pure heaven. Plus, they're ready in just minutes, making it the perfect dish for busy weeknights. I once literally cooked it every night for a week straight - it's that addictive!

Trim the enoki mushrooms and separate into 20 small bundles. Place a piece of the thinly sliced steak on a board or plate, then place a bundle of enoki at one end of the piece of steak and roll up, leaving each end of the enoki bundle exposed, until you have a neat parcel. Repeat with the remaining beef and mushrooms.

In a small bowl, combine all the ingredients for the sauce with 2 tablespoons water. Stir until the sugar has dissolved, then set aside.

Heat the oil in a large frying pan over a medium-high heat. Once hot, add the onion and stir-fry for 1 minute, then arrange the beef-and-enoki bundles on top and sear for 1 minute on each side until the beef is browned.

Pour over the sauce and cover the pan with a lid. Reduce the heat to low and leave the beef to simmer in the sauce for 2-3 minutes until the sauce is glossy and the beef is cooked through and tender.

Scatter over the julienned spring onion and sesame seeds, then spoon over rice to serve.

Vietnamese Summer Rolls

Makes: 12–15

Prep time: 25 minutes **Cook time:** 20 minutes

- 100g (3½oz) dried rice vermicelli (the thinner the better)
- 12–15 × 22cm (8½in) Vietnamese rice papers
- bunch of mint, leaves picked
- bunch of coriander (cilantro), leaves picked
- bunch of Vietnamese perilla, leaves picked (optional)
- handful of fresh edible flowers (optional)
- 250g (9oz) cooked prawns, halved
- 100g (3½oz) gio dac biet (Vietnamese pork roll), thinly sliced and cut into strips
- 1 carrot, finely julienned
- ½ large cucumber, finely julienned
- 4–5 iceberg lettuce leaves

FOR THE SWEET CHILLI DIPPING SAUCE

- 1 tablespoon white rice vinegar
- 2 tablespoons Thai sweet chilli sauce
- 2–3 drops fish sauce
- ½ tablespoon lime juice

FOR THE PEANUT DIPPING SAUCE

- 3 tablespoons crunchy peanut butter
- 2 tablespoons hoisin sauce
- 2 tablespoons light soy sauce
- 1 tablespoon white rice vinegar
- 1 tablespoon caster (superfine) sugar
- 1 tablespoon crushed salted peanuts

Beautiful, delicate, jewel-like rolls made from Vietnamese rice paper and filled with a mixture of beanthread noodles, fragrant herbs, crunchy vegetables and a little meat: these are a Vietnamese staple. Rice paper is something I always have in my pantry. When dry, the sheets are quite stiff, but when passed through water, they become translucent, stretchy and soft. In this recipe, I've used gio dac biet, a Vietnamese pork roll, which adds a nice texture and flavour to the rolls, but it isn't essential, so you can leave it out if you can't find it. For the fresh herbs, I love using mint and coriander, but you can vary these based on your own personal taste. I've offered two dipping sauces for the summer rolls: one is lighter, a classic nước chấm Vietnamese sauce, and the other is a peanutty, hoisin-rich dipping sauce with a really bold flavour. My top tip would be to wrap these rolls as tightly as you can so they hold together when eaten. I've included some edible flowers to make them prettier, but that's optional; I usually only do this if I am serving them as a starter for a dinner party.

Soak the rice vermicelli in a bowl of boiling water for 3 minutes, then drain and rinse under cold water. Set aside.

Prepare a large, shallow bowl of cold water for the rice paper and have it ready.

Place a clean damp tea towel on your chopping board. Dip a sheet of rice paper into the bowl of water, making sure it gets completely wet, then remove and place on the damp cloth. Add the fillings in a neat line across the lower third of the rice paper, adding the herbs and flowers first so that they face outwards for presentation. Continue filling with the prawns, pork roll, carrot, cucumber and some vermicelli.

Fold the rice paper in on both sides - it might stick to the cloth slightly, so be careful not to rip it - then fold the bottom up and roll the filling forward until it is tightly sealed (see page 105). Repeat with the next wrapper, and keep going until all your filling is used up.

Now make your sauces. For the sweet chilli dipping sauce, simply combine all the ingredients in a small bowl and mix well. Taste and adjust as needed.

For the peanut dipping sauce, combine the peanut butter and hoisin sauce in a small bowl, mixing them into a paste, then add the soy sauce, vinegar and sugar. Slowly add 3 tablespoons warm water to loosen and lastly add the peanuts. Mix well. Set aside both sauces until needed.

continued →

continued →

Place the finished summer rolls on a bed of iceberg lettuce leaves so that they don't stick to the plate. If you are not eating straight away, cover the rolls with a damp tea towel or some clingfilm to prevent them from drying out. Use any extra flowers to garnish the platter and serve with your sauces for dipping.

TIPS

- If you are not a fan of prawns, you can substitute with thin slices of grilled beef, chicken or pork belly.
- To create a vegan or vegetarian version, swap the prawns for some pressed tofu or sliced avocado.
- Rice paper is so versatile. I like to use it to make rice paper dumplings. Fill them with minced pork and veggies, then pan-fry until lovely and crispy.
- You can also cut rice paper sheets into thick slices and use them as noodles. They are delicious stir-fried or added to soups.

Serves: 2–3

Sichuan Dry-Fried Green Beans with Pork

Prep time: 15 minutes **Cook time:** 15 minutes

150g (5½oz) minced pork
1 teaspoon light soy sauce
1 teaspoon Shaoxing wine (see page 22)
½ teaspoon granulated sugar
¼ teaspoon salt
¼ teaspoon ground white pepper
4 tablespoons neutral oil
300g (10½oz) long green beans, trimmed and cut into 5cm (2in) lengths
3 dried red chillies, snipped into 1cm (½in) pieces (use more or less, depending on how spicy you like it)
½ teaspoon Sichuan peppercorn powder
2 garlic cloves, minced
1 teaspoon minced fresh ginger
1 spring onion (scallion), finely sliced, to serve

FOR THE SEASONING SAUCE

1 tablespoon light soy sauce
½ tablespoon dark soy sauce
1 teaspoon Chinese black vinegar (see page 24)
½ teaspoon caster (superfine) sugar
¼ teaspoon salt

Green beans stir-fried with dried chillies, Sichuan pepper and minced pork: a classic dish in Sichuan cuisine. In restaurants, the green beans are usually deep-fried, but at home, I prefer to blister them slightly by pan-searing them in hot oil. It's a typical dish that I always order in Sichuan restaurants; I love the texture of the beans and the mala (numbing and hot) flavour of the Sichuan pepper. I prefer to use Sichuan pepper powder instead of whole Sichuan peppercorns, as I don't like the crunch of the peppercorns in the final dish. Don't worry, the end result isn't as spicy as you might imagine. That said, if you are feeling brave, feel free to go wild with the dried chillies.

Place the pork mince into a bowl and add the light soy sauce, Shaoxing wine, sugar, salt and white pepper. Mix to combine, then set aside until needed.

In a small bowl, combine the ingredients for the seasoning sauce. Stir and set aside.

Heat 2 tablespoons of the oil in a wok or large frying pan over a medium-high heat. Add the green beans. Sear for 5-6 minutes until blistered and slightly wrinkled, then remove the beans to a plate and set aside.

Add the remaining 2 tablespoons oil to the wok, still over a medium-high heat. Add the dried chillies and stir-fry for 30 seconds until fragrant, then add the Sichuan peppercorn powder, garlic and ginger, and stir-fry for another 30 seconds. Add the minced pork and cook for 4-5 minutes until browned and slightly crispy.

Pour in the seasoning sauce and mix well until the pork is evenly coated. Now return the green beans to the pan and stir-fry everything together for 2 minutes until heated through and well mixed.

Scatter over the sliced spring onion to serve.

TIPS

* I like to serve this with some jasmine rice or biang biang noodles (see page 59).
* To make a vegetarian version of this dish, swap the pork for some finely diced shiitake mushrooms.

Chinese Crispy Stuffed Lotus Root with Pork and Prawn

Makes: about 20

Prep time: 30 minutes **Cook time:** 10 minutes

1 tablespoon white vinegar
600g (1lb 5oz) fresh lotus roots
neutral oil, for frying
sweet chilli sauce, to serve

FOR THE FILLING

60g (2¼oz) dried shiitake mushrooms
15g (½oz) dried shrimp (see page 26)
175g (6oz) minced pork
175g (6oz) raw prawns, peeled, deveined and finely chopped
2 teaspoons cornflour (cornstarch)
100g (3½oz) tinned water chestnuts, finely diced
1 spring onion (scallion), finely chopped
1cm (½in) piece of fresh ginger, peeled and minced
1 tablespoon Shaoxing wine (see page 22)
2 tablespoons light soy sauce
1 teaspoon sesame oil
1 teaspoon caster (superfine) sugar
½ teaspoon ground white pepper
½ teaspoon salt

FOR THE BATTER

40g (1½oz) plain (all-purpose) flour
40g (1½oz) cornflour
½ teaspoon salt
¼ teaspoon Chinese five-spice
70ml (2¼fl oz) lager

This is a traditional Chinese dish, made by sandwiching a filling of pork and prawn between two slices of lotus root before shallow-frying. Lotus roots are exactly that: the roots of the lotus flower. When you slice into them, the slices look like wheels. My uncle cooks with lotus roots a lot, including them in Chinese-style bone-broth soups and a braised pork belly and taro dish, but my favourite way to eat lotus root is this recipe, which was a family favourite when I was growing up. It is a true delicacy that you rarely find in restaurants; it's more of a homecooked dish.

Prepare a large bowl of cold water and add the white vinegar. Peel the lotus roots and slice into 3-4mm (⅛in) rounds, adding the slices to the acidulated water to prevent them discolouring while you prepare the filling. Set aside.

For the filling, soak the dried mushrooms and dried shrimp in a bowl of hot water for 15-20 minutes, then drain and chop very finely. Set aside.

Combine the pork, prawns and cornflour in a large bowl, mixing vigorously for 2 minutes, then add the shiitake mushrooms and shrimp, along with the rest of the filling ingredients. Mix for a further 2-3 minutes until sticky.

Now, drain the lotus roots and pat dry using paper towels - don't skip this step, or you will have trouble frying them!

Take a slice of lotus root and top it with about 2 teaspoons of the filling mixture, spreading it out to form a thin layer. Top with a second slice of lotus root to form a sandwich. Press gently to seal, then repeat until all the lotus-root slices are used up.

Pour the neutral oil into a wok or deep-sided saucepan to a depth of about 2cm (¾in). Place the pan over a medium-high heat until the oil reaches about 150°C (300°F).

While the oil is heating, make the batter by whisking together the flour, cornflour, salt and five-spice in a large bowl. Gradually stir in the lager and 70ml (2¼fl oz) water until a smooth, slightly thick batter forms.

Working in batches, use chopsticks or a pair of tongs to dip the stuffed lotus-root sandwiches into the batter before carefully transferring them to the hot oil. Fry, turning occasionally, for 6-7 minutes until golden brown and tender. Remove the cooked lotus-root sandwiches from the oil and drain on paper towels or a wire rack while you cook the rest.

Serve hot, with some sweet chilli sauce for dipping.

Simple Kimchi

Makes: a 1-litre (1-quart) jar

Prep time: 15 minutes **Active time:** 2 hours **Fermentation time:** 2–5 days

30g (1oz) flaky sea salt
1 head of Chinese leaf (about 1–1.2kg/2lb 4oz–2lb 11oz), chopped into large bite-sized pieces
5 large garlic cloves, minced
1 teaspoon freshly grated ginger
3 tablespoons gochugaru (Korean red pepper flakes, see page 19)
2 tablespoons Korean soy sauce (see page 21) or light soy sauce
1 tablespoon caster (superfine) sugar
3 spring onions (scallions), finely sliced

Kimchi in Korea is huge! It is eaten all the time, with any meal, and it forms a significant part of the culture. It's traditionally made in large earthenware pots, which you can see lined up on the rooftops of most buildings in Korea. Kimchi is delicious and is also said to be very good for you and your gut. I remember attending my Korean friends' wedding in Hawaii. At the pre-wedding dinner, the bride's mum served some homemade kimchi that she had made in her hotel room! That's where the inspiration for this simple kimchi recipe comes from. Here, we will be using napa or Chinese leaf, which is the most common type, but kimchi can be made with many other vegetables. The longer you leave it to ferment - perhaps 2-5 days - the better the kimchi tastes (just make sure to leave space at the top of the jar when packing the mixture to ensure it doesn't explode during fermentation). So, happy kimchi-making - it's not as difficult as you may think!

Dissolve the salt in a bowl containing 500ml (2 cups) cold water, then submerge the cabbage in the water. To keep the cabbage submerged, you can place a plate slightly smaller than the diameter of your bowl on top of the cabbage and weigh it down with a heavy pan. Soak for 1½–2 hours, turning every 30 minutes, then rinse thoroughly in cold water and drain well. Soaking the cabbage in this manner helps draw out the moisture and makes for a better kimchi.

In a bowl, combine the garlic, ginger, gochugaru, soy sauce, sugar and spring onions, then add the drained cabbage and use gloved hands to massage the mixture thoroughly into the leaves, ensuring the cabbage is evenly coated.

Pack the mixture tightly into a sterilised 1-litre (1-quart) jar, pressing down to remove any air pockets. Remember to leave 2-3cm (¾–1¼in) space at the top of the jar to ensure it doesn't explode during fermentation!

Cover the jar with the lid and leave the kimchi at room temperature for 2-5 days, depending on the warmth of your room and your desired tanginess. Keep tasting the kimchi as it ferments to check in on how you like it - just remember to use a clean, metal utensil to taste - and don't double-dip, as this could introduce bacteria that might spoil your kimchi.

Once the kimchi is fermented to your liking, transfer the jar to the fridge to preserve. Use within 2-3 months.

Makes: 4

Chinese Spring Onion Pancakes

Prep time: 15 minutes **Cook time:** 10 minutes, plus resting

250g (9oz) plain (all-purpose) flour
1½ teaspoons salt
4 tablespoons neutral oil, plus extra for frying
4 spring onions (scallions), very finely chopped
chilli oil, to serve

I first tried spring onion pancakes during my master's year at Lancaster University. One of my Chinese housemates made them for a shared dinner. It was the first time I'd seen someone make these pancakes, and it looked surprisingly simple: just flour, water and spring onions. What really caught my attention was the rolling technique. She rolled the dough into a log, coiled it, and flattened it again. That gave the pancakes a unique texture and shape unlike other flatbreads. I really enjoyed these pancakes, and they pair so well with stews. They're also great as a snack or as a breakfast dish, which is how they're often eaten in China.

Place the flour and 1 teaspoon of the salt into the bowl of a stand mixer fitted with a dough hook and mix for a few seconds to combine. Then, with the motor running, pour in 180ml (5¾fl oz) just-boiled water. Mix until the dough comes together in a smooth ball.

Remove the dough from the food processor and knead briefly, then place into a large bowl. Cover with a clean tea towel and leave to rest at room temperature for 1 hour.

Meanwhile, in a small bowl combine the sliced spring onions with the remaining ½ teaspoon salt. Mix and set aside for at least 10 minutes.

When you're ready to cook, divide the dough into 4 equal pieces. Roll the first piece into a very thin rectangle measuring about 13 × 20cm (5 × 8in), then lightly brush all over with oil and sprinkle with some of the spring onions. Starting from the long side, roll the dough tightly into a log, then coil the log into a spiral, like a cinnamon roll. Flatten gently with your palm, then roll out into a 13-15cm (5-6in) round pancake. Repeat with the remaining dough pieces.

Heat 1-2 tablespoons oil in a non-stick frying pan over a medium heat. Add the first pancake and fry for 2-3 minutes per side, pressing gently with a spatula, until golden brown and crisp. Set aside to keep warm and repeat with the remaining pancakes. Once they're all cooked, slice into wedges and serve hot, drizzled with some chilli oil.

Pickled Daikon

Makes: 2 medium jars

Prep time: 15 minutes **Cook time:** 5 minutes, plus 30 minutes for salting

75g (2¾oz) granulated sugar
120ml (½ cup) white vinegar
120ml (½ cup) white rice vinegar

FOR THE VEGETABLES

400g (14oz) daikon radish, peeled and thickly julienned
1 carrot, peeled and thickly julienned
½ cucumber, deseeded and thickly julienned
1 tablespoon salt

Daikon is also known as white radish. This Asian vegetable is very versatile, and is often used in stews, as well as being pickled and grated for sushi. In this recipe, we'll make a quick pickle. This is something my uncle Hoi makes a lot; it's crunchy, sharp and sweet all at the same time. It's such a treat. I always keep a jar of pickles in my fridge. Many Asian restaurants serve a small dish of this pickled daikon before dinner to help awaken your palate before all the food arrives. I like to add carrots and cucumbers to my pickled daikon for some colour and extra crunch.

In a large heatproof bowl, mix the sugar with 250ml (1 cup) boiling water. Stir until the sugar is fully dissolved, then mix in the vinegars and set aside to cool to room temperature.

In a separate large bowl, combine the daikon, carrot and cucumber sticks and sprinkle with the salt, tossing together to combine and distribute the salt evenly throughout the vegetables. This is an important step to ensure your vegetables remain crunchy. It also helps to drain the water from the vegetables so that they can better absorb the pickling liquid.

Let the vegetables sit for 15–20 minutes, then rinse thoroughly under cold running water. Drain well and lightly pat dry with paper towels.

Divide the vegetables between 2 sterilised jars, then pour the cooled pickling liquid over the top to submerge. Cover the jars with their lids, then refrigerate. For a mild pickle, let it sit for 24 hours. For a stronger flavour, wait 48 hours. The pickles will keep in the fridge for up to a month, and will keep developing in flavour the longer they are left.

Thai Basil Pork Stir-Fry

Serves: 2

Prep time: 10 minutes **Cook time:** 10 minutes

300g (10½oz) minced pork
2 tablespoons Thai light soy sauce (see page 21)
2 tablespoons Thai sweet soy sauce (optional, see page 21)
1 tablespoon Thai soybean paste (optional, see page 22)
1 teaspoon granulated sugar
2 tablespoons neutral oil
3–4 garlic cloves, minced
1–2 red bird's-eye chillies, finely chopped, depending on how spicy you like it
100g (3½oz) Thai basil, leaves picked

FOR THE SAUCE
1 tablespoon oyster sauce
1 tablespoon Thai light soy sauce
1 teaspoon Thai fish sauce
1 teaspoon granulated sugar

TO SERVE (OPTIONAL)
steamed jasmine rice
crispy fried eggs

This is a classic in Thailand, where it's known as pad kra pow. The use of Thai basil transforms this dish from a normal stir-fry to something truly fragrant and amazing. I usually serve it with steamed jasmine rice and a crispy fried egg, but it also works wonderfully as a filling for bao buns or even tacos. I often make extra to enjoy the next day. Feel free to adjust the amount of chilli, depending on your spice tolerance.

Place the pork mince into a large bowl and add the soy sauce, sweet soy sauce, Thai soybean paste and sugar. Mix well and set aside.

In a small bowl, combine the sauce ingredients with 1 tablespoon water and stir well, adding more water if it is a little too thick.

Heat the oil in a wok or deep-sided frying pan over a medium-high heat. Add the pork mince and stir-fry for 4–5 minutes until browned and fully cooked, then add the garlic and chillies and fry for about 30 seconds until fragrant. Now pour in the sauce, stirring everything well to coat. Turn off the heat, toss in the basil leaves, and stir until just wilted.

Serve with steamed jasmine rice and crispy fried eggs, or your chosen accompaniments.

TIPS

- You can use crumbled tofu here to replace the minced pork if you'd like a vegetarian version.
- For a lighter option, serve with some baby gem lettuce leaves and fill them with the stir-fry.

Light Bites & Snacks

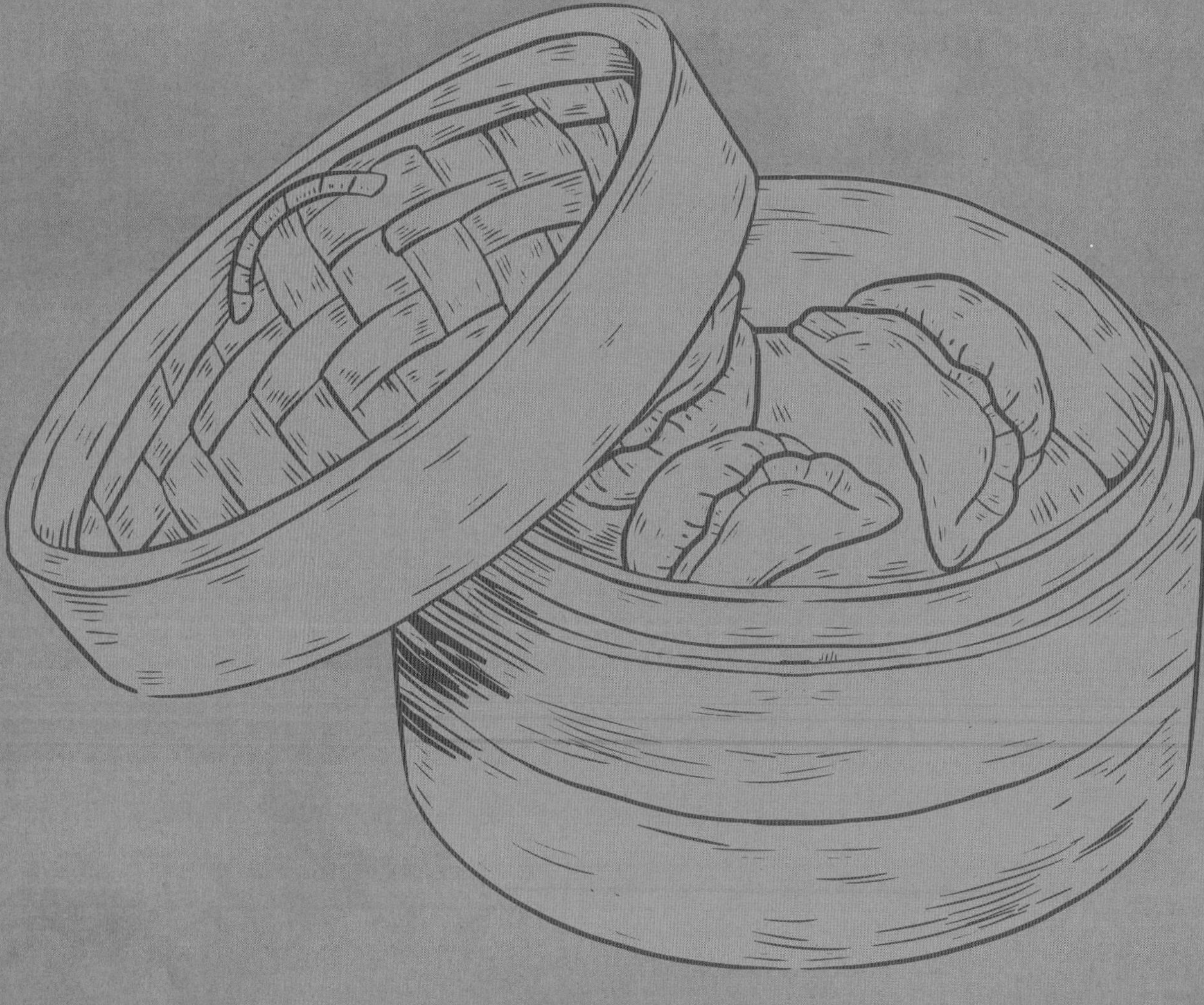

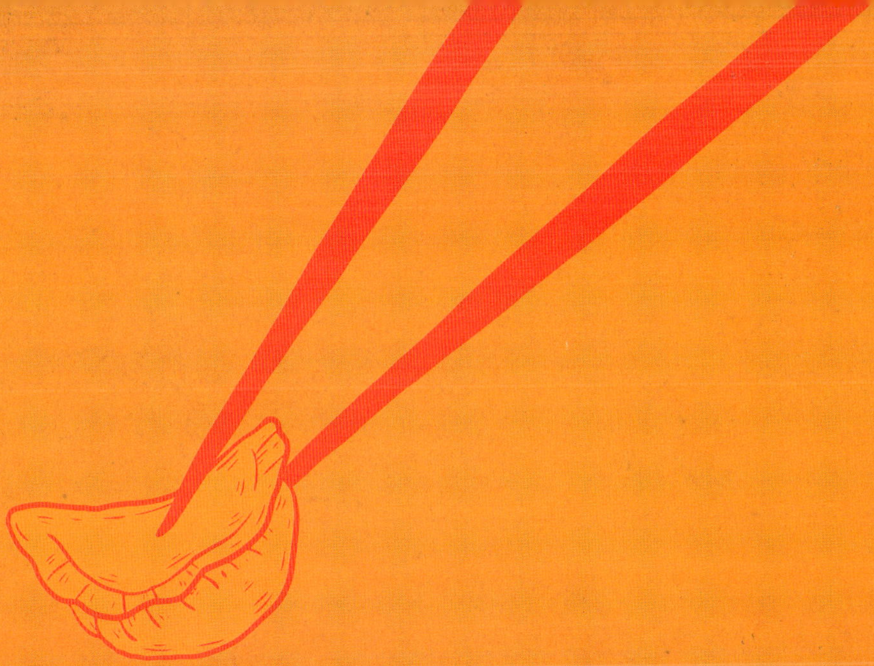

Sesame Prawn Toast 101

Korean Tteokbokki Rice Cakes 102

Crispy Vietnamese Spring Rolls 104

Korean Fried Chicken 107

Classic Chinese Dumplings 108

Japanese Chicken Gyoza 112

Vietnamese Lemongrass Pork Chop Bánh Mì 114

Five-Spiced Pork Belly with Steamed Bao Buns 116

K-Toast: Korean Ham-and-Cheese Toastie 120

Chinese Cumin Lamb Skewers 121

Sesame Prawn Toast

Makes: 20

Prep time: 20 minutes **Cook time:** 10 minutes

- 400g (14oz) raw prawns, peeled and deveined
- 2 garlic cloves
- 1cm (½ in) piece of fresh ginger
- 3 spring onions (scallions)
- 1 egg white
- 2 tablespoons light soy sauce
- 1 tablespoon sesame oil
- 1 tablespoon Shaoxing wine (see page 22)
- mix of toasted black and white sesame seeds, for coating
- 5 slices thickly sliced white bread
- neutral oil, for frying
- sea salt

TO SERVE

- sweet chilli sauce
- freshly chopped coriander (cilantro)

Sesame prawn toast needs no introduction. It's been a staple on Chinese restaurant and takeaway menus for years. I absolutely love it, and making it at home is incredibly satisfying, especially since you can whip up a generous batch and make loads if you want to. In this recipe, I've combined prawns with spring onions, garlic and ginger, which infuse the prawn toast with a wonderfully rich flavour. Personally, I always go for a generous coating of sesame seeds, but if you prefer a lighter touch, simply sprinkle them on instead of dunking. One of the best parts of making it yourself is the freedom to enhance the prawn mixture with extra flavours and ingredients like chilli, water chestnuts and coriander.

Roughly chop half the prawns into small chunks and set aside in a bowl.

Combine the garlic, ginger and spring onions in the bowl of a food processor and blitz until finely chopped. Add the remaining prawns and blitz again until you have a smooth paste.

Spoon the contents of the food processor into the bowl of chopped prawns, then add the egg white, soy sauce, sesame oil and Shaoxing wine. Mix well to combine - the mixture should look slightly liquidy.

Dollop 2 tablespoons of the prawn mixture on to each bread slice and spread it thickly - it should be about 1cm (½in) thick. Cut each bread slice into 4 triangles.

Put the sesame seeds on a plate and press the prawn side of the triangles into the mix to coat evenly. Alternatively, sprinkle the sesame seeds over the prawn mixture for a lighter coating.

Pour the oil into a frying pan to a depth of 1-2cm (½-¾ in). Place over a medium-high heat until the oil reaches 175°C (340°F). Working in batches, add the triangles, prawn-side down, and fry in the hot oil for 2-3 minutes, then flip and fry on the bread side for 30-60 seconds until golden brown.

Remove from the pan and drain on a plate lined with paper towels while you fry the remaining prawn toasts. Sprinkle with a pinch of flaky sea salt to finish, and serve with sweet chilli sauce, topped with freshly chopped coriander.

Korean Tteokbokki Rice Cakes

Serves: 2

Prep time: 15 minutes **Cook time:** 30 minutes

- 300g (10½oz) fresh Korean rice cakes, preferably cylindrical (see tip)
- 1 piece (about 10g/⅓oz) of kombu (see page 26)
- 5g (⅛oz) dried anchovies (see page 26)
- 2 tablespoons gochujang (see page 24)
- 2 tablespoons caster (superfine) sugar
- ½ teaspoon gochugaru (Korean red pepper flakes, see page 19)
- 1 garlic clove, minced
- ¼ teaspoon salt
- 1 onion, finely sliced
- 100g (3½oz) Korean fish cakes, sliced into small squares

TO SERVE

- 2 spring onions (scallions), finely sliced
- 1 tablespoon toasted white sesame seeds
- sesame oil, for drizzling

I first had tteokbokki - chewy, sweet and spicy rice cakes - when I visited Korea as a teenager with my mum. What initially drew me in was their bright red-orange colour. I remember seeing people eating them on every street corner in Seoul. When I first tried them, I was surprised to find that they weren't as spicy as I'd expected, but I was completely hooked on that addictive chewy texture and the sweet and spicy gochujang sauce - what's not to like? The beauty of this recipe is that it creates a perfect base that you can customise. Add fish cakes, throw in some ramen noodles, sprinkle cheese on top, or even try them deep-fried - crispy on the outside, chewy on the inside!

Soak the rice cakes in a bowl of warm water for 20-30 minutes. This softens them to make sure they cook evenly.

Meanwhile, place the kombu into a large saucepan and pour over 500ml (2 cups) cold water. Add the anchovies, then place the pan over a medium-high heat and bring to the boil. Boil for 15 minutes, then strain the stock through a piece of muslin or a fine sieve into a separate clean pan.

Place this pan of stock over a low heat and add the gochujang, sugar, gochugaru, garlic and salt, and whisk together to combine.

Drain the soaked rice cakes and add them to the saucepan, along with the gochujang sauce. Bring to the boil, then add the sliced onion and fish cake sheets. Stir gently to coat everything in the sauce, then reduce the heat to a low simmer. Continue to cook, stirring frequently, for 10-15 minutes until the rice cakes are soft and chewy, and the sauce is thick and glossy.

Serve the tteokbokki in bowls, sprinkled with the sliced spring onions and sesame seeds. Top with a drizzle of sesame oil to finish.

TIPS

- Korean rice cakes can be found in chilled or ambient form in most Asian supermarkets.
- If you can't find Korean fish cake sheets, use Chinese fish cakes or Japanese white fish cakes (kamaboko), which can be found in the freezer section of most Asian supermarkets. Thinly slice them to imitate the Korean type.

Crispy Vietnamese Spring Rolls

Makes: 24

Prep time: 35 minutes, plus resting **Cook time:** 10 minutes

- 50g (1¾oz) dried beanthread noodles (see page 12)
- 10g (⅓oz) dried wood ear or black fungus mushrooms (see page 26)
- 450g (1lb) minced pork
- 1 large carrot, julienned
- 1 shallot, finely chopped
- 1 garlic clove, minced
- 1 teaspoon freshly grated ginger
- 1 egg white
- 2 tablespoons fish sauce
- 1 tablespoon vegetable oil
- ½ teaspoon salt
- ½ teaspoon ground white pepper
- 3 teaspoons granulated sugar
- neutral oil, for frying
- iceberg lettuce leaves, to serve

FOR THE NƯỚC CHẤM

- 3 tablespoons fish sauce
- 3 tablespoons fresh lime juice
- 2 tablespoons caster (superfine) sugar
- 1 garlic clove, very finely diced
- 1 small red bird's-eye chilli, thinly sliced

My fondest memories of Vietnamese spring rolls come from visiting a Vietnamese family who are close friends of my parents. They invite us over often, and there are always enormous platters of freshly deep-fried spring rolls waiting for us. What makes them truly special is how they are served, with a big bowl of fresh, crisp iceberg lettuce alongside an incredible dipping sauce - a lovely, vinegary nước chấm with soy and fish sauce that is both tangy and savoury. The first time I saw this set-up, I was completely puzzled. Iceberg lettuce with spring rolls? I had no idea what to do, until they showed me the magic: you wrap each crispy spring roll in the cool lettuce, dip it in that amazing sauce, and take a bite. The contrast is absolutely perfect: the hot, crispy exterior giving way to the flavourful filling, all wrapped in refreshing lettuce.

For the nước chấm, mix all the ingredients together in a small bowl with 3 tablespoons water. Set aside until needed.

Soak the noodles in a bowl of just-boiled water for 10 minutes. Drain well and rinse in cold water, then, using scissors, chop into short pieces.

In a separate bowl, soak the wood ear mushrooms in just-boiled water for 15 minutes until they have expanded in size. Drain, pat dry and finely chop.

In a large bowl, mix the chopped noodles with the mushrooms, then add the pork, carrot, shallot, garlic, ginger, egg white, fish sauce, vegetable oil, salt and pepper, along with 1 teaspoon of the sugar. Stir well until evenly mixed.

In a shallow bowl, dissolve the remaining 2 teaspoons sugar in 250ml (1 cup) warm water. The sugar will help make the rice paper rolls nice and golden.

To assemble, dip a rice paper wrapper in the sugared water for 5-10 seconds, then place on a flat surface. Add about 40g (1½oz) of the filling mixture near the edge of the rice paper wrapper, then fold the closest edge up and over the filling. Roll up tightly, folding in the sides as you go - the wrapper should stick to itself. Place the wrapped rolls on a piece of oiled baking paper to keep them from sticking. Repeat until all the rolls are filled.

Refrigerate the rolls for at least 1 hour to help them firm up and slightly dry out, then remove from the fridge and let them sit at room temperature for 15 minutes before frying.

When you're ready to fry, pour neutral oil into a large, deep-sided frying pan to a depth of 5cm (2in). Place over a medium-high heat and heat the oil to 160°C (315°F). Fry the spring rolls in small batches for 5–6 minutes until lightly golden. Don't let them touch each other at first, or they will stick together. Remove from the oil and leave to drain on a wire rack while you cook the remaining rolls.

Now increase the heat slightly and bring the oil to 175°C (340°F). Return the spring rolls to the pan, working in batches once more, and fry for 1½–2 minutes until crispy and golden brown. Serve straight away, alongside a bowl of crispy iceberg lettuce leaves and the nước chấm.

1.

2.

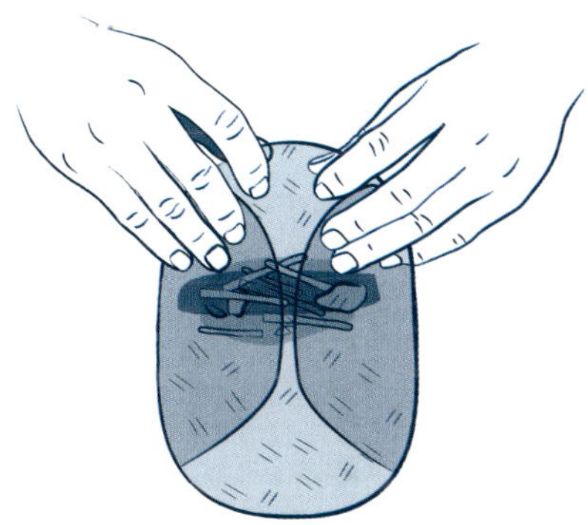

3.

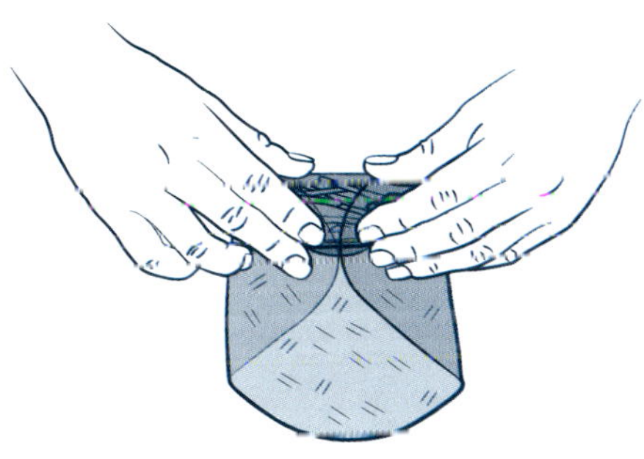

4.

TIP

✱ These reheat brilliantly in an air fryer, so if you like you can pre-fry all the rolls in advance and just reheat them before serving.

Korean Fried Chicken

Serves: 2

Prep time: 30 minutes, plus marinating **Cook time:** 20 minutes

250ml (1 cup) buttermilk
½ teaspoon salt
1 teaspoon freshly grated ginger
4 boneless, skinless chicken thighs, cut into 2.5cm (1in) pieces
100g (3½oz) plain (all-purpose) flour
50g (1¾oz) cornflour (cornstarch)
¼ teaspoon freshly ground black pepper
neutral oil, for frying
1 tablespoon toasted sesame seeds, to serve

FOR THE SAUCE

85g (3oz) gochujang (see page 24)
3 tablespoons tomato ketchup
2 tablespoons mirin (see page 25)
1 tablespoon dark soy sauce
2 tablespoons honey
1 tablespoon soft light brown sugar
4 garlic cloves, very finely chopped
2 tablespoons Korean apple vinegar (see page 25) or white rice vinegar

TO SERVE

Simple Kimchi (see page 92)
steamed short-grain rice

My first taste of authentic Korean fried chicken was during a visit to Seoul when I met up with an old school friend. She took me to this amazing Korean fried chicken restaurant, and I'll never forget that experience - crispy fried chicken paired with ice-cold Korean beer felt like the perfect combination I never knew I needed. What struck me most was the incredible variety of options. There were so many different styles and toppings to choose from. You could go for the sauced version, like we're making here, or try the one with crispy garlic flakes mixed right into the batter. They even served deep-fried tteokbokki rice cakes alongside the chicken. The chicken itself was absolutely amazing - so much crunchier than any fried chicken I'd had before, with that signature double-frying technique that makes it so special. But it was the sauce that really made it unforgettable: sweet, spicy and sticky. One bite, and I understood why Korean fried chicken has become such a global obsession!

In a bowl, combine the buttermilk, salt and grated ginger. Add the chicken thigh pieces and stir, ensuring they're fully coated. Cover and leave to marinate for at least 30 minutes, or overnight in the fridge.

To make the sauce, combine the gochujang, ketchup, mirin, soy sauce, honey and brown sugar in a small saucepan over a medium heat. Bring to a gentle simmer and cook, stirring occasionally, for 3–4 minutes until the sugar has fully dissolved. Stir in the garlic and simmer for 1–2 minutes more, then remove from the heat. Whisk in the vinegar and set aside.

Combine the flour, cornflour and black pepper in a large mixing bowl, then remove the chicken from the marinade and let any excess drip off. Dredge each piece of chicken in the flour mixture and press the coating into the meat for maximum crunch.

Now, pour neutral oil into a large, deep-sided pan to a depth of 2.5cm (1in). Place over a medium-high heat and heat the oil to 140°C (275°F). Working in batches, fry the coated chicken pieces for 6–8 minutes, then transfer to a wire rack to drain while you cook the rest.

Once all the chicken has been cooked, increase the heat slightly and bring the oil temperature up to 180°C (350°F). Still working in batches, return the chicken to the pan and fry for 2–3 minutes until it is golden brown and reaches an internal temperature of 74°C (165°F).

Toss the hot fried chicken in the gochujang sauce until well coated, then sprinkle with the sesame seeds. Serve with kimchi and rice.

Classic Chinese Dumplings

Makes: 24

Prep time: 30 minutes **Cook time:** 20 minutes

300g (10½oz) plain (all-purpose) flour or high-gluten wheat flour (see tip), plus extra for dusting

FOR THE FILLING

1 spring onion (scallion), cut into 2.5cm (1in) lengths and bashed
2.5cm (1in) piece of fresh ginger, bashed
1 teaspoon Sichuan peppercorns, crushed
200g (7oz) minced pork
100g (3½oz) raw prawns, peeled, deveined and very finely chopped
2 teaspoons light soy sauce
1 teaspoon sesame oil
1 teaspoon granulated sugar
1 teaspoon salt
½ teaspoon ground white pepper
100g (3½oz) Chinese chives (garlic chives or gau choi), finely chopped

FOR THE DIPPING SAUCE

4 tablespoons light soy sauce
2 tablespoons Chinese black vinegar (see page 24)
½ teaspoon sesame oil
1cm (½in) piece of fresh ginger, sliced into thin matchsticks
1 spring onion, finely sliced

I often make these as a fun weekend activity with my kids. There's a lot of work involved in rolling out the dumplings, so having a little production line going is handy. A classic Chinese dumpling has a thicker wrapper compared to a Japanese gyoza. Typically, you boil them, but if there are any leftovers, I like to keep them in the fridge to pan-fry the next day - this gives them a lovely crispy base. These dumplings are one of my dad's favourite foods. He can devour a plateful in the blink of an eye ... come to think of it, so can I! The traditional accompaniment is a tangy and warming Chinese black vinegar and shredded ginger dipping sauce.

Combine all the ingredients for the dipping sauce in a small bowl and set aside.

For the filling, pour 90ml (3fl oz) just-boiled water into a separate bowl, and add the bashed spring onion and ginger. Sprinkle in the Sichuan peppercorns, stir and set aside to cool.

Tip the flour into a large bowl and add 150ml (5fl oz) warm water, mixing all the while with chopsticks or a metal spoon. Now add 3 tablespoons room-temperature water and stir until no more liquid can be seen. Knead the dough until smooth, then place into a clean bowl. Cover with a clean tea towel and set aside to rest for 30 minutes.

Meanwhile, combine the minced pork and chopped prawns in a mixing bowl. Add the soy sauce, sesame oil, sugar, salt and white pepper, and stir vigorously to mix everything together to form a paste-like mixture. Strain the cooled infused water, removing the aromatics, then gradually add the infused water to the bowl. Mix well in a clockwise motion until all the water has been incorporated. Finally, add the chopped Chinese chives and mix briefly to combine. Cover and keep in the fridge until you're ready to assemble the dumplings.

To make the dumplings, remove the dough from the bowl and knead on a floured surface for a minute or so until smooth. Form the dough into a large ball and make a hole in the middle so that it looks like a doughnut. Use your hands to even the dough out in a circular motion, then tear one side to turn the doughnut into a log. Roll out the log to make it longer, trying to keep it as even as possible. Now start to divide it into pieces about 2.5cm (1in) long, pulling each piece from the log and rolling to make little dough balls. The dough should yield 22-24 dumplings.

Use a rolling pin to flatten each dough ball into a thin disc about 10cm (4in) in diameter, dusting with flour if the dough gets sticky. Cover any pieces of dough that you're not using with a clean tea towel to prevent them from drying out.

Take a dough disc and place a spoonful of filling in the centre. Bring the sides up and around the filling to form a little parcel. Crimp the seams to seal and set aside on a lined tray. Repeat until all the filling and dough discs are used up, leaving a little space between the dumplings on the tray and sprinkling some flour over them so they don't stick together. Cover with a clean tea towel to stop them drying out.

Bring a large saucepan of water to the boil. Working in batches of about 8, place the dumplings into the boiling water. Add a small cup of cold water to the pan and allow the water to come back to the boil. Do this 3 more times, and when the dumplings float to the top, the filling is cooked. This will take about 6–8 minutes in total. Repeat with the rest.

Serve the dumplings immediately, alongside the dipping sauce.

TIPS

* Using high-gluten wheat flour (also known as dumpling flour) creates a more elastic dough, which is easier to work with.
* You can freeze the dumplings once they are made. Freeze on a tray, spaced well apart, for 2 hours until firm, then transfer into a freezer bag. This stops them sticking together.

Japanese Chicken Gyoza, page 112

Classic Chinese Dumplings, page 108

Japanese Chicken Gyoza

Makes: 30–35 dumplings

Prep time: 30 minutes **Cook time:** 10 minutes

Japanese gyoza, or dumplings, feature a thin wrapper and a flat base. My preferred cooking method is to pan-steam them, which means the gyozas are first pan-fried and then, with the addition of water, steamed in the same pan. This gives you a lovely soft gyoza with a satisfyingly crispy base. I've included a simple dipping sauce here; and I sometimes like to add a few fresh chopped chillies for a touch of spice and colour. Gyoza freeze really well, so I like to batch-prepare these and keep them in the freezer (see tip). They make a perfect light bite, lunch or snack for unexpected visitors.

150g (5½oz) white cabbage, roughly chopped
½ onion, roughly chopped
1 small carrot, peeled and roughly chopped
1 spring onion (scallion), roughly chopped
2 teaspoons freshly grated ginger
300g (10½oz) boneless, skinless chicken thighs, roughly chopped
285g (10¼oz) packet of frozen gyoza dumpling wrappers, defrosted
1 tablespoon neutral oil

FOR THE SEASONING

2 tablespoons Japanese soy sauce (see page 21) or light soy sauce
1 tablespoon mirin (see page 25)
½ teaspoon salt
1 teaspoon granulated sugar
½ teaspoon sesame oil
1 teaspoon cornflour (cornstarch)

FOR THE DIPPING SAUCE

2 tablespoons Japanese soy sauce or light soy sauce
1 tablespoon white wine vinegar
drop of sesame oil
1 teaspoon toasted white sesame seeds

Add the cabbage, onion, carrot, spring onion and ginger to a food processor. Pulse for about 20 seconds until you have very small pieces that still have a bit of texture. Transfer to a large bowl.

Now add the chicken to the food processor and pulse for 15-20 seconds, again trying to retain some texture. Add the chicken to the bowl with the vegetables and combine.

Add all the seasoning ingredients to the chicken and vegetable mixture, and mix again thoroughly.

To make the gyoza, take a gyoza wrapper in one hand and spoon a heaped teaspoon of the filling into the centre. Wet the edges of the wrapper, then pull up both sides and pinch together in the middle. Make little folds on either side to seal it tightly. Make sure the gyoza has a flat base by lightly rolling it on a flat surface, then place on to a baking tray lined with a clean tea towel or some baking paper (this will keep them from sticking). Repeat until all the filling has been used up.

Heat the oil in a non-stick frying pan over a medium heat and add the gyoza to the pan, making sure they are positioned base-down. You'll need to work in batches. Fry for 1-2 minutes until the bases have turned a golden brown colour. Add 3 tablespoons water to the pan and immediately cover with a lid. Leave to steam for 4-5 minutes, then remove the lid and cook for a further 2 minutes until all the water has evaporated. Transfer to a warm serving plate and repeat with the remaining gyoza.

Combine all the ingredients for the dipping sauce in a small bowl, and serve alongside the gyoza.

1.

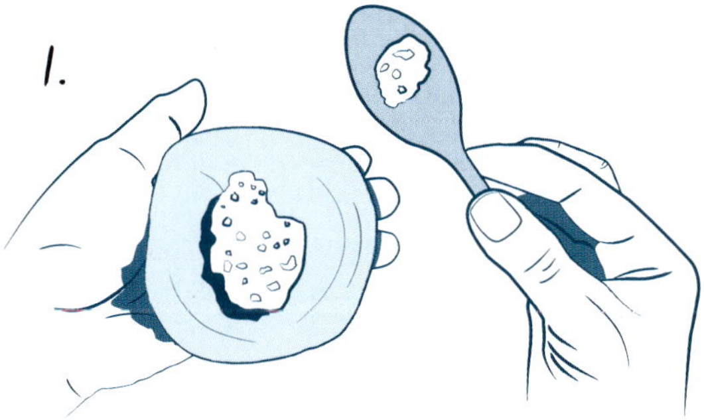

2.

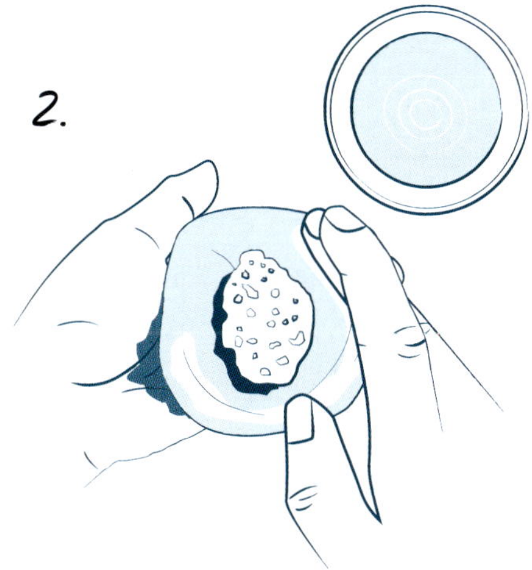

3.

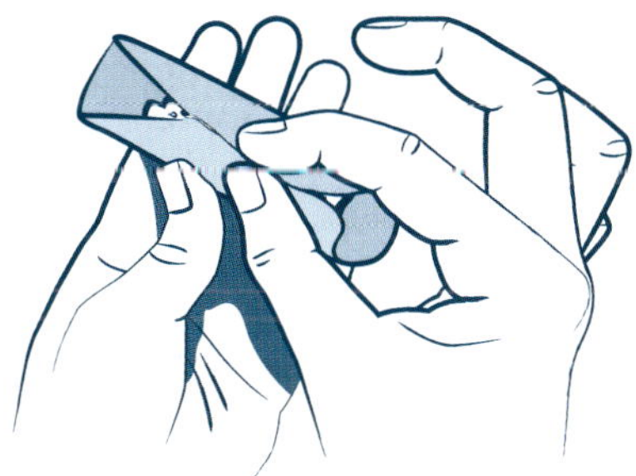

4.

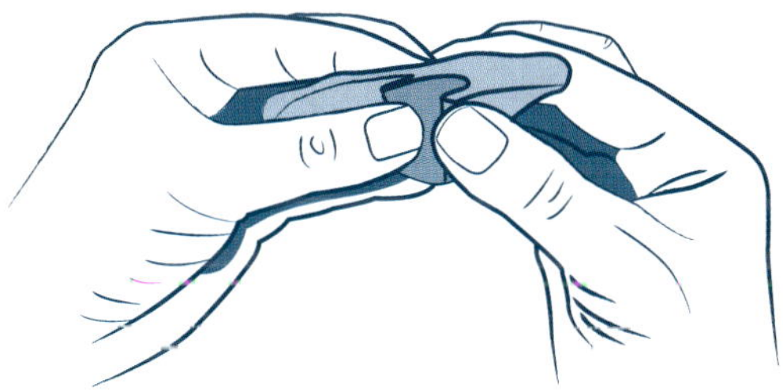

5.

TIP

✱ To cook gyoza from frozen, there is no need to defrost them first. Either boil for 8–10 minutes or steam-fry them from frozen as described opposite, adding an extra 3–4 minutes to the cooking time.

Serves: 4

Vietnamese Lemongrass Pork Chop Bánh Mì

Prep time: 10 minutes, plus marinating **Cook time:** 20 minutes

- 4 boneless pork chops
- 4 small baguettes
- 75g (2¾oz) chicken liver pâté (optional)
- 50g (1¾oz) mayonnaise
- 100g (3½oz) Pickled Daikon (see page 96), well drained
- 1 large red chilli, finely sliced
- large handful of coriander (cilantro)

FOR THE MARINADE

- 4 lemongrass stalks, white parts only, finely minced
- 3 garlic cloves, minced
- 2 shallots, finely diced
- 2 tablespoons soft light brown sugar
- 1½ tablespoons fish sauce
- 1½ tablespoons Vietnamese soy sauce (see page 21) or light soy sauce
- 1 tablespoon vegetable oil
- ½ teaspoon ground white pepper
- ½ teaspoon salt

I fondly remember my first introduction to bánh mì, which in my mind is like the original fusion dish. I stepped out of my hotel in Hanoi, turned down a side street to a bustling food cart and ordered what everyone else was having: a newspaper-wrapped French baguette with an explosion of delicious flavours within. Thinly sliced lemongrass pork, pickled veg, lovely fresh coriander and a sprinkling of fresh red chilli. It was the best filled roll I'd ever had.

Tenderise the pork chops by placing them between 2 sheets of baking paper and bashing them lightly with a meat mallet or rolling pin until they are roughly 5mm (¼in) thick.

To make the marinade, bash the lemongrass, garlic and shallots using a large pestle and mortar until a thick paste forms and the lemongrass has broken down. Alternatively, you can do this in a small food processor to speed things up. Add the sugar, fish sauce, soy sauce, oil, white pepper and salt, and mix everything together.

Rub this marinade all over the pork chops, turning them to coat evenly. Cover and leave to marinate at room temperature for at least 30 minutes. Alternatively, you can marinate the pork in the fridge overnight.

When you're ready to cook, lightly oil a non-stick frying pan (or a griddle pan, if you have one) and place over a medium-high heat. Cook the chops for 4–5 minutes per side until nicely charred and cooked through, then remove from the pan and allow to rest for 5 minutes.

To assemble the bánh mì, place the baguettes in an air fryer and spritz with a tiny bit of water, then air-fry at 180°C (350°F) for 4 minutes. Alternatively, cook in an oven preheated to 180°C fan (350°F/gas mark 4) for 5 minutes.

Slice the warmed baguettes open lengthways, leaving a hinge. Spread the bottom half of each baguette with the pâté, if using, and the other half with mayo. If you're not using pâté, just spread both sides with the mayo.

Slice the pork and divide it among the baguettes. Load up each one with the pickled daikon, sliced red chilli and a healthy amount of coriander, then gently close the baguettes, pressing down lightly. Slice each one in half and serve immediately.

Makes: 8

Five-Spiced Pork Belly with Steamed Bao Buns

Prep time: 30 minutes, plus proving **Cook time:** 1½ hours

2 tablespoons neutral oil
4cm (1½in) piece of fresh ginger, thinly sliced
400g (14oz) deboned raw pork belly strips, chopped into 5cm (2in) pieces
2 cinnamon sticks
2 star anise

FOR THE BAO BUNS

240g (8¾oz) low-gluten wheat flour (see tip), plus extra for dusting
1 tablespoon caster (superfine) sugar
½ teaspoon salt
½ teaspoon baking powder
1 teaspoon active dried yeast
1 tablespoon vegetable oil, plus extra for brushing
3 tablespoons warm milk

FOR THE BRAISING SAUCE

1 tablespoon light soy sauce
1 tablespoon dark soy sauce
1 tablespoon of chu hou (five-spice) paste (see page 22)
1 tablespoon Shaoxing wine (see page 22)
40g (1½oz) rock sugar (see page 27), or soft light brown sugar

TO SERVE

2 spring onions (scallions), finely sliced
1 red chilli, finely sliced
50g (1¾oz) salted peanuts, crushed in a pestle and mortar
small handful of coriander (cilantro) leaves, finely chopped

These bao buns (pictured overleaf) are unbelievably moreish. The filling features pork belly braised in a rich five-spiced cooking liquor. While the pork is braising and filling your kitchen with wonderful aromas, you can prepare your steamed bao buns. I typically use a stand mixer fitted with a dough hook to make the dough - it's very straightforward. The buns can be made in advance and frozen for later use. You can, of course, buy frozen bao buns in the supermarket, but I prefer the warm, yeasty flavour of the homemade ones. Once you have made these, you will realise just how versatile they are and will want to experiment with different delicious fillings. Breaded prawns, teriyaki salmon, deep-fried chicken - the world is your bao bun!

Start with the bao buns. Add all the ingredients to the bowl of a stand mixer, along with 100ml (3½oz) warm water. Mix with the dough hook for 3 minutes until combined. (Alternatively, mix by hand in a bowl.) Transfer the dough to a floured surface and knead for 3-4 minutes until smooth. Roll out the dough to a thickness of about 3mm (⅛in) height. Use a round cutter or pint glass to cut out rounds from the dough - a 9cm (3½in) cutter will make 8 bao buns.

Brush the bao buns with vegetable oil, then fold each one into a half-moon so the oiled side is in the middle - this will keep them from sticking too much. Place each bun on a square of baking paper and arrange on a baking tray, spacing them well apart. Cover with a clean tea towel and leave to prove for 1½-2 hours, or until they double in size.

Meanwhile, get started on your pork belly. Heat the oil in a wok or large frying pan over a medium heat. Once hot, add the ginger pieces and pork belly. Fry the pork belly for 3-4 minutes on each side until slightly browned. Add the cinnamon and star anise and stir for a minute or two.

Combine all the braising sauce ingredients in a jug with 650ml (22½fl oz) water. Pour this mixture into the pan. Cover the pan with a lid and simmer, still over a medium heat, for 50-55 minutes, until the liquid has mostly evaporated and you are left with a sticky, dark, sweet sauce that coats the pork belly.

When your bao buns have finished proving, transfer them to a steamer, still on their baking paper squares. Steam for 8 minutes, working in batches if needed. A bamboo or pot steamer will work here, so use whatever you have.

Let the steamed bao buns rest for 5 minutes, then fill them with the pork belly, spring onions, red chilli, peanuts and coriander. Enjoy!

TIPS

* Low-gluten wheat flour is used to make the bao soft and light and helps stop them becoming too dense. If you prefer, you can just use plain (all-purpose) flour.
* You can freeze any leftover steamed bao buns by placing them on a tray and freezing for a couple of hours. After this time, they can be transferred into a freezer bag. To reheat, steam them from frozen for about 8 minutes until piping hot throughout.

Five-Spiced Pork Belly with Steamed Bao Buns, page 116

K-Toast: Korean Ham-and-Cheese Toastie

Serves: 4

Prep time: 15 minutes **Cook time:** 10 minutes

4 teaspoons salted butter, plus extra for the omelette
8 thick slices of white bread
4 slices of ham
1 teaspoon caster (superfine) sugar
4 slices of cheese, either American-style cheese singles or any mild Cheddar
4 tablespoons tomato ketchup, plus extra to taste
4 tablespoons Japanese mayonnaise (see page 25) or regular mayonnaise, plus extra to taste

FOR THE OMELETTE

80g (2¾oz) white cabbage, finely shredded
1 carrot, peeled and finely julienned
½ small onion, finely sliced
1 spring onion (scallion), finely sliced
2 eggs, beaten
salt and freshly ground black pepper

K-toast is short for Korean-style toast, which is Korea's take on a classic ham-and-cheese toastie. Inside, you'll find ham and cheese with ketchup, as well as - and now for the Korean bit - a cabbage, carrot and onion omelette! There is also a special ingredient: a sprinkling of sugar. You might not typically think to include sugar in a sandwich, but in this case, it tastes delicious. K-toast is really popular in Korea, especially in the street markets like Namdaemun in Seoul. When I first tasted this sandwich, I fell in love with it. I sometimes like to ramp up the Korean flavours by adding a layer of kimchi as well.

Begin by preparing the omelette. In a bowl, mix together the cabbage, carrot, onion, spring onion and eggs. Season with salt and pepper and set aside.

Heat a non-stick frying pan over medium heat and add a small amount of butter. Spoon 5 tablespoons of the omelette mixture into the pan and form it into a small, thin, rectangular omelette - you're aiming to get it the same size as a slice of bread, so the omelette fits well inside your sandwich when you assemble it. Cook for 2 minutes on each side until golden brown, then transfer to a plate and repeat with the remaining mixture - you should get 4 omelettes in total.

In the same pan, melt 1 teaspoon of the butter, then place 2 bread slices in the pan and toast for 1-2 minutes on each side until golden brown. Set aside and repeat with the remaining butter and bread slices.

Now add the ham slices to the pan and sear quickly on both sides for about 30 seconds, just to warm through.

To assemble your first sandwich, take a slice of toasted bread and top it with a cooked omelette. Sprinkle ¼ teaspoon of the sugar over the omelette, then top with a slice of ham and a slice of cheese. Drizzle with ketchup and mayonnaise - as much or as little as you'd like - then top with a second slice of bread. Transfer the sandwich to the pan and toast, still over a medium heat, for about a minute on each side to warm through.

Serve immediately, and repeat to make the remaining sandwiches.

Chinese Cumin Lamb Skewers

Serves: 6 as a starter

Prep time: 20 minutes, plus marinating **Cook time:** 15 minutes

500g (1lb 2oz) lamb shoulder or leg, with a good fat cap, cut into 2.5cm (1in) cubes

FOR THE MARINADE

2 tablespoons light soy sauce
1 tablespoon Shaoxing wine (see page 22)
1 tablespoon neutral oil, plus extra for brushing
¼ teaspoon salt
½ teaspoon granulated sugar
1 teaspoon ground cumin
1 teaspoon chilli flakes
½ teaspoon Sichuan peppercorn powder
2 garlic cloves, minced
1 teaspoon grated ginger

FOR THE SPICE MIX

1 tablespoon whole cumin seeds
1 tablespoon ground cumin
2 teaspoons chilli flakes
½ teaspoon flaky sea salt

I remember walking through the streets of Beijing, passing countless food stalls that filled the air with the most mouthwatering smells and wonderful sounds. What caught my attention was a small, simple stand with a charcoal grill and the irresistible aroma of grilled lamb skewers seasoned with cumin. The flavour combination is absolutely unbeatable. Traditionally, the skewers alternate between chunks of meat and fat, which adds flavour as the fat melts during grilling. Personally, I prefer less fat, so in this recipe I've used small pieces of lamb shoulder. For the marinade, I've used a mix of Sichuan pepper powder, cumin, garlic, ginger and a few herbs. I've given instructions for cooking them in a griddle pan, but if you can cook them on the barbecue, they are even better.

In a large bowl, combine the lamb pieces with the marinade ingredients. Mix well, cover and marinate in the fridge for at least 2 hours, or preferably overnight.

When you're ready to cook, thread the marinated lamb pieces on to metal skewers (or soak wooden skewers in water for 30 minutes before using).

For the spice mix, toast the whole cumin seeds in a dry frying pan over a medium heat for about 1 minute until fragrant, then tip into a bowl. Add the ground cumin, chilli flakes and salt. Stir and set aside.

Place a griddle pan over a medium-high heat and brush lightly with oil. Cook the skewers for about 8-10 minutes, turning occasionally until nicely charred on the edges and cooked through.

During the last minute of grilling, sprinkle the spice mix generously over the skewers. Serve piping hot.

TIP

✱ If you'd prefer to cook these on the barbecue, cook them over a high heat for 6-8 minutes until nicely charred and cooked through.

Soups & Salads

Tom Yum Soup 125

Hot-and-Sour Soup 126

Wonton Soup 129

Thai Beef Salad 130

Wakame Seaweed Salad 132

Asian Cucumber Salad 132

Asian-Style Coleslaw 133

Chicken and Sweetcorn Soup 137

Salmon Miso Soup 138

Cold Sesame Ramen Noodle Salad 139

Tom Yum Soup

Serves: 2

Prep time: 10 minutes **Cook time:** 15 minutes

- 3cm (1¼in) piece of galangal (see page 16), thickly sliced
- 5 makrut lime leaves (fresh or frozen), torn into pieces
- 1 banana shallot, finely sliced
- 3 lemongrass stalks, white parts only, cut into 5cm (2in) pieces and lightly crushed
- 12g (½oz) coriander (cilantro) roots (see tip), washed and chopped into 5cm (2in pieces), plus finely chopped leaves for garnish
- 3 garlic cloves, peeled and lightly crushed
- 200g (7oz) raw prawns, peeled and deveined
- 80g (2¾oz) oyster or chestnut mushrooms, sliced
- 3 tablespoons fish sauce
- 2 tablespoons coconut milk
- 2½ tablespoons nam prik pao (Thai chilli paste, see page 24)
- 2 tablespoons lime juice
- 1 teaspoon salt
- 2–3 red bird's-eye chillies, finely sliced, to serve (optional)

Tom yum soup holds such a special place in my heart because of my annual trips to Thailand with my dad for Thaifex, which is a huge Thai food exhibition in Bangkok. There's this incredible restaurant called Somboon, where they serve the most amazing tom yum soup in a stainless-steel hot pot, which is kept bubbling hot by little flames underneath. What I love most about this soup is how perfectly balanced it is. Despite having that signature spicy kick, the flavours feel surprisingly light and refreshing. That bright, zingy lime flavour cuts through everything, creating a clean taste that's so comforting. The magic really comes from all those gorgeous fresh aromatics - the galangal, lemongrass and fresh coriander all working together to create a fragrant base. What makes this recipe even better is its versatility. While it's perfect on its own, I love using it as a base and adding noodles to make a more substantial meal.

Pour 1 litre (4 cups) water into a large saucepan and place over a medium heat. Add the galangal, lime leaves, shallot, lemongrass, coriander roots and garlic. Bring to the boil, then reduce the heat to a simmer and allow to infuse for 2–3 minutes.

Add the prawns and mushrooms, and simmer for 4 minutes, then stir in the fish sauce, coconut milk, nam prik pao, lime juice and salt. Simmer for a further minute.

Ladle the soup into bowls, leaving the aromatics in the pan, and serve garnished with some chopped coriander leaves and the sliced chillies, if using.

TIPS

- If you can't find coriander root, you can use the stems of the plant instead, cutting 10cm (4in) from the base of the stem/plant.
- I've gone for a creamy version of tom yum soup by adding coconut milk; if you prefer a clear version, just leave it out.
- To make this into a more substantial meal, try adding ho fun (flat white rice) noodles.

Hot-and-Sour Soup

Serves: 4

Prep time: 25 minutes **Cook time:** 15 minutes

Hot-and-sour soup is a Shanghainese specialty. If you have never tried it, you simply must! I don't know anyone who has tried it and not loved it. The hot element comes from a Chinese chilli bean paste known as toban sauce, while the sourness comes from a Chinese black vinegar. Beyond just the hot-and-sour flavour, this soup is very textural, with crunchy wood ear mushrooms, tender pork and luxuriously silky tofu. Restaurants usually serve hot-and-sour soup with a small ramekin of red vinegar, allowing you to adjust the sourness to your own taste.

50g (1¾oz) dried shiitake mushrooms
50g (1¾oz) dried wood ear or black fungus mushrooms (see page 26)
1 teaspoon neutral oil
1cm (½in) piece of fresh ginger, finely sliced into matchsticks
1 litre (4 cups) chicken or vegetable stock
50g (1¾oz) carrot, julienned
40g (1½oz) bamboo shoots, finely sliced into matchsticks
4 tablespoons Chinese black vinegar (see page 24)
2 tablespoons light soy sauce
1 teaspoon dark soy sauce
½–1 teaspoon Chinese toban sauce (chilli bean paste, see page 22)
½ teaspoon ground white pepper
1 tablespoon cornflour (cornstarch)
1 egg, lightly beaten
200g (7oz) silken tofu, cut into thin strips

FOR THE PORK

100g (3½oz) pork fillet, thinly sliced
¼ teaspoon Shaoxing wine (see page 22)
¼ teaspoon caster (superfine) sugar
salt and ground white pepper

TO SERVE

2 spring onions (scallions), sliced
handful of roughly chopped coriander (cilantro)
Chinese red vinegar (see page 25)

Begin by preparing the pork. Place the sliced pork in a bowl and add the Shaoxing wine, sugar and a pinch each of salt and white pepper. Mix well and set aside to marinate while you prepare the other ingredients.

Place the shiitake mushrooms and wood ear mushrooms in another bowl and pour over enough just-boiled water to cover. Leave to rehydrate for 10 minutes, then finely slice.

Heat the oil in a large, deep-sided saucepan over a medium-high heat. Once hot, add the ginger and stir-fry for 20 seconds, then add the marinated pork and stir-fry for 1-2 minutes. Pour in the stock and bring everything to a simmer.

Add the mushrooms and carrot and simmer for a minute more, then add the bamboo shoots, Chinese black vinegar, soy sauces, toban sauce and white pepper. Taste and adjust the seasoning - it should be slightly tangy and a little bit spicy.

In a small bowl, mix the cornflour with 2 tablespoons water. Stir this mixture into the soup, then continue stirring slowly until the soup thickens slightly.

Remove the pan from the heat and slowly drizzle the beaten egg into the soup while gently stirring in one direction. This will create silky egg ribbons. Finally, add the tofu and gently stir, taking care not to break up the tofu too much.

Ladle the soup into bowls and garnish with chopped spring onions and coriander. Serve with Chinese red vinegar on the side for everyone to season their own bowls.

TIP

✱ To make a vegetarian version, use vegetable stock and omit the pork.

醬油
Tung Chun
紅浙醋
VINEGAR
CHINOIS
(500毫升)
NET 500 g

Wonton Soup

Serves: 4–6

Prep time: 25 minutes **Cook time:** 50 minutes

1 tablespoon neutral oil
300g (10½oz) raw chicken wings
5cm (2in) piece of fresh ginger, peeled and thickly sliced
4 spring onions (scallions), 2 cut into 5cm (2in) pieces and 2 finely sliced
1 teaspoon salt
¼ teaspoon ground white pepper
2 green pak choi, trimmed and halved

FOR THE WONTONS

200g (7oz) raw prawns, peeled, deveined and chopped into 1cm (½in) pieces
150g (5½oz) minced pork
70g (2½oz) tinned water chestnuts, very finely chopped
1 tablespoon light soy sauce
1½ teaspoons sesame oil
1 teaspoon cornflour (cornstarch)
1 teaspoon salt
1 teaspoon granulated sugar
½ teaspoon ground white pepper
200g (7oz) packet frozen wonton wrappers

To me, wontons and Hong Kong go hand in hand. There is something about the delicacy of the flavours, the size of the bowl and the theatre of seeing this dish prepared that always reminds me of my time in Hong Kong. Every neighbourhood there has a number of small, casual wonton restaurants, usually with a steam-filled glass kiosk at the front, in which a chef is busy preparing the wontons, peering out past a stack of bowls. Fillings can vary, but traditional Hong Kong-style wontons are filled with prawn and a little bit of pork. The soup broth is just as important. Traditionally, it is made with dried flounder fish, but I have adapted my recipe to use chicken stock, which pairs beautifully with the warmth of ginger - oh-so-comforting!

Heat the oil in a large saucepan over a medium heat and stir-fry the chicken wings for 3 minutes until lightly browned. Add 1 litre (4 cups) water, along with the ginger and large spring onion pieces, and simmer for about 25 minutes. Strain through a sieve into a clean pan and stir in the salt and white pepper.

To prepare the wonton filling, combine the chopped prawns and pork mince in a bowl. Add the water chestnuts, soy sauce, sesame oil, cornflour, salt, sugar and white pepper, and mix well to combine.

To fill the wontons, place a wonton wrapper on a plate or in the palm of your hand and add 1 heaped teaspoon of the filling mixture. Wet the edges of the wrapper with a little water and fold over diagonally, pinching two of the corners together, then bring the two other corners together so that all four corners meet in the middle. It's important to make sure the wonton is properly sealed, or else water will get in, which will make the wonton flavourless. Continue making wontons until all the filling is used up.

To cook the wontons, bring a large saucepan of water to the boil and add the wontons, working in batches. Cook for 8-10 minutes until they float to the top of the water, then scoop out and set aside while you cook the rest.

Meanwhile, bring the broth back to the boil. Add the pak choi and cook for 3-4 minutes until tender.

To serve, divide the wontons and pak choi between bowls. Top up with a couple of ladlefuls of the broth, and finally garnish with some sliced spring onions.

TIP

✱ If you don't have pak choi, you can use whatever leafy green veg you'd like - choy sum, tenderstem broccoli, Chinese leaf or Chinese spinach will all work well.

Thai Beef Salad

Serves: 4

Prep time: 20 minutes **Cook time:** 20 minutes

200g (7oz) vermicelli rice noodles
2 thick-cut sirloin steaks
2 tablespoons neutral oil
pinch of salt
2 garlic cloves, very finely chopped
1cm (½in) piece of fresh ginger, very finely chopped
1 lemongrass stalk, white parts only, very finely sliced
1–2 small red bird's-eye chillies, finely sliced (use more or less depending on how spicy you like it)
3 tablespoons light soy sauce
2 tablespoons fish sauce
1 tablespoon soft light brown sugar
1 teaspoon sesame oil
juice of 1 lime, plus lime wedges to serve
1 red onion, finely sliced
cherry tomatoes, halved
½ head frisée lettuce (curly endive)
½ cucumber, deseeded and finely sliced into half-moons
handful of coriander (cilantro) leaves
handful of mint leaves
handful of Thai basil leaves

To call this a salad is maybe a little bit of a stretch, but stay with me - it's really, really good. It has noodles, cucumbers, lettuce, cherry tomatoes and onions, all topped with beautiful slices of seared beef. The dressing is where this salad really comes to life: it's packed with bold Thai flavours including fish sauce, garlic, ginger, lemongrass, chilli and lime. This is a great dish to serve at dinner parties or summer barbecues.

Cook the vermicelli noodles according to the packet instructions, then drain and set aside.

Place a frying pan over a high heat. Rub the steaks with 1 tablespoon of the oil and season with a pinch of salt. Cook for 3-4 minutes on each side until the meat reaches 54°C (129°F) for medium-rare, then remove from the pan and leave to rest.

Add the remaining 1 tablespoon oil to the same pan and allow it to get very hot. Add the garlic, ginger, lemongrass and chilli(es). Cook for about a minute, then add the soy sauce, fish sauce, sugar, sesame oil and lime juice, stirring to combine. Now add the red onion, tomatoes and drained vermicelli noodles, swirling the pan around to heat everything through. Remove from the heat.

Arrange the lettuce and cucumber on a serving platter, then spoon the contents of the pan on top, drizzling over any juices left in the pan. Now, very thinly slice the steak and drape it over the veg and noodles. Tear the herbs and sprinkle them over the top. Serve straight away, with some extra lime wedges on the side for squeezing.

TIP

* If you're serving this at a barbecue, prepare all the other ingredients in advance, then gently sear the steaks on the barbecue and assemble.

Wakame Seaweed Salad

Serves: 4 as a side salad

Prep time: 15 minutes **Cook time:** 20–30 minutes

- 40g (1½oz) dried wakame (see page 26)
- 1 spring onion (scallion), thinly sliced
- ½ cucumber, julienned
- 2 teaspoons toasted sesame seeds

FOR THE DRESSING

- 3 tablespoons light soy sauce
- 2 tablespoons sesame oil
- 1½ tablespoons white rice vinegar
- 1 teaspoon caster (superfine) sugar
- 1 teaspoon mirin (see page 25)
- ¼ teaspoon freshly grated ginger
- pinch of salt

Seaweed salad is a staple side dish in many Japanese restaurants. This simple and classic dish features dried wakame seaweed, known for its unique crunchy texture. The light dressing enhances the flavours, while the addition of cucumber and sesame seeds creates a refreshing and versatile salad that complements a variety of dishes beautifully.

Place the dried wakame in a large bowl of cold water and soak for 5-10 minutes, or until fully rehydrated. It will expand significantly and should yield about 300g (10½oz) rehydrated seaweed. Drain and gently squeeze out any excess water, then, if the seaweed is in large pieces, slice it into thin, noodle-like strips - using scissors is helpful here. Set aside in a large bowl.

While the wakame soaks, combine the dressing ingredients in a small bowl and whisk until well combined.

Add the spring onion and julienned cucumber to the bowl with the seaweed, then pour the dressing over the top and toss gently to coat evenly.

Let the salad chill in the fridge for 15-30 minutes before sprinkling with the sesame seeds and serving.

Asian Cucumber Salad

Serves: 4 as a side salad

Prep time: 15 minutes **Cook time:** 15 minutes

- 1 large cucumber
- 1 teaspoon salt
- 3 tablespoons Chinese black vinegar (see page 24)
- 1 tablespoon light soy sauce
- 1 teaspoon caster (superfine) sugar
- 2 garlic cloves, finely chopped
- small handful of coriander (cilantro), finely chopped, plus extra to serve
- ½ red chilli, deseeded and finely chopped
- 1 tablespoon toasted sesame seeds

This is a traditional Chinese appetiser called pai huang gua, which means 'smashed cucumbers'. The act of smashing the cucumber before chopping helps it to soak up all the lovely dressing. To keep the cucumber chunks super crunchy, we salt them to remove as much moisture as possible. This salad has a lovely umami flavour, with that lively kick of garlic and coriander which I absolutely love.

Smash the cucumber with the side of your cleaver or a rolling pin, then roughly chop the cucumber into cubes. Place all the chopped cucumber pieces into a sieve over a bowl. Sprinkle with the salt and set aside for 15-20 minutes. The salt helps draw the water out of the cucumber, giving it a bit more crunch.

Tip the drained cucumber into a bowl and add the vinegar, soy sauce, sugar, garlic, coriander and chilli. Mix well to combine, then transfer to a serving dish and sprinkle with the sesame seeds and extra chopped coriander to serve. Eat immediately or keep in the fridge for up to a day before serving.

Asian-Style Coleslaw

Serves: 4–6

Prep time: 15 minutes **Cook time:** 10 minutes

300g (10½oz) white cabbage, very finely sliced
150g (5½oz) red cabbage, very finely sliced
1 carrot, peeled and julienned
2 spring onions (scallions), thinly sliced
2 pinches of salt
small handful of coriander (cilantro), finely chopped, plus extra to serve
1 tablespoon toasted white sesame seeds, plus extra to serve

FOR THE DRESSING

2 tablespoons white rice vinegar
1 tablespoon light soy sauce
1 tablespoon sesame oil
1 tablespoon sriracha
1 tablespoon honey
1 teaspoon freshly grated ginger
1 small garlic clove, finely minced
juice of 1 lime

Homemade coleslaw is so different from the shop-bought type, and I love it because you can add more of whatever vegetable you like. This coleslaw has no mayo, which makes it lighter and more zingy. The red cabbage isn't essential, but I love the colour that it brings. This recipe is definitely one to add to your repertoire: it complements so many dishes and is amazing as part of a barbecue.

Combine the white and red cabbage, carrot and spring onions in a large mixing bowl and sprinkle with the salt. Massage it in with your hands and set aside.

In a small bowl or jar, whisk together the dressing ingredients until well combined, then pour the dressing over the vegetables and add the coriander and sesame seeds. Toss everything together until evenly coated, then let the slaw sit for at least 10–15 minutes before serving.

Transfer into a serving bowl and sprinkle with some extra coriander and sesame seeds to serve.

Wakame Seaweed Salad, page 132

Asian Cucumber Salad, page 132

Asian-Style Coleslaw, page 133

Chicken and Sweetcorn Soup

Serves: 4

Prep time: 5 minutes **Cook time:** 25 minutes

- 1 litre (4 cups) chicken stock
- 2.5cm (1in) piece of fresh ginger, peeled and sliced into 3 big pieces
- 1 garlic clove, peeled and left whole
- 2 spring onions (scallions), white and green parts separated, whites cut into 5cm (2in) lengths, greens finely sliced
- 2 skinless chicken breasts
- 300g (10½oz) sweetcorn kernels (fresh, tinned or frozen)
- ½ teaspoon salt
- ¼ teaspoon ground white pepper
- 1 tablespoon cornflour (cornstarch)
- 1 egg, beaten
- small handful of coriander (cilantro) leaves, finely chopped, to garnish (optional)

When I was growing up, we used to make this soup using tinned creamed corn. For those of you unfamiliar with creamed corn, it's like a can of concentrated soup, to which you add water to dilute it. I learned to make this soup when I was very young, and it has become a pantry staple for me. Here, we are making our own creamed corn - it's delicious and really quick to prepare. Once you have the soup up to temperature, you turn off the heat and stir in a beaten egg, which creates strands of white ribbon running through the soup. In Chinese, we call this dan fa, which translates as 'egg flower'.

Pour the chicken stock into a medium saucepan and add the ginger slices, garlic clove and spring onion whites. Bring to a gentle simmer over a medium heat, then add the whole chicken breasts. Simmer gently, but don't boil, for 10-12 minutes, or until the chicken is just cooked through.

Remove the chicken from the pan, leave to cool slightly, then shred into small strips using two forks and set aside. Remove the ginger, garlic clove and spring onion from the stock with a slotted spoon and discard.

Add 225g (8oz) of the sweetcorn to the hot stock and bring the liquid back to a simmer. Cook for 3-4 minutes (a bit longer if using frozen corn), until everything is hot, then blitz the soup with a hand blender for 30 seconds-1 minute. You don't want to create a smooth soup; you just want to begin to break down a few of the sweetcorn kernels. Now stir in the remaining 75g (2¾oz) sweetcorn and season with the salt and white pepper.

In a small bowl, mix the cornflour with 2 tablespoons water. Stir this mixture into the soup, and continue stirring slowly until slightly thickened.

Return the shredded chicken to the soup and warm through for a couple of minutes, then turn off the heat. Slowly drizzle the beaten egg into the soup while gently stirring in one direction. This will create silky egg ribbons.

Taste and adjust the seasoning with salt or more white pepper if needed, then ladle the soup into bowls and garnish with the finely sliced spring onion greens and some finely chopped coriander, if you like.

TIP

✱ Try adding crabsticks for extra flavour and texture.

Salmon Miso Soup

Serves: 2

Prep time: 15 minutes **Cook time:** 45 minutes

- 1 tablespoon dried wakame (see page 26)
- 1 litre (4 cups) dashi stock (see page 25)
- 60g (2¼oz) shiitake mushrooms, finely sliced
- 200g (7oz) skinless salmon fillets, cut into 1cm (½in) dice
- 150g (5½oz) silken tofu, cut into 1cm (½in) dice
- 3 tablespoons white miso paste
- 2 spring onions (scallions), finely sliced

The main base of the miso soup is dashi broth, for which you can buy a powder or make your own using kombu and katsuobushi (also known as bonito flakes or dried tuna flakes; see page 26). You might recognise katsuobushi as the wafer-thin feather-like garnish on sushi rolls or takoyaki. I love miso soup. It's served with almost all set meals in Japan, and I just adore its warming umami comfort. Here, I'm adding little pieces of raw salmon to poach in the soup, which are beautifully tender and bring an extra flavour element.

Put the wakame in a bowl and cover with 150ml (5fl oz) cold water. Set aside until needed.

Prepare your dashi stock and bring to a simmer in a large saucepan. Add the sliced shiitake mushrooms and salmon, and cook for 2–3 minutes until the salmon pieces are cooked through.

Turn off the heat and add the tofu to the pan. Drain the wakame, which should now be rehydrated, and add this to the pot as well.

In a small bowl, combine the miso paste with a ladleful of the hot dashi. Carefully mix the two together until you have a smooth mixture with no lumps, then stir this back into the pan.

Divide the soup into bowls, and serve topped with the sliced spring onions.

TIPS

* Instead of making your own dashi stock, you can buy dashi stock powder in most Asian supermarkets. Simply follow the packet instructions to make up 1 litre (4 cups) of stock.
* This recipe is lovely, simple and clean, but if you want to inject some more salmon flavour, you can ask your fishmonger for salmon steaks on the bone and poach these in the broth for 10 minutes. Once they're cooked, you can remove them from the broth and flake the salmon flesh before stirring it back in.

Cold Sesame Ramen Noodle Salad

Serves: 2

Prep time: 15 minutes **Cook time:** 15 minutes

100g (3½oz) dried ramen noodles
100g (3½oz) cooked chicken breast, shredded
¼ cucumber, deseeded and julienned
¼ head of iceberg lettuce, shredded
2 spring onions (scallions), julienned
2 large vine tomatoes, deseeded and sliced into thin matchsticks
1 tablespoon toasted white sesame seeds
1 large nori sheet, cut into thin strips
small handful of coriander (cilantro) leaves (optional)

FOR THE GOMA DRESSING

2 tablespoons toasted white sesame seeds
2 tablespoons Japanese mayonnaise (see page 25)
1½ tablespoons rice wine vinegar
1 tablespoon tahini
1 tablespoon Japanese soy sauce (see page 21) or light soy sauce
1 tablespoon mirin (see page 25)
2 teaspoons caster (superfine) sugar
1 teaspoon sesame oil
pinch of salt

I often enjoy this salad at a Japanese restaurant in Hong Kong, China, overlooking Victoria Harbour. It's a simple meal, consisting of cold ramen noodles with fresh tomatoes and cucumber. What truly enhances it is the exquisite sesame sauce, which is what keeps me going back to this restaurant, again and again. In this recipe, I've recreated that sauce, often known in Japan as a goma dressing. If you are planning to prepare this dish in advance, I recommend keeping the dressing separate until you're ready to serve. The goma dressing is also lovely on other salads, so it's nice to make up some extra and keep it in the fridge.

Cook the ramen noodles according to the packet instructions, then drain and rinse under cold water until completely cool. Drain well once more, then set aside.

To make the dressing, grind the toasted sesame seeds using a pestle and mortar until they form a rough paste, then transfer to a bowl. Add the remaining dressing ingredients and whisk to combine. Add 2-3 tablespoons water to loosen the dressing to a pourable consistency, if necessary, then taste and adjust the seasoning.

Toss the cooled ramen noodles with the dressing until evenly coated, then add the chicken, cucumber, lettuce, spring onions and tomatoes and toss to combine. Transfer the noodles to a large serving platter and serve sprinkled with the sesame seeds, nori strips and coriander leaves, if using.

TIP

✱ You can buy ready-made goma dressing at most Asian supermarkets if you want to save time.

Curries & Stews

Thai Green Prawn Curry 143

Korean Kimchi Tofu Stew 144

Japanese Pork Katsu Curry 147

Malaysian Beef Rendang 148

Spicy Sichuan Boiled Fish Stew 151

Lamb Massaman Curry 152

Vietnamese Beef Bò Kho 153

Chicken Adobo 155

One-Pot Thai Red Curry Dumplings 156

Chicken Tikka Masala 158

Chinese Chicken Curry 159

Thai Green Prawn Curry

Serves: 4

Prep time: 15 minutes **Cook time:** 20 minutes

400g (14oz) tin coconut milk
100g (3½oz) courgette (zucchini), sliced into thick half-moons (I like to use baby courgettes if they are in season)
50g (1¾oz) bamboo shoots
300g (10½oz) raw prawns, peeled and deveined
100g (3½oz) green beans, halved
2 tablespoons fish sauce
15g (½oz) palm sugar (jaggery), or soft light brown sugar
handful of Thai basil leaves, plus extra to serve
large handful of coriander (cilantro), chopped, plus extra to serve

FOR THE CURRY PASTE

1 teaspoon coriander seeds
½ teaspoon cumin seeds
½ teaspoon white peppercorns
2 lemongrass stalks, white parts only, cut into 2.5cm (1in) pieces and bashed
thumb-sized piece of galangal (see page 16), peeled and sliced
5 makrut lime leaves (fresh or frozen)
1 tablespoon fish sauce
4 small green bird's-eye chillies
2 banana shallots, roughly chopped
4 garlic cloves, peeled
large handful of coriander stems

TO SERVE

500g (1lb 2oz) steamed jasmine rice
2–3 red bird's-eye chillies, thinly sliced
1 lime, cut into wedges

Thailand is famous for its curries, including red curry, yellow curry and massaman curry, to name just a few, but my favourite is the green curry. While you can buy ready-made curry paste, I always prefer making it from scratch; the smell of all the fresh herbs and spices blitzed together is absolutely intoxicating. Of all the ingredients used, the two most important, in my opinion, are the Thai basil and palm sugar. I'm using prawns here, but the curry works really well with chicken, pumpkin or tofu too. This is my go-to curry for party food, whether it's a large gathering or a small dinner party, as it's a guaranteed crowd-pleaser. I typically make a big batch of just the curry sauce a day in advance, then reheat it on the day of the event with the protein added. This is also a handy way to make two versions of the same curry.

Begin by making the curry paste. Toast the coriander seeds, cumin seeds and peppercorns in a dry frying pan over a medium heat for a few minutes until fragrant, then tip into a spice grinder and blitz until you have a coarse powder. Add this to a blender, along with the rest of the curry paste ingredients, and blend until smooth.

Don't shake the tin of coconut milk. Scoop the coconut cream from the top of the tin and add it to a wok over a medium heat - this coconut cream will act as the oil, so there should be no need for extra oil. Stir in the curry paste and fry for 4–5 minutes until fragrant.

Pour in the remaining coconut milk and a splash of water if needed, then add the courgettes and bamboo shoots. Simmer for 4 minutes, then add the prawns and green beans and cook for a further 2–3 minutes. Stir in the fish sauce and palm sugar, and taste for seasoning, adding more fish sauce or sugar as needed.

Just before serving, stir in the Thai basil and coriander. Serve the curry alongside some cooked jasmine rice, topped with the sliced chilli, with lime wedges on the side for squeezing.

TIP

✱ To make a vegan version, use vegan fish sauce and omit the prawns.

Korean Kimchi Tofu Stew

Serves: 4

Prep time: 10 minutes **Cook time:** 25 minutes

1 teaspoon sesame oil
200g (7oz) pork belly, chopped into 4cm (1½in) pieces
1 onion, sliced
2 garlic cloves, minced
250g (9oz) kimchi, chopped, juices reserved
1 tablespoon gochugaru (Korean red pepper flakes, see page 19)
1 tablespoon gochujang (see page 24)
1 tablespoon Korean soy sauce (see page 21) or light soy sauce
500ml (2 cups) chicken or vegetable stock
100g (3½oz) silken tofu, cubed
2 spring onions (scallions), finely sliced

I find myself craving this stew constantly, especially during the winter months. Growing up in Ireland, I was used to the traditional Irish stew that my friends' families would serve - beef or lamb with carrots and potatoes. This Korean stew is completely different, but equally comforting in its own way. It uses smooth silken tofu that melts in your mouth, a savoury pork belly base and tangy, fermented kimchi. It's the perfect balance of spicy, sour and savoury that just warms you from the inside out. I love tweaking it - sometimes I'll throw in frankfurters for a bit of smokiness. The aroma of this stew bubbling away just makes me so happy!

Heat the sesame oil in a large, heavy-based saucepan over a medium-high heat. Add the pork belly and fry for 6-7 minutes on each side until lightly browned, then add the onion and garlic and cook, stirring, for another 3 minutes.

Stir in the chopped kimchi and its juices, along with the gochugaru, gochujang and soy sauce. Cook for 1 minute until everything is fragrant, then pour in the stock and bring to the boil. Reduce the heat to low and simmer for 15-20 minutes until the pork is tender and cooked through.

Add the tofu cubes and cook for an additional 2-3 minutes to warm through, then serve the stew in bowls, garnished with the sliced spring onions.

TIPS

- If you have dolsots at home (traditional Korean stone bowls), this recipe will fill two of them.
- Serve with some steamed short-grain rice to make it a full meal.

Japanese Pork Katsu Curry

Serves: 2

Prep time: 15 minutes **Cook time:** 35–40 minutes

2 boneless pork chops
30g (1oz) plain (all-purpose) flour
1 large egg
60g (2¼oz) panko breadcrumbs
500–700ml (17–24fl oz) neutral oil, for frying
salt and freshly ground black pepper

FOR THE CURRY SAUCE

1 tablespoon neutral oil
2 onions, finely diced
½ apple, peeled and finely grated
3 garlic cloves, minced
2cm (¾in) piece of fresh ginger, grated
2 tablespoons plain flour
2 teaspoons Japanese curry powder or mild curry powder
3 tablespoons Japanese soy sauce (see page 21)
1 teaspoon dark soy sauce
2 teaspoons Worcestershire sauce
2 teaspoons tomato paste (concentrated purée)
2 teaspoons caster (superfine) sugar
pinch of salt

TO SERVE

300g (10½oz) cooked Japanese short-grain rice or jasmine rice
Japanese pickles

The first time I had katsu curry was in Wagamama in Dublin, while I was studying at Trinity College. We would go there as a group, and the katsu curry quickly became the most popular dish among our friends. In fact, katsu curry is probably the most popular curry in Japan as well. It's got a fruity flavour and is not spicy at all, which makes it perfect for family dinners. Make sure the panko coating on the pork chops is crispy and golden. Serve on a bed of fluffy Japanese sushi rice, with Japanese pickles on the side. Yum!

Start by making the curry sauce. Heat the oil in a medium-sized saucepan over a medium heat. Add the onions and apple and cook for 8–10 minutes until lightly golden and soft, then add the garlic and ginger and stir-fry for 1–2 minutes. Sprinkle in the flour and curry powder and stir constantly for 1–2 minutes to coat. Now gradually add 600ml (scant 2½ cups) water, stirring well to avoid any lumps forming.

Take off the heat and use a hand blender to blitz the sauce until really smooth, then stir in the soy sauces, Worcestershire sauce, tomato paste, sugar and salt. Return to the heat and simmer for 2–3 minutes, then keep warm over a low heat while you prepare the pork.

Place each pork chop between 2 pieces of baking paper or clingfilm and use a meat mallet or rolling pin to gently bash the meat to an even thickness of about 1cm (½in). Season both sides with salt and pepper.

Tip the flour into a shallow bowl. Beat the egg in a second bowl, and put the panko in a third. Dredge each piece of pork in the flour, then dip in beaten egg, and finally coat in the panko breadcrumbs. Set aside.

Heat the oil in a deep-sided frying pan or wok over a medium-high heat until it reaches 175°C (340°F). Fry the coated pork for 4–5 minutes per side until golden and cooked through, then remove to a wire rack or a plate lined with paper towels to drain. Season with a little more salt, and allow to rest for a few minutes before slicing.

To serve, place a mound of steamed rice and some sliced katsu pork on each plate. Top with the hot curry sauce and serve the pickles on the side.

TIP

* This recipe also works brilliantly with chicken thighs. I like to make a vegetarian version, too, using pumpkin korokke, croquettes made with mashed kabocha (Japanese squash).

Malaysian Beef Rendang

Serves: 4–6

Prep time: 20 minutes **Cook time:** 3 hours

3 tablespoons neutral oil
800g (1lb 12oz) chuck steak or boneless beef short ribs, cut into 2.5cm (1in) chunks
400ml (14fl oz) coconut milk
300ml (10½fl oz) chicken stock
1 cinnamon stick
2 star anise
2 makrut lime leaves, torn
1 tablespoon kecap manis (see page 22)
1 tablespoon Babas curry powder (see tip)
100g (3½oz) desiccated (shredded) coconut
1 tablespoon tamarind paste (see page 24)
1 tablespoon palm sugar (jaggery) or soft light brown sugar
salt

FOR THE SPICE PASTE
4–6 dried red chillies
4 banana shallots, roughly chopped
4 garlic cloves, roughly chopped
thumb-sized piece of fresh ginger, peeled and roughly chopped
thumb-sized piece of galangal (see page 16), roughly chopped
2 lemongrass stalks, white parts only, roughly chopped
1 teaspoon ground coriander
1 teaspoon ground cumin
½ teaspoon ground turmeric

TO SERVE
500g (1lb 2oz) steamed jasmine rice
small handful of coriander (cilantro), roughly chopped
small handful of crispy fried onions or shallots
sliced cucumber and chopped tomato

I love any opportunity to travel to Malaysia. The food scene there is incredible, with a real fusion between Chinese, Indian and everything in between. It's a true melting pot. Rendang, with its blend of Asian herbs and Indian spices, must be one of the most famous curries in Malaysian cuisine. There are regional variations - some have more coconut, others have a mix of different spices, and every chef has their own closely guarded secret recipe - but I have never tried one that I didn't love! Rendang isn't a very saucy dish; it's a drier style of curry where the spices cling to the beef and are absorbed into the meat, making the flavour more intense.

Begin by making the spice paste. Soak the dried chillies in a bowl of hot water for 10 minutes until soft, then drain and transfer to a blender. Add all the other spice paste ingredients and blend for 2–3 minutes until you have a smooth paste, adding a splash of water if needed to help it blend.

Heat the oil in a large heavy-based saucepan over a medium heat. Once hot, add the spice paste and fry for 8–10 minutes until fragrant, stirring often. The paste should begin to turn a deeper, richer colour, and the oil will start to separate from the paste.

Add the beef and stir to coat it in the paste, then pour in the coconut milk and stock. Add the cinnamon stick, star anise, lime leaves, kecap manis and curry powder and stir. Bring to a gentle simmer, then reduce the heat to low and cook, uncovered, for 2½ hours, stirring occasionally to prevent sticking. The sauce should slowly reduce and thicken to coat the beef in a rich sauce.

Meanwhile, in a dry frying pan, toast the desiccated coconut over a medium heat for 3–4 minutes, stirring constantly, until golden brown and nutty. Let it cool, then grind to a coarse paste using a pestle and mortar or spice grinder, and set aside until needed.

When the beef has been cooking for 2½ hours, stir in the coconut paste, tamarind and sugar, and season to taste with salt. Continue simmering until the sauce is thick and dark and the beef is meltingly tender. This can take another 30–45 minutes, so stir frequently near the end to prevent burning.

Serve the rendang with some steamed rice, chopped coriander, crispy fried onions or shallots, sliced cucumber and chopped tomato.

TIP

✱ Babas is a famous Malaysian spice brand, and its curry powder is a special blend that works beautifully here. If you can't get a hold of it, use mild curry powder instead.

Spicy Sichuan Boiled Fish Stew

Serves: 4

Prep time: 25 minutes, plus marinating **Cook time:** 40 minutes

500g (1lb 2oz) white fish (such as hake, haddock or cod), skinless and boneless, thinly sliced
50g (1¾oz) dried beanthread noodles (see page 12)
200g (7oz) Chinese leaf, cut into 2.5cm (1in) pieces
75g (2¾oz) beansprouts
1 tablespoon neutral oil
4 garlic cloves, sliced
thumb-sized piece of fresh ginger, peeled and thinly sliced
2 spring onions (scallions), white and green parts separated, whites cut into 2.5cm (1in) pieces, greens finely sliced
2 tablespoons Sichuan peppercorns, lightly crushed
4–6 dried red chillies
2 tablespoons doubanjiang (chilli bean paste, see page 22)
1 tablespoon chilli flakes
1 litre (4 cups) chicken or fish stock
1 tablespoon Shaoxing wine (see page 22)
1 tablespoon light soy sauce
2 star anise
1 cinnamon stick

FOR THE MARINADE

1 tablespoon Shaoxing wine
½ teaspoon salt
¼ teaspoon ground white pepper
1 tablespoon cornflour (cornstarch)

TO FINISH

3 tablespoons neutral oil
1 teaspoon Sichuan peppercorns, lightly crushed
1 teaspoon chilli flakes
large handful of coriander (cilantro), roughly chopped

If you're a fan of both fish and spicy food, this is the stew for you. In Chinese, it's known as shui zhu yu. Essentially, we're creating a very spicy broth in which we cook thinly sliced fish fillets. I particularly enjoy this dish because the fish isn't boiled for long; it's just lightly poached in the spicy broth. The base is filled with vegetables that absorb the broth beautifully. In restaurants, you can often find variations, such as a spicy beef stew (shi zhu niu rou) or a mix of pork, duck blood and vegetables (mao xue wang). However, the fish version is my favourite due to its texture and lightness - it really hits the spot.

Combine the marinade ingredients in a shallow bowl. Add the fish and stir to coat, then leave to marinate for 15-30 minutes.

Soak the beanthread noodles in a bowl of just-boiled water for 20 minutes, then drain.

When you're ready to cook, fill a large wok with boiling water and place over a high heat. Add the cabbage and beansprouts and briefly blanch for 2-3 minutes until just tender. Drain and transfer to a large serving bowl, and top with the drained beanthread noodles.

Return the empty wok to a medium heat and add the 1 tablespoon oil. Add the garlic, ginger, spring onion whites, Sichuan peppercorns and dried chillies. Stir-fry for 30-60 seconds until fragrant, then add the doubanjiang and chilli flakes. Cook for another 1-2 minutes until aromatic, then add the stock, Shaoxing wine and soy sauce. Bring everything to a boil, then toss in the star anise and cinnamon stick. Reduce the heat to low and simmer gently for 10 minutes, adding a little more stock if it reduces too much.

After 10 minutes, carefully lower the marinated fish slices into the broth - don't stir, or you will break up the fish, and you want to keep the slices intact. Let the fish cook, undisturbed, for 2-3 minutes, or until just opaque and tender, then ladle the cooked fish and broth over the cabbage and noodles in the serving bowl.

To finish, heat the 3 tablespoons neutral oil in a small saucepan over a medium heat until it shimmers. Sprinkle the crushed Sichuan peppercorns, chilli flakes and coriander over the top of the stew, then drizzle the hot oil over the spices and coriander to awaken them - it should sizzle and become fragrant. Finally, scatter over the sliced spring onion greens and serve.

Lamb Massaman Curry

Serves: 4

Prep time: 20 minutes **Cook time:** 1 hour

If you like Indian and Thai curries, massaman curry is the one for you! It combines a beautiful blend of Indian curry spices like cumin, coriander and cardamom with aromatic Thai herbs like lemongrass and galangal. The result is truly stunning. This recipe is great to make ahead of time, as the flavour just builds. Sometimes, I turn it into a pie by transferring the curry into an ovenproof dish, topping with some puff pastry and baking. If you are not a fan of lamb, this recipe also works really well with beef.

3 tablespoons neutral oil
2 small onions, finely sliced
900g (2lb) boneless lamb shoulder, cut into bite-sized pieces
3 potatoes, peeled and chopped into bite-sized pieces
2 carrots, peeled and chopped into bite-sized pieces
400g (14oz) tin coconut milk
200ml (7fl oz) beef stock
40g (1½oz) palm sugar (jaggery) or soft light brown sugar
1 tablespoon fish sauce
2 tablespoons tamarind concentrate (see page 24)
100g (3½oz) roasted salted peanuts
½ teaspoon salt
steamed jasmine rice, to serve

FOR THE MASSAMAN PASTE

5 small dried red chillies
1 tablespoon cumin seeds
1 tablespoon coriander seeds
4 cloves
8 green cardamom pods
½ teaspoon salt
2 banana shallots, roughly chopped
5 garlic cloves, crushed
5cm (2in) pieces of galangal (see page 16), peeled and sliced
3 lemongrass stalks, white parts only, finely sliced
¼ teaspoon ground cinnamon
¼ teaspoon ground turmeric
½ teaspoon ground white pepper
1 teaspoon shrimp paste or 1 tablespoon fish sauce

Begin by making the spice paste. In a small bowl, soak the dried chillies for 10-15 minutes until soft.

Meanwhile, in a small frying pan, dry-fry the cumin seeds, coriander seeds, cloves and cardamom pods over a low heat for 2 minutes until fragrant. Transfer to a blender.

Drain the chillies and add these to the blender too, along with the remaining massaman paste ingredients. Blend to form a coarse paste.

To make the curry, heat the oil in a large, heavy-based saucepan over a medium heat. Once hot, add the spice paste and fry for 8-10 minutes until fragrant, darker in colour and slightly sticky in texture.

Add the onions and stir to coat in the paste for 2 minutes, then add the lamb and cook for 3 minutes more, stirring to make sure all the sides get seared and coated with the paste.

Add the potatoes, carrots, coconut milk, stock, palm sugar, fish sauce, tamarind, peanuts and salt. Reduce the heat to low-medium and cover with a lid. Simmer for 20 minutes, then remove the lid and simmer for a further 30 minutes, or until the lamb is tender and the sauce has reduced.

Serve the massaman with some steamed rice.

TIP

✱ This is the perfect recipe for the pressure cooker. Cook on high for 30 minutes.

Vietnamese Beef Bò Kho

Serves: 4

Prep time: 20 minutes, plus marinating **Cook time:** 2½–3 hours

1kg (2lb 4oz) chuck steak or brisket, cut into 2.5cm (1in) chunks
1 tablespoon neutral oil, plus extra if needed
1 onion, sliced
4 garlic cloves, minced
2.5cm (1in) piece of fresh ginger, sliced
2 tablespoons tomato paste (concentrated purée)
2 lemongrass stalks, white parts only, bruised
1 star anise
1 cinnamon stick
250ml (1 cup) coconut water (see tip)
1 tablespoon fish sauce
1 tablespoon Vietnamese soy sauce (see page 21) or light soy sauce
1 teaspoon palm sugar (jaggery) or soft light brown sugar
½ teaspoon freshly ground black pepper
2 carrots, peeled and cut into large chunks

FOR THE MARINADE
2 tablespoons fish sauce
1 tablespoon hoisin sauce
1 teaspoon Chinese five-spice
1 teaspoon granulated sugar
¼ teaspoon salt
¼ teaspoon freshly ground black pepper

TO SERVE
large handful of coriander (cilantro) or Thai basil leaves
1 red chilli, thinly sliced
1 lime, cut into wedges
1 red onion, very thinly sliced
Vietnamese bánh mì rolls or crusty baguettes

Bò kho is a deliciously fragrant Vietnamese soupy stew. It's rich in aromatics, has a lovely deep red colour thanks to the tomato paste and finishes with a comforting warmth. The carrots soak up all the wonderful flavours of the stewing liquid, while the coconut water brings its own twist with a subtle sweetness. I love to do what the Vietnamese do and soak up the stew with a hot, crusty baguette. This is a perfect winter-warming dish with a gently spiced flavour.

Combine all the marinade ingredients in a bowl. Add the beef and stir to coat, then set aside to marinate for 30 minutes-1 hour at room temperature, or overnight in the fridge.

When you're ready to cook, heat the oil in a large, heavy-based casserole dish with a lid set over a medium-high heat. Working in batches, sear the beef for 2-3 minutes until browned, then remove from the pot and set aside on a plate.

Reduce the heat to low, adding another drizzle of oil to the casserole dish if needed, and add the onion, garlic and ginger. Cook, stirring, for 2-3 minutes, then add the tomato paste and cook for a few minutes more until it has darkened a little in colour.

Return the beef to the casserole dish, along with the lemongrass, star anise and cinnamon. Stir everything together, then add 500ml (2 cups) water and the coconut water, along with the fish sauce, soy sauce, sugar and pepper. Increase the heat and bring to the boil, then reduce the heat to low, cover the casserole dish with a lid and simmer very gently for 1½-2 hours, or until the beef is very tender.

Once the beef is tender, add the carrots and cook for a further 30 minutes until they are tender and the beef is meltingly soft. Taste and adjust the seasoning, then divide between bowls. Serve the herbs, sliced chilli, lime wedges and sliced red onion on the side for everyone to add themselves, and make sure you have plenty of bánh mì or crusty bread for mopping up the sauce.

TIPS

* If you prefer, you can use a pressure cooker for the simmering stage and cook on high for 1 hour.
* Coconut water is the clear liquid from inside young coconuts. Sweet and refreshing, it's most commonly sold as a drink, but adds a subtle sweetness to dishes like this.

Chicken Adobo

Serves: 4

Prep time: 10 minutes, plus marinating **Cook time:** 50 minutes

- 1kg (2lb 4oz) bone-in, skin-on chicken thighs and drumsticks
- 120ml (½ cup) Filipino white cane vinegar (see page 25) or distilled white vinegar
- 80ml (⅓ cup) Filipino soy sauce (see page 21 and tip)
- 8 garlic cloves, peeled and bashed with the back of a knife
- 2 bay leaves
- 1 teaspoon black peppercorns, lightly bashed using a pestle and mortar
- 1 tablespoon neutral oil
- 1 onion, finely sliced
- 2 tablespoons soft light brown sugar

TO SERVE

- 500g (1lb 2oz) steamed rice
- 2 spring onions (scallions), finely sliced

Chicken adobo is a relatively recent recipe in my repertoire, following a business trip to the Philippines, where chicken adobo is one of their national dishes. It's quite similar to a teriyaki but with the addition of vinegar, which really adds a unique touch. There are different types of adobos, but my version is soy-based. In this recipe, I've specified to marinate for at least two hours, but it's better overnight. It's definitely worth it, as the chicken becomes so lovely and tender. Some of the most delicious parts of this dish are the cooked-down onions and the background hit of black pepper.

Score each of the chicken pieces a few times with a knife to allow the marinade to absorb better, then place them in a large ziplock bag and add the vinegar, soy sauce, garlic cloves, bay leaves and peppercorns. Place the bag on a tray and marinate in the refrigerator for at least 2 hours, but preferably overnight. You don't have to marinate it if you are in a hurry, but it makes such a difference to the texture, as the vinegar really softens the meat.

When you're ready to cook, remove the chicken from the marinade and reserve the marinade. Pat the chicken with paper towels to dry it slightly; this will help it to brown when you sear it.

Heat the oil in a heavy-based casserole dish with a lid. Working in batches, add the chicken pieces, skin-side down. Brown for 6–8 minutes until lightly golden, then turn and brown on the other side for another 6–8 minutes. Set aside on a plate. Now add the onion to the casserole dish and stir-fry for 2–3 minutes, then pour in the reserved marinade, including all the aromatics. Return the chicken to the pan, then add the sugar and 200ml (7fl oz) water and stir to combine. Bring the mixture to a gentle boil, then immediately reduce the heat to low and cover the pot loosely with a lid.

Simmer for 30–40 minutes, turning the chicken halfway through, until the chicken is tender and slightly caramelised and the liquid has thickened to a rich, deep brown sauce that clings to the chicken pieces.

Remove the bay leaves and serve the chicken adobo with rice, topped with sliced spring onions.

TIPS

- ✱ If you can't get hold of Filipino soy sauce, then use 40ml (1¼fl oz) each of light soy sauce and dark soy sauce.
- ✱ If you're making this for kids, you can leave out the black peppercorns.
- ✱ Adobo tastes amazing the next day, so I recommend you make extra!

One-Pot Thai Red Curry Dumplings

Serves: 4

Prep time: 10 minutes **Cook time:** 30 minutes

This is such a simple dish to whip up, and a great way to elevate the humble dumpling. It's a bit like a pasta bake, but with dumplings. You start by making a Thai red curry sauce in a baking tray, then adding your dumplings and veg and letting it bake away in the oven while you relax and help the kids with their homework! You can enjoy this straight from the baking tray or make it go even further by serving it on a bed of noodles in a bowl. This is serious comfort food.

2–3 heads of baby pak choi, halved or quartered
100g (3½oz) enoki mushrooms
16 dumplings, frozen or fresh – choose your favourite kind or make your own (see page 108)

FOR THE SAUCE
2 garlic cloves, minced
1 teaspoon freshly grated ginger
2 tablespoons light soy sauce
2 tablespoons Thai red curry paste
1 teaspoon toasted sesame oil
1 tablespoon white rice vinegar
350ml (12fl oz) chicken or vegetable stock
400g (14oz) tin coconut milk

TO SERVE
2 spring onions (scallions), thinly sliced
handful of coriander (cilantro) leaves, roughly chopped
1–2 teaspoons crispy chilli oil
1 teaspoon toasted white sesame seeds
1 lime, cut into wedges
cooked ramen noodles

Preheat the oven to 180°C fan (350°F/gas mark 4).

In a large baking dish, combine all the sauce ingredients and stir until smooth and well blended.

Nestle the halved pak choi and trimmed enoki mushrooms into the sauce, then place the dumplings on top, arranging them evenly across the dish. Bake for 30 minutes, or until the dumplings are tender and fully cooked through.

Top with the sliced spring onions, coriander leaves, a drizzle of chilli oil and a sprinkling of toasted sesame seeds. Serve warm, ladled into small bowls, with lime wedges for squeezing and ramen noodles.

Chicken Tikka Masala

Serves: 4

Prep time: 10 minutes, plus marinating **Cook time:** 40 minutes

- 500g (1lb 2oz) boneless, skinless chicken thighs, cut into bite-sized pieces
- 2 tablespoons neutral oil or ghee
- 2 onions, finely sliced
- 4 garlic cloves, minced
- 1 tablespoon freshly grated ginger
- 2 teaspoons ground cumin
- 2 teaspoons paprika
- 1 teaspoon garam masala
- 1 teaspoon ground coriander
- 1 teaspoon Kashmiri chilli powder
- 1 teaspoon granulated sugar
- 300ml (10½fl oz) passata
- 100ml (3½oz) double (heavy) cream
- ½ teaspoon salt

FOR THE MARINADE

- 100g (3½oz) natural yoghurt
- 2 tablespoons lemon juice
- 2 teaspoons garam masala
- 2 teaspoons ground cumin
- 1 teaspoon paprika
- 1 teaspoon ground turmeric
- 1 teaspoon salt
- ½ teaspoon Kashmiri chilli powder
- 3 garlic cloves, minced
- 1 tablespoon freshly grated ginger

TO SERVE

- handful of coriander (cilantro)
- 500g (1lb 2oz) cooked basmati rice
- 4 naan breads, warmed and brushed with melted butter

My dad moved to England from Hong Kong, China, when he was 16 to study. It was the 1960s, and the Indian restaurant scene was blossoming all across the UK. It was here that he developed a love for Indian cuisine, a love that he passed to me too. The story goes that tikka masala was born during this time, when a chef blended a skewered barbecue chicken with the British desire for a saucier dish. I don't remember the first time I tried tikka masala, but it was probably on one of our trips back to the UK to visit my parents' friends in Manchester. It's always been a dish that I get serious cravings for. It's unmistakably Indian in flavour, mild and slightly sweet. I just love it - and being able to make it yourself, just the way you like it, feels like such a treat!

Combine all the marinade ingredients in a large bowl and mix well. Add the chicken and stir to coat. Marinate for at least 30 minutes, or overnight in the fridge.

When you're ready to cook, heat a large deep-sided saucepan over a medium-high heat. Add 1 tablespoon of the oil or ghee and, working in batches, cook the marinated chicken for 6-8 minutes until golden brown. It doesn't need to be fully cooked through at this point. Remove and set aside on a plate.

Heat the remaining tablespoon of oil or ghee in the same pan over a medium heat. Add the onions and cook for 7-8 minutes, stirring occasionally, until they are a deep golden colour. Add the garlic and ginger and cook for another minute, then add the spices and cook for a further minute until fragrant. Now add the sugar, passata and 100ml (3½oz) water. Stir well and simmer for 10 minutes, stirring occasionally.

Return the chicken to the pan and simmer for another 20 minutes until the chicken is cooked through and tender. Finally, stir in the cream and bring the sauce back to the boil, then season with the salt.

To serve, garnish the curry with coriander leaves and serve with basmati rice and naan bread.

Chinese Chicken Curry

Serves: 2

Prep time: 15 minutes, plus marinating **Cook time:** 15 minutes

400g (14oz) boneless, skinless chicken thighs, cut into 2.5cm (1in) pieces
1 tablespoon madras curry powder
½ teaspoon ground ginger
½ teaspoon Chinese five-spice
½ teaspoon ground turmeric
2 tablespoons neutral oil
1 onion, finely sliced
1 carrot, peeled and thinly sliced
300ml (10½fl oz) chicken stock
50g (1¾oz) frozen peas
½ teaspoon salt
1 teaspoon granulated sugar
2 teaspoons cornflour (cornstarch)

FOR THE MARINADE

2 teaspoons light soy sauce
1 teaspoon sesame oil
1 teaspoon granulated sugar
¼ teaspoon ground white pepper
1 teaspoon Shaoxing wine (see page 22)
1 teaspoon cornflour

TO SERVE

handful of coriander leaves (cilantro), roughly chopped
1 red chilli, finely sliced
250g (9oz) steamed jasmine rice

Every Chinese restaurant and takeaway has their own recipe for this classic dish. My Chinese cheffy friends have told me about adding everything from apple to lots of onion - and even banana skin. My version is very simple to make, and you should definitely make extra for dipping chips into or drizzling over rice and noodles. I like mine with frozen peas, and I always use boneless chicken thighs because the meat has more flavour and is more tender than chicken breasts. There's a really nice depth of flavour with this curry, and it's not that spicy, so it's perfect for the whole family.

Combine all the marinade ingredients in a bowl. Add the chicken and stir to coat, then set aside to marinate for 15-20 minutes.

In a separate small bowl, combine the curry powder, ginger, five-spice and turmeric, then set aside.

Heat the oil in a wok over a high heat. Once it's shimmering, add the onion and carrot. Stir-fry for 3-4 minutes, then add the marinated chicken and stir-fry for a further 3 minutes. Sprinkle with the spice mix and stir-fry for 2 minutes more until fragrant.

Pour the stock into the pan, along with the peas, and let the curry simmer for 2-3 minutes. Season with the salt and sugar.

In a small bowl, mix the cornflour with 3 tablespoons water. Add this mixture to the curry a little at a time, stirring it in slowly, to thicken the curry to the consistency that you like.

Serve the curry topped with coriander and red chilli slices, with steamed rice on the side.

Chinese Takeaway Classics

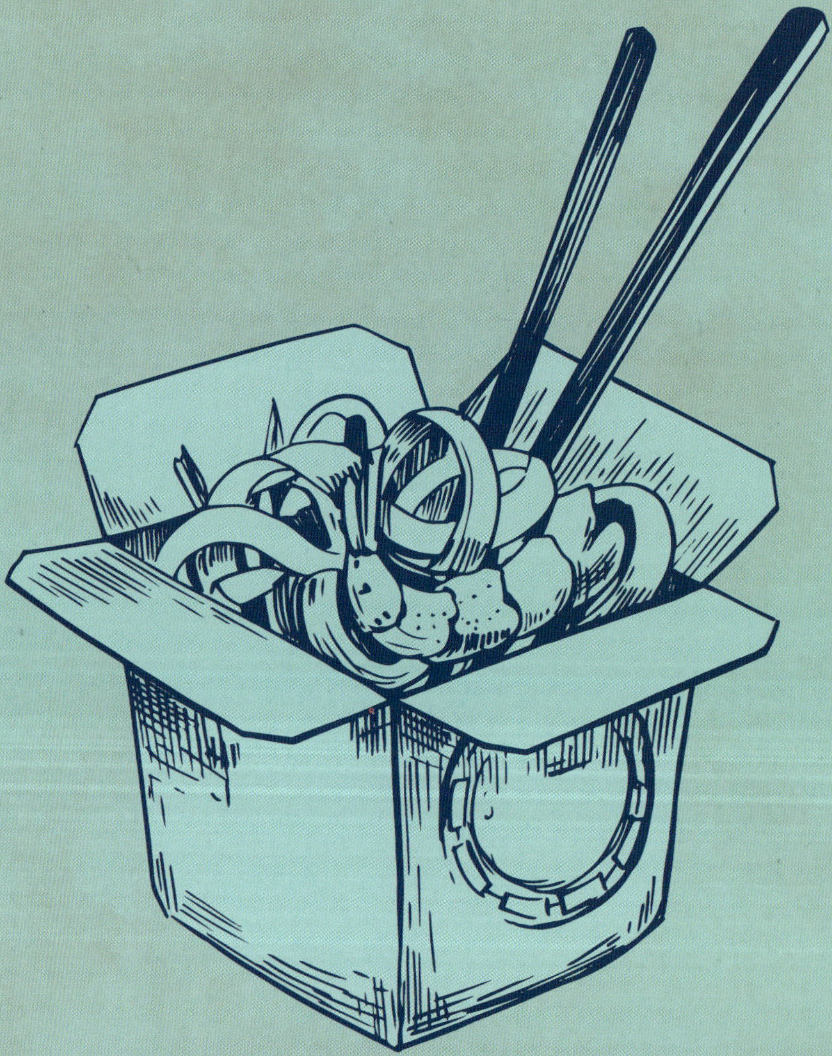

Salt-and-Chilli King Prawns 163

Aromatic Duck Pancakes 164

Black Bean Beef 167

Sweet-and-Sour Pork 168

Kung Pao Chicken 171

Satay Chicken 172

Teriyaki Chicken 173

Duck in Plum Sauce 175

Beef with Broccoli in Oyster Sauce 176

Crispy Tofu in Chilli Garlic Sauce 177

Salt-and-Chilli King Prawns

Serves: 2 as a main, 4 as a starter/side

Prep time: 10 minutes **Cook time:** 20 minutes

- 400g (14oz) raw king prawns, peeled and deveined
- 1 egg white, lightly whisked
- ¼ teaspoon salt
- ¼ teaspoon ground white pepper
- 1 tablespoon neutral oil, plus extra for shallow-frying
- ½ red onion, finely sliced
- 2 garlic cloves, finely chopped
- 2 spring onions (scallions), cut into 1cm (½in) pieces
- 1 large red chilli, finely sliced on the diagonal
- small handful of coriander (cilantro), roughly chopped, to serve (optional)

FOR THE BATTER

- 3 tablespoons cornflour (cornstarch)
- 2 tablespoons plain (all-purpose) flour
- ½ teaspoon salt
- ¼ teaspoon ground white pepper

FOR THE SPICE MIX

- 2 teaspoons caster (superfine) sugar
- 1 teaspoon chilli flakes
- 2 teaspoons salt
- ½ teaspoon Chinese five-spice
- ¼ teaspoon chilli powder
- ¼ teaspoon ground black pepper

My husband Tom absolutely loves this dish, and it's easy to see why. The prawns really are the star here, with a super-light, dry batter that provides the perfect texture for the warm, spicy, salty mix to stick to. The salt-and-chilli mixture adds just enough of a kick to tickle your taste buds without overpowering them. These prawns are a great addition to any dinner table, offering something different in both texture and flavour that's sure to impress your guests!

Pat the prawns dry with paper towels, then add to a bowl. Add the egg white, salt and white pepper, and mix well to combine.

In another bowl, mix together the dry batter ingredients. Add the prawns and mix well.

Pour neutral oil into a deep-sided frying pan to a depth of 2cm (¾in). Heat until it reaches 180°C (350°F), then, working in batches, fry the prawns for 1–2 minutes per side until golden, crispy and cooked through. Once cooked, remove from the hot oil, and set aside to drain on a plate lined with paper towels.

In a small bowl, mix together the ingredients for the spice mix and set aside.

Heat the 1 tablespoon oil in a clean frying pan or wok over a medium heat. Add the red onion and stir-fry for 1 minute, then add the garlic, spring onions and chillies, and stir-fry for a further 1 minute. Add the crispy prawns to the pan, along with 1–2 teaspoons of the spice mix. Toss together for 1–2 minutes until everything is well combined. Taste and add more spice mix if necessary.

Serve immediately on a platter, garnished with the chopped coriander, if using.

TIPS

- ✱ Any leftover spice mix will keep in an airtight jar in the cupboard for up to a month.
- ✱ Toss some cooked chips into the stir-fry and make it into a 'spice bag', a hugely popular Irish Chinese creation available in all Chinese takeaways in Ireland.

Aromatic Duck Pancakes

Serves: 4 as a starter

Prep time: 20 minutes, plus chilling time **Cook time:** 1 hour 30 minutes

2.6kg (5lb 12oz) whole duck
1 tablespoon salt
2 teaspoons Chinese five-spice
3cm (1½in) piece of fresh ginger, peeled and sliced
2 spring onions (scallions), cut into 2.5cm (1in) pieces
4 star anise
4 bay leaves
2 cinnamon sticks

FOR THE GLAZING LIQUID
70ml (2¼fl oz) white wine vinegar
3 tablespoons maltose or golden syrup

FOR THE SWEET HOISIN SAUCE
90ml (3fl oz) hoisin sauce
30g (1oz) granulated sugar

TO SERVE
24 Chinese-style pancakes, warmed according to the packet instructions
½ cucumber, cut into thin matchsticks
8 spring onions, finely shredded

Duck pancakes have always been a huge favourite in my family. It's hardly surprising: who doesn't love the combination of succulent, aromatic duck with fresh cucumber, spring onions, sweet hoisin sauce and wafer-thin pancakes? They are so fun to make, and perfect for little kiddies too! Whenever I am in Beijing, I love to take the opportunity to go to a specialty Peking duck restaurant, where they pride themselves on producing the crispiest, most golden duck skin. In fact, in these restaurants, they carve and serve just the skin, which can be enjoyed either dipped in sugar, or served in pancakes and bao buns.

Place the duck on a wire rack set over a large roasting tray and pour a full kettle of just-boiled water all over the duck - this helps to render the fat and also tighten the skin, which helps it crisp up later. Carefully pour off the water in the tray and place the duck, still on the wire rack, back into the tray.

In a small bowl, combine the salt, Chinese five-spice, ginger, spring onions, star anise, bay leaves and cinnamon sticks, and stir to coat the aromatics in the salt and spices. Rub this mixture around the cavity of the duck, then place the aromatics into the cavity. Tilt the duck on its end and use a skewer to 'sew up' the open end of the duck - this helps the duck steam-cook from the inside while the skin remains crispy.

In a separate bowl, mix together the glazing liquid ingredients - you may need to warm the maltose or syrup first, as it can be very sticky! Use a brush to baste the liquid all over the duck 3-4 times, then cover the duck with foil and place in the fridge to dry for 6 hours, or, for best results, overnight - the longer you can leave it, the more the duck skin will crisp up when cooking.

When you're ready to cook, preheat the oven to 190°C fan (375°F/gas mark 5). Remove the duck from the fridge and remove the foil. Prop up the wire rack at one end of the roasting tray to hold the duck at an angle. Roast for about 1 hour, then let it rest for 15 minutes.

Meanwhile, combine all the ingredients for the hoisin sauce in a saucepan, along with 100ml (3½fl oz) water. Place over a medium heat and bring to the boil, then reduce the heat and simmer for a couple of minutes to thicken. Pour into a bowl and set aside until needed.

When the duck is ready, remove the meat from the bones and shred or slice, then place it on a serving platter. Serve with the hoisin sauce, pancakes and the cucumber and shredded spring onions.

TIP

✱ You can strain the leftover duck fat into a jar and use it wherever you would use oil or fat - it's great for roasting potatoes or frying meat. It will keep in the fridge for up to 2 months.

Black Bean Beef

Serves: 2

Prep time: 10 minutes, plus marinating **Cook time:** 10 minutes

- 20g (¾oz) fermented black beans (see page 24)
- 300g (10½oz) beef sirloin, thinly sliced
- 1 teaspoon cornflour (cornstarch)
- 3 tablespoons neutral oil
- 4 garlic cloves, finely sliced
- ½ small white onion, cut into 2.5cm (1in) pieces
- ¼ green pepper (capsicum), cut into 2.5cm (1in) pieces
- ¼ red pepper(capsicum), cut into 2.5cm (1in) pieces
- 250g (9oz) steamed jasmine rice, to serve

FOR THE MARINADE

- 1 teaspoon bicarbonate of soda (baking soda)
- 1 tablespoon light soy sauce
- ½ teaspoon sesame oil
- ¼ teaspoon ground white pepper
- 1 teaspoon granulated sugar

FOR THE SEASONING SAUCE

- 1 tablespoon light soy sauce
- ½ teaspoon dark soy sauce
- 1 teaspoon granulated sugar

Black bean beef is a quick and simple dish to make. The key to the flavour is the fermented black beans (see page 24). These are like tiny flavour bombs; you only need a small amount to make this dish sing. This recipe combines black bean and garlic, two flavours that work really well together. This pairing appears in many other dishes I love (including my uncle Hoi's top-secret recipe for steamed black bean spare ribs!). My top tip here is not to overcook the black beans, as they can become a bit bitter. Just fry them for a minute, then set them aside.

In a bowl, combine the fermented black beans with 3 tablespoons hot water and set aside to rehydrate for 10 minutes, then drain.

Meanwhile, combine all the marinade ingredients in another bowl. Add the sliced beef and stir to combine, then set aside to marinate for 15-20 minutes.

In a separate bowl, combine all the seasoning sauce ingredients with 100ml (3½oz) cold water. Stir well and set aside. In another small bowl, mix the cornflour with 2 tablespoons water. Set aside.

When you're ready to cook, heat 1 tablespoon of the oil in a wok over a high heat. Once shimmering, add the garlic and the drained black beans. Stir-fry for 1 minute until the aromas are released, then remove from the wok and set aside in a bowl. Remember, it's important that you don't overcook or burn the beans as the sauce may taste bitter.

Return the empty wok to the heat and add 1 tablespoon of the oil. Once hot, add the beef and stir-fry for 3-4 minutes, then remove to a separate plate and set aside.

Heat the remaining 1 tablespoon oil in the wok over a medium heat. Once shimmering, stir-fry the onion and peppers for 3-4 minutes until the vegetables are soft but still a little crunchy. Return the garlic and black bean mixture to the pan and stir, then pour in the seasoning sauce and stir-fry for another minute before returning the beef to the wok. Mix well, then reduce the heat to medium-low and slowly pour the cornflour mixture into the pan, stirring all the while. Cook for a further 1-2 minutes until the sauce has thickened.

Serve the black bean beef with steamed jasmine rice.

TIP

✱ A nice alternative to serving it with rice is to fold the black bean beef through some thick hor fun rice noodles or egg noodles.

Sweet-and-Sour Pork

Serves: 2

Prep time: 25 minutes **Cook time:** 20 minutes

300g (10½oz) pork fillet, cut into 2.5cm (1in) pieces
1 egg white
½ teaspoon salt
⅓ teaspoon ground white pepper
2 tablespoons neutral oil, plus extra for shallow-frying the pork
30g (1oz) plain (all-purpose) flour
30g (1oz) cornflour (cornstarch), plus 1 teaspoon for thickening
1cm (½in) piece of fresh ginger, peeled and finely sliced
1 small onion, cut into 2.5cm (1in) pieces
1 carrot, peeled and finely sliced
½ green pepper (capsicum), cut into 2.5cm (1in) pieces
½ red pepper, (capsicum), cut into 2.5cm (1in) pieces
100g (3½oz) tinned pineapple chunks
2 spring onions (scallions), finely sliced, to serve (optional)

FOR THE SWEET-AND-SOUR SAUCE

100ml (3½oz) soft light brown sugar
100ml (3½oz) white rice vinegar
100ml (3½oz) tomato ketchup
100ml (3½oz) pineapple syrup from the tinned pineapple, or pineapple juice

As a child, sweet-and-sour was hands down my favourite Chinese restaurant dish. Come to think of it, it probably still is - and I've definitely passed my love for it on to my kids! In Europe, we tend to think that sweet-and-sour is a very Westernised version of Chinese food, but actually this is an original dish from the Canton region of China, and it is just as popular there as it is here. In this recipe, I'm making sweet-and-sour pork, but it works equally well with chicken, prawns or even fish - a favourite dish of my grandmother's. She once took me to a restaurant in Hung Hom, Hong Kong, where we shared an entire fish, beautifully presented with the head and tail still attached, the flesh perfectly fried and coated with a glossy red sweet-and sour-sauce. It was perfection!

Place the pork pieces in a bowl, then add the egg white, salt and white pepper. Stir to combine and set aside.

In a medium-sized bowl, combine all the sweet-and-sour sauce ingredients and stir to combine. Set aside.

Pour oil into a wok to a depth of about 4cm (1½in) and place over a medium-high heat. Heat the oil until it reaches 175°C (340°F).

In another bowl, mix together the plain flour and cornflour. Working in batches so you don't overcrowd the pan, dip the pork pieces into the flour mix and then add them to the hot oil. Fry for 4-5 minutes on each side until cooked through and golden. Set aside to drain on a plate lined with paper towels. Safely dispose of the used oil and wipe out the wok to clean.

Place the wok back over a high heat and add the 2 tablespoons neutral oil. Add the ginger, onion, carrot and green and red peppers, and stir-fry for 2 minutes. Now add the pineapple chunks and the sweet-and-sour sauce, stirring to combine.

In a small bowl, mix the 1 teaspoon cornflour with 2 tablespoons water. Slowly pour this mixture into the wok, stirring all the while. Cook for a further 2-3 minutes until the sauce has thickened, then add the fried pork and mix well, coating it with the sauce.

Spoon the sweet-and-sour pork into bowls and serve topped with the sliced spring onions, if using.

Kung Pao Chicken

Serves: 2

Prep time: 15 minutes, plus marinating **Cook time:** 10 minutes

- 400g (14oz) skinless, boneless chicken thighs, cut into 1cm (½in) chunks
- 4 tablespoons neutral oil
- 50g (1¾oz) raw cashew nuts
- 8g (⅓oz) small dried Chinese chillies, snipped into 1cm (½in) pieces using scissors
- 1 teaspoon Sichuan peppercorns
- ½ small onion, cut into 1cm (½in) chunks
- 4cm (1½in) piece of fresh ginger, peeled and julienned
- 4 spring onions (scallions), cut into 2cm (¾in) pieces
- 2 garlic cloves, finely sliced
- 250g (9oz) steamed jasmine rice, to serve

FOR THE MARINADE

- 1 tablespoon light soy sauce
- 1 tablespoon dark soy sauce
- 1 tablespoon Shaoxing wine (see page 22)
- 1 teaspoon sesame oil
- ½ teaspoon ground white pepper
- 1 teaspoon cornflour (cornstarch)

FOR THE KUNG PAO SAUCE

- 1 teaspoon cornflour
- 3 tablespoons light soy sauce
- 3 tablespoons Chinese black vinegar (see page 24)
- 40g (1½oz) soft light brown sugar

Spicy, aromatic, tangy and sweet: it has to be kung pao chicken. I've played around with this recipe for a long time, and I love this version. The black vinegar has a slight treacly flavour, which brings a nice complexity and a lovely balance of flavours with the soy and sugar. The dried chillies and Sichuan peppercorns are essential, although you can adjust the quantity depending on how brave you are feeling! The Sichuan peppercorns bring that distinctive numbing, tingling feeling that is part of the character of the dish - and I haven't even mentioned the cashew nuts yet! Trust me, the more the merrier.

Combine all the marinade ingredients in a bowl. Add the chicken, then mix well and set aside to marinate for 15-20 minutes.

To make the kung pao sauce, mix the cornflour with 2 tablespoons water in a small bowl. Add all the other kung pao sauce ingredients, mix well and set aside.

Heat the oil in a wok over a high heat. Once shimmering, add the cashew nuts and toast them in the oil for 2 minutes until they are slightly golden in colour. Remove them from the wok using a slotted spoon and set aside on a plate.

Add the dried chillies, Sichuan peppercorns, onion and ginger to the hot wok with the leftover oil from the cashew nuts. Stir to combine, then add the marinated chicken and stir-fry for 3-4 minutes until the chicken is nearly cooked.

Pour in the kung pao sauce, followed by the toasted cashew nuts, spring onion and garlic. Stir well for 2 minutes until the sauce and ingredients are well combined and the sauce has thickened to coat the chicken.

Spoon the kung pao chicken into bowls and serve alongside some steamed jasmine rice.

TIP

✱ If you can handle your spice, feel free to add extra chillies to taste. Traditionally, kung pao is quite spicy; I've taken the spice down a notch in this version so it's more family-friendly.

Satay Chicken

Serves: 2

Prep time: 15 minutes, plus marinating **Cook time:** 15 minutes

- 400g (14oz) boneless, skinless chicken thighs, diced into 2.5cm (1in) pieces
- 2 tablespoons neutral oil
- 1 white onion, cut into 2.5cm (1in) pieces
- 2 garlic cloves, finely diced
- 1 small carrot, peeled and thinly sliced
- ½ green pepper (capsicum), cut into 2.5cm (1in) pieces
- ½ red pepper (capsicum), cut into 2.5cm (1in) pieces
- 1 teaspoon mild curry powder (I like to use Babas curry powder – see page 148)
- 2 tablespoons shop-bought satay sauce (see tip)
- 2 tablespoons crunchy peanut butter
- 300ml (10½fl oz) chicken stock
- ¼ teaspoon granulated sugar
- ½ tablespoon kecap manis (see page 22)
- 1 teaspoon cornflour (cornstarch) (optional)
- 250g (9oz) steamed jasmine rice, to serve

FOR THE MARINADE

- 1 tablespoon light soy sauce
- 1 teaspoon Shaoxing wine (see page 22)
- ½ tablespoon kecap manis
- 1 teaspoon granulated sugar
- ¼ teaspoon salt
- 1 teaspoon cornflour
- pinch of ground white pepper

Satay chicken always reminds me of Singapore. When I was working in Hong Kong, China, I was seconded to Singapore for three months, and the food scene there really blew me away. It's a true melting pot of cuisines from all around the world. I didn't realise before, but satay in Singapore is off the charts! There is even a street in the central business district called Satay Street where, every evening, they close off the road and the whole area comes alive with countless stalls lined up one after another, each grilling up endless varieties of skewers - chicken, lamb, beef or pork - the smoky aroma filling the air. That's what I think of when someone mentions satay: those perfectly charred skewers, served with fresh cucumber slices and dipped in a rich and sweet peanut sauce. This recipe takes all those satay flavours and transforms them into something more accessible for the home kitchen.

Combine all the marinade ingredients in a bowl. Add the diced chicken, stir to combine and set aside for 15–20 minutes to marinate.

Heat 1 tablespoon of the oil in a non-stick wok over a high heat. Once shimmering, add the chicken and cook for 4–5 minutes until nearly done, then remove to a plate and set aside.

Add the remaining 1 tablespoon oil to the wok and reduce the heat to medium-high. Add the onion and garlic. Stir-fry for 30 seconds, then add the carrot and green and red peppers and stir-fry for a minute more. Sprinkle the curry powder over the vegetables and stir to combine, then add the satay sauce and peanut butter. Stir-fry for 1 minute until all the peanut butter has melted, then return the cooked chicken to the wok, along with the chicken stock, sugar and kecap manis. Cook for 2–3 minutes until the chicken is cooked through.

If you would like the sauce thicker, mix the cornflour with 2 tablespoons water in a small bowl, then slowly add this mixture to the pan, stirring over low heat until the sauce is the consistency you'd like.

Serve the satay chicken with steamed jasmine rice.

TIP

✱ When it comes to shop-bought satay sauce, my favourite brand is Jimmy's - it's from Hong Kong, China, and is super tasty.

Teriyaki Chicken

Serves: 2

Prep time: 15 minutes **Cook time:** 10 minutes

400g (14oz) boneless, skinless chicken thighs, cut into 2.5cm (1in) pieces
2 tablespoons cornflour (cornstarch)
¼ teaspoon salt
¼ teaspoon ground white pepper
2 tablespoons neutral oil
1 onion, finely sliced

FOR THE TERIYAKI SAUCE

50ml (1¾fl oz) light soy sauce
50ml (1¾fl oz) sake (see page 25)
2 tablespoons mirin (see page 25)
3 tablespoons soft light brown sugar

TO SERVE

1 tablespoon toasted white sesame seeds
1 spring onion (scallion), finely sliced
300g (10½oz) cooked Japanese short-grain rice

I always think of teriyaki as being the perfect gateway into the world of Japanese cuisine.

It's a well-balanced mix of sweet, salty and umami flavours, covering the chicken with a deep, glossy glaze without being overly sticky. It's delicious and appetising. I'm using chicken thigh meat here once again, because of its tenderness and flavour. This teriyaki sauce also works really well on the barbecue: skewered chicken yakitori (skewers), cooked over the grill and brushed with teriyaki sauce is absolutely irresistible.

Place the chicken into a bowl and add the cornflour, salt and white pepper. Mix well to combine.

Combine all the teriyaki sauce ingredients in a separate small bowl and set aside.

Heat the oil in a large frying pan over a medium heat. Once hot, add the chicken and cook for 5 minutes to slightly brown, then add the sliced onion and cook for a further minute. Pour over the teriyaki sauce and simmer for 3–4 minutes until the sauce thickens slightly.

Spoon the teriyaki chicken into bowls and sprinkle with sesame seeds and finely sliced spring onions. Serve with steamed rice.

Duck in Plum Sauce

Serves: 2

Prep time: 15 minutes **Cook time:** 25 minutes

2 skin-on, boneless duck breasts
pinch of salt
1 tablespoon neutral oil
steamed jasmine rice, to serve

FOR THE PLUM SAUCE

6 Chinese preserved plums in brine (about 120g/4¼oz), stoned and roughly chopped (see tip)
6cm (2½in) piece of fresh ginger, peeled and thickly sliced
2 star anise
2 cinnamon sticks
4 bay leaves
120g (4¼oz) rock sugar (see page 27) or soft light brown sugar
2 teaspoons white rice vinegar
2 teaspoons cornflour (cornstarch)

Even though this is a takeaway classic, I love serving it as a dinner-party dish. The whole duck breast, with crisp skin and tender flesh, carefully sliced and served with this beautiful, fruity homemade plum sauce always feels so elegant - almost fine dining! You can, of course, buy plum sauce in a bottle, but trust me, the homemade version is divine. It's fruitier, has a more complex flavour and is not nearly as gloopy. The preserved plums are key here. We have always stocked them in our shop, but the first time I came across them beyond our shelves was in Hong Kong, where they are used in a drink mixed with lemonade called ham ling tsat. In this recipe, I've balanced the saltiness with sugar, star anise, cinnamon and ginger.

Using a sharp knife, gently score the skin of both duck breasts in a criss-cross pattern. Rub the salt all over the duck, making sure to work it into the cuts.

Heat the oil in a large frying pan over medium-high heat. Place the duck breasts in the pan, skin-sides down, and cook for about 5 minutes, or until the skin starts to crisp up. Flip to cook on the other side for another 5 minutes until the duck reaches an internal temperature of 54°C (129°F). Transfer the duck breasts to a plate, lightly cover with a clean tea towel, and allow to rest.

Carefully pour the duck fat from the pan (see tip on page 164), leaving about 2 tablespoons in the pan. Place over a medium heat and add the plums and ginger. Fry for 2 minutes, then add the star anise, cinnamon stick and bay leaves. Fry for 40 seconds until fragrant, then add the rock sugar, vinegar and 200ml (7fl oz) water. Bring everything to a gentle simmer and cook for 5-7 minutes to melt the sugar.

In a small bowl, mix the cornflour with 2 tablespoons water. Add half of this mixture to the pan, mix well and simmer for 1-2 minutes. The sauce should thicken slightly. If it isn't thick enough, add the remaining cornflour mixture, stir well and bring back to the boil. Once you're happy with the consistency, season the sauce with salt to taste, then remove the star anise, bay leaves and cinnamon sticks.

Thickly slice the rested duck breasts. Transfer the plum sauce to a shallow serving dish and arrange the sliced duck on top. Serve with steamed jasmine rice.

TIP

* You can find preserved plums in brine in Asian supermarkets.

Serves: 4

Beef with Broccoli in Oyster Sauce

Prep time: 15 minutes **Cook time:** 15 minutes

- 450g (1lb) beef sirloin, very thinly sliced
- 1 small head of broccoli (about 250g/9oz), cut into small florets
- 2 tablespoons neutral oil
- 3 garlic cloves, finely sliced
- cooked noodles or steamed jasmine rice, to serve

FOR THE MARINADE

- 2 teaspoons light soy sauce
- 1 teaspoon Shaoxing wine (see page 22)
- ¼ teaspoon sesame oil
- 1 teaspoon caster (superfine) sugar
- 1 teaspoon bicarbonate of soda (baking soda)
- ¼ teaspoon ground white pepper
- pinch of salt

FOR THE SAUCE

- 1 teaspoon cornflour
- 4 tablespoons premium oyster sauce
- 1 tablespoon dark soy sauce
- 2 teaspoons caster sugar

This dish is a staple on many takeaway menus - and also in my mum's kitchen. I think it is probably the first dish I ever learned to cook, standing beside my mum at the stove. It was a Chinese household, so there was always a bottle of oyster sauce on the counter. I remember her showing me how to make a really simple oyster sauce glaze, using oyster sauce, water and cornflour. The key step in this recipe is tenderising the beef with a little bicarbonate of soda. It gives a restaurant-quality feel but is easy to recreate in your own home. The tender beef is paired with lovely, crunchy broccoli that soaks up all the beautiful sauce. It's a great midweek meal with plenty of veg.

Combine all the marinade ingredients in a bowl. Add the beef strips and stir to coat, then set aside.

Now make the sauce. In a separate small bowl, mix the cornflour with 4 tablespoons water. Add the remaining sauce ingredients and mix well to combine. Set aside.

Place a large wok over a medium-high heat and pour in some freshly boiled water. Add the broccoli and cook for 4 minutes until just tender, then drain and set aside.

Empty and wipe out the wok, then place it over a medium heat. Add the oil and, when hot, add the garlic. Cook for 30 seconds, then add the marinated beef and cook for 4–5 minutes. Now add the broccoli and the sauce, and cook for 1–2 minutes more until the sauce thickens and becomes glossy.

Serve immediately with noodles or jasmine rice.

Serves: 2 as a main, 4 as a starter/side

Crispy Tofu in Chilli Garlic Sauce

Prep time: 20 minutes **Cook time:** 25 minutes

400g (14oz) firm tofu
3 tablespoons cornflour (cornstarch)
½ teaspoon Chinese five-spice
½ teaspoon salt
neutral oil, for frying
1 tablespoon toasted white sesame seeds

FOR THE SAUCE
1 tablespoon neutral oil
4 garlic cloves, finely chopped
1cm (½in) piece of fresh ginger, peeled and grated
1 tablespoon sambal oelek (see tip)
1 tablespoon light soy sauce
1 tablespoon chilli garlic sauce (I like the Lee Kum Kee brand)
1 tablespoon white rice vinegar
1 tablespoon caster (superfine) sugar
1 teaspoon cornflour

Chilli garlic sauce is a classic flavour in Chinese takeaways, and in this recipe, we're using tofu for a vegan twist. Pressing the tofu removes all the excess water, which allows for the creation of wonderfully crispy cubes. If you prefer, you can substitute the tofu for your preferred meat, as the sauce is so versatile. It's not overly spicy - perfect for those who enjoy a hint of heat without being overwhelmed.

Place the tofu between two layers of paper towels, then place on a plate or chopping board. Place a second plate or board on top of the wrapped tofu, then add something heavy - a tin of beans, a cookbook - on top. Let the tofu sit under this pressure for 10 minutes. The paper towels will soak up the water that's released, and you're on the right path for crispy tofu!

Cut the pressed tofu into 2.5cm (1in) cubes, then toss in a bowl with the cornflour, five-spice and salt until evenly coated.

Pour oil into a frying pan to a depth of about 1-2cm (½-¾in). Heat over a medium-high heat until shimmering, then add the tofu cubes and fry for 2-3 minutes per side until golden and crisp. Set aside on a plate lined with paper towels to drain.

To make the sauce, heat the 1 tablespoon oil in a wok over a medium heat. Add the garlic and ginger, and stir-fry for 30 seconds until fragrant. Now add the sambal oelek, light soy sauce, chilli garlic sauce, vinegar, sugar and 2 tablespoons water. Stir well and bring to a simmer.

In a small bowl, mix the cornflour with 1 tablespoon water, then stir this mixture into the wok to thicken the sauce.

Add the crispy tofu to the sauce and toss gently to coat, then cook for 1-2 minutes until the tofu is glazed and sticky.

Spoon the tofu into bowls and serve garnished with the sesame seeds.

TIP

* Sambal oelek is a medium-spicy coarse chilli paste made with red chillies, salt and vinegar. It has a unique tangy flavour and is great added to stir-fries or used as a dipping sauce.

Sweet Treats

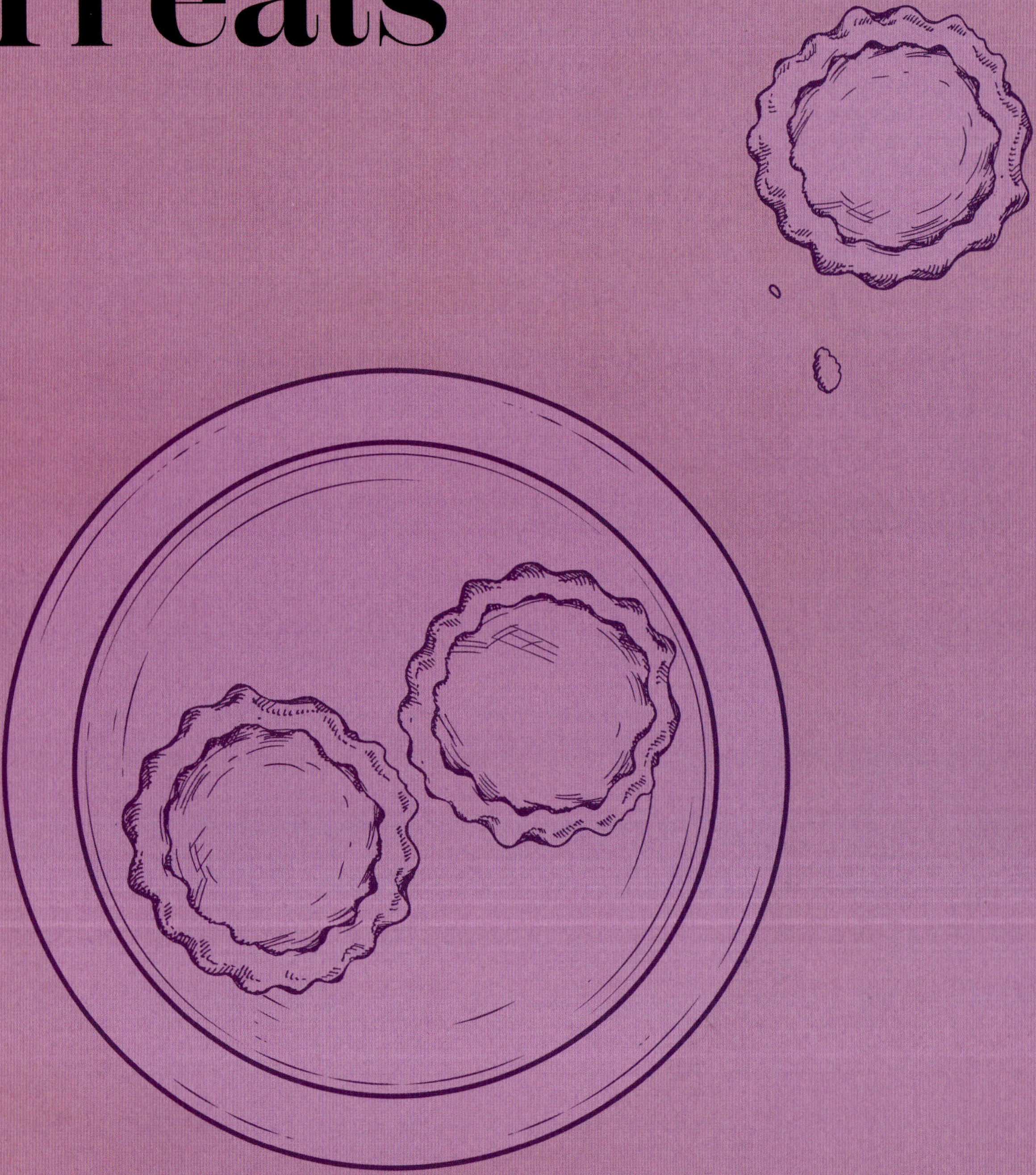

Banana and Apple Fritters 181

Miso Caramel Banoffee Pie 182

Hokkaido-Style Cheese Tarts 184

Onde Onde Cake 188

Filipino Leche Flan 190

Matcha Basque Cheesecake 191

Brown Sugar Bubble Tea Ice Cream 193

Halo-Halo Ice-Cream Sundae 194

Thai Mango Sticky Rice 197

Korean Red-Bean Doughnuts 198

Banana and Apple Fritters

Serves: 4

Prep time: 10 minutes **Cook time:** 10 minutes

neutral oil, for deep-frying
2 ripe bananas
2 large cooking apples

FOR THE BATTER
120g (4¼oz) plain (all-purpose) flour
60g (2¼oz) cornflour (cornstarch)
1 teaspoon baking powder
1 teaspoon bicarbonate of soda (baking soda)
2 teaspoons vanilla bean paste

TO SERVE
golden syrup, for drizzling
2 tablespoons toasted white sesame seeds
vanilla ice cream

Wow, these are such a blast from my childhood. Every time I had a Chinese restaurant meal growing up, I always made sure to leave space for the banana fritter dessert. Hot, crispy, golden nuggets of banana drizzled with golden syrup. Even thinking about it makes my mouth water. These aren't just for kids; I've served them as a fun dessert at dinner parties, and they've always gone down an absolute treat. Over time, I've added apple to this dessert as well. My kids love apples, and any time we visit my parents' house, they pinch Bramley apples from the tree and ask me to make apple fritters when we get home.

In a mixing bowl, combine all the batter ingredients with 200ml (7fl oz) cold water and whisk until you get a smooth, slightly thick batter the texture of double (heavy) cream.

Pour the oil into a large, deep-sided saucepan to a depth of 5cm (2in). Place over a medium-high heat and heat the oil to 175°C (340°F).

Peel the bananas and top and tail each one, then slice lengthways. Cut each slice in half. Peel and core the apples, then slice into 5mm (¼in) rounds.

Working in batches, dip the banana and apple slices into the batter, ensuring they are well coated, then carefully place into the hot oil and fry until golden and crispy - this will take 2 minutes for the banana slices and 6 minutes for the apple slices. Remove from the oil and drain on a plate lined with paper towels to absorb any excess oil.

When they're ready, drizzle the fritters with golden syrup and sprinkle with the sesame seeds. Serve alongside some vanilla ice cream.

Miso Caramel Banoffee Pie

Serves: 8–10

Prep time: 20 minutes **Cook time:** 30 minutes, plus chilling time

neutral oil, for greasing
3 bananas, sliced
350ml (12fl oz) double (heavy) cream
1 tablespoon icing (confectioners') sugar
1½ teaspoons vanilla bean paste
75g (2¾oz) dark chocolate shards, to decorate

FOR THE CRUST

125g (4½oz) plain (all-purpose) flour
2 tablespoons cocoa powder
50g (1¾oz) soft light brown sugar
¼ teaspoon salt
115g (4oz) salted butter, melted
1 teaspoon vanilla bean paste

FOR THE MISO CARAMEL

397g (14oz) tin caramel condensed milk
60ml (¼ cup) golden syrup
60ml (¼ cup) double (heavy) cream
50g (1¾oz) salted butter, diced
1 heaped tablespoon white miso paste

I absolutely love this dessert. I've been a big banoffee-pie fan ever since I tasted it as a teenager at a restaurant beside our shop in Dublin. Miso, typically a savoury ingredient, is a fantastic addition to a caramel sauce. The miso brings just the right amount of saltiness, like in a salted caramel, while also delivering a wonderful umami back note. It feels to me like a 'grown-up' banoffee pie. What I also love about my version is the pastry base, which is infused with cocoa powder, adding a slight bitterness that complements the miso caramel beautifully.

Preheat the oven to 190°C fan (375°F/gas mark 5). Lightly grease a loose-bottomed, deep-sided 22cm (8½in) tart tin with neutral oil.

Begin by preparing the crust. In a bowl, sift together the flour, cocoa powder, sugar and salt, then pour in the melted butter and vanilla. Stir until the mixture resembles damp sand and begins to clump together. You can add 1-2 teaspoons cold water, if needed, to bring it together.

Transfer the mixture to the lined tart tin and press it evenly across the bottom and up the sides using your fingers or the back of a spoon. Bake for 15-18 minutes, or until set and slightly firm to the touch. Remove from the oven and allow to cool completely in the tin.

Meanwhile, combine all the miso caramel ingredients in a medium saucepan over a medium-high heat. Cook, stirring, for about 2 minutes, until everything is melted and well combined. Bring the mixture to a gentle simmer, then reduce the heat to low and continue to simmer for about 5 minutes, stirring frequently, until the caramel is glossy and slightly thickened. Remove from the heat and set aside to cool.

To assemble the pie, arrange the banana slices in the bottom of the tart case so the base is covered with a layer of banana. Pour over the miso caramel and place the pie in the fridge to set for 2 hours, or overnight if you have the time.

When you're ready to serve, carefully remove the tart from the case and place on a serving plate.

In a large bowl, whisk the double cream, icing sugar and vanilla bean until soft peaks form, then spoon this mixture over the miso caramel. Decorate with the chocolate shards before slicing and serving.

Hokkaido-Style Cheese Tarts

Makes: 9

Prep time: 25 minutes, plus chilling **Cook time:** 35 minutes

FOR THE PASTRY CASES

70g (2½oz) salted butter, softened, plus extra for greasing
1½ tablespoons caster (superfine) sugar
1 teaspoon vanilla bean paste
1 egg, separated
125g (4½oz) plain (all-purpose) flour, plus extra for dusting

FOR THE FILLING

100g (3½oz) cream cheese, at room temperature
100g (3½oz) mascarpone, at room temperature
25g (1oz) Parmesan cheese, finely grated
30g (1oz) salted butter
50ml (1¾fl oz) milk
2 tablespoons double (heavy) cream
1 egg
60g (2¼oz) caster (superfine) sugar
2 tablespoons cornflour (cornstarch)
1 teaspoon lemon juice
½ teaspoon vanilla bean paste

TO FINISH

1 egg
1 tablespoon milk
icing (confectioners') sugar, for dusting

You will need 9 × 7cm (2¾in) fluted tart tins and baking beans or rice

Hokkaido-style cheese tarts have taken Asia by storm. If you haven't been lucky enough to try these yet, here is your chance! If you enjoy a classic baked cheesecake, you'll find these delicious (pictured overleaf). They are quite hard to describe, because they sit somewhere between a savoury cheese tart and a baked cheesecake. The filling includes cream cheese, Parmesan, mascarpone and vanilla - trust me, it works!

Preheat the oven to 180°C fan (350°F/gas mark 4) and lightly grease the tart tins with butter.

Begin by preparing the pastry. Combine the butter and sugar in a medium bowl and, using an electric hand whisk, cream together for 2-3 minutes until light and fluffy. Add the vanilla and egg yolk (reserve the white for later) and whisk again until combined, then sift in the flour and use a spatula to fold it into the mix until a dough forms. Bring the dough together in a disc, wrap in clingfilm and place in the fridge to rest for 15 minutes.

After 15 minutes, remove the dough from the fridge and, on a lightly floured work surface, roll out to a thickness of about 5mm (¼in). Using a 9cm (3½in) round cutter, cut out 9 rounds and use these to line the prepared tart tins, pressing the dough into the tins so it covers the bases and sides. Prick the bases with a fork, then leave to chill in the fridge for 30 minutes.

Cut out 9 × 9cm (3½in) discs of baking paper. Crumple these up, then flatten them out and press one into each of the tart tins, on top of the chilled pastry case. Fill each case with baking beans or rice, then blind-bake for 15 minutes. Carefully remove the baking beans or rice and baking paper, and bake for a further 10 minutes until the pastry cases are lightly golden brown. Brush each pastry case with the egg white, then bake for a further 2 minutes. Remove from the oven and leave to cool.

To make the filling, combine the cream cheese, mascarpone, Parmesan, butter, milk and cream in a saucepan and set over a low-medium heat. Allow everything to melt together, stirring constantly until smooth.

In a separate bowl, whisk together the egg, sugar, cornflour, lemon juice and vanilla until smooth. Slowly add a little of the warm cream-and-cheese mixture to the egg mixture and whisk to temper it, then pour in the rest, whisking everything to combine. Be careful not to over-whisk, as this will create air bubbles, and you want a nice, smooth filling.

Return the mixture to the saucepan and cook gently for a few minutes, stirring constantly, until it thickens slightly. Remove from the heat and let it cool slightly, then transfer the filling to a piping bag.

Increase the oven temperature to 230°C fan (450°F/gas mark 8) and pipe the cheese filling into the cooled pastry cases.

To finish, make an egg wash by combining the egg with the 1 tablespoon milk, then carefully brush this over the top of each tart. Sift a tiny bit of icing sugar over each one, then bake for 5-8 minutes, or until the tops are slightly brûléed and golden brown.

Let the tarts cool for at least 5-10 minutes before serving warm. If you prefer, you can chill them for a firmer, fudgier texture.

TIPS

- If you don't have a piping bag, you can use a food-storage bag and snip one of the corners with scissors to create a makeshift piping bag.
- If you want a deeply golden brûléed tart, you can use a blow torch on these once they are fully cooked. This is entirely optional - they are still delicious without this step.

Hokkaido-Style Cheese Tarts, page 184

Onde Onde Cake, page 188

Onde Onde Cake

Serves: 10–12

Prep time: 20 minutes **Bake:** 1 hour

butter, for greasing
4 pandan leaves (see page 17), washed and cut into 1cm (¾in) pieces
80ml (2½fl oz) coconut milk
4 large eggs, separated
40ml (1¼fl oz) vegetable oil
90g (3oz) caster (superfine) sugar
80g (2¾oz) low-gluten flour
20g (¾oz) plain (all-purpose) flour
1 teaspoon baking powder
a few drops of lemon juice
desiccated coconut or fresh or frozen grated coconut (defrosted if frozen), for coating (see tip)

FOR THE FILLING

50g (1¾oz) gula melaka, or coconut sugar
2 pandan leaves, rolled and tied into a knot
120g (4¼oz) fresh or frozen grated coconut (defrosted if frozen)

FOR THE TOPPING

200g (7oz) coconut whipping cream (see page 27)
50g (1¾oz) cream cheese
1 tablespoon icing (confectioners') sugar

I first had this cake during a recent trip to Malaysia. We were celebrating my uncle's birthday in a Chinese restaurant in Selangor in Kuala Lumpur. At the end of the meal, they brought out his favourite cake: onde onde cake (pictured on previous page). It looked like a regular, white-dusted cake, but when they cut into it, it had glorious layers of super-soft green pandan-flavoured sponge with a sweet and salty coconut filling, coated with freshly shaved coconut. I just remember falling in love with it. I think I must have had three or four slices ... purely for research purposes, of course! One of the special ingredients in this recipe is a Malaysian sugar called gula melaka. I sometimes melt it to make a syrup to enjoy with sago and coconut. But here, we're using it to create the sweet coconut filling.

Preheat the oven to 125°C fan (250°F/gas mark 1). Grease the bases and sides of 2 × 20cm (8in) cake tins with melted butter, then line the bottoms with rounds of baking paper.

In a blender, combine the chopped pandan leaves and coconut milk with 1 tablespoon water, and blend until fine. Strain the mixture through a sieve into a bowl - it should yield 60ml (2fl oz) pandan liquid. Add the egg yolks, oil and 20g (¾oz) of the caster sugar. Whisk until smooth, then sift in the low-gluten flour, plain flour and baking powder, and stir until there are no lumps left.

In a separate bowl, whisk the egg whites with an electric hand whisk. Add a few drops of lemon juice and whisk until foamy, then gradually add the remaining 70g (2½oz) sugar until you have a glossy white meringue with medium-stiff peaks.

Fold a third of the meringue into the pandan batter, then gently fold in the remaining meringue, preserving as much air as possible.

Divide the batter between the prepared tins and bake for 30 minutes, then increase the oven temperature to 150°C fan (300°F/gas mark 2) and bake for another 10 minutes, or until a skewer inserted into the centre comes out clean.

Remove the cakes from the oven and allow to cool for 5 minutes, then remove from the cake tins and transfer to a wire rack to cool fully. The cakes will shrink slightly, so don't be alarmed - this is just the nature of chiffon cake.

Now prepare the filling. In a small saucepan, combine the gula melaka or coconut sugar and pandan leaves with 3 tablespoons water. Place over a medium heat until the sugar fully dissolves, then add the grated coconut and stir for 2-3 minutes until the water is absorbed and the mixture thickens. Set aside to cool completely.

To make the topping, combine all the ingredients in a bowl and whisk with an electric whisk for 10 minutes until you have lovely soft peaks. The consistency should be like that of thick yoghurt.

Place one of the cooled cakes on a board or plate and spread with half of the topping and all of the filling. Top with the second cake, then spread the remaining topping over the top and sides. Press the desiccated or grated fresh coconut on to the top and sides of the cake to finish.

This is best eaten on the day it's made.

TIPS

* If using frozen grated coconut, then you will need to defrost and squeeze any excess liquid from the coconut before using it to coat the cake.
* If you find the filling too sweet, you can add ¼ teaspoon salt to balance the sweetness. It will transform it to be something similar to a salted caramel.
* If you can't source low-gluten flour, use plain flour. It will still work, but the cake will be slightly denser.

Filipino Leche Flan

Makes: 6

Prep time: 10 minutes **Cook time:** 1 hour 15 minutes, plus chilling time

- 125g (4½oz) caster (superfine) sugar
- 10 egg yolks
- 397g (14oz) tin condensed milk
- 410g (14½fl oz) tin evaporated milk
- 1 teaspoon vanilla bean paste

You will need 6 × 10cm (4in) flan dishes or ramekins

I first tried leche flan while visiting a Filipino friend. Her mum made this for dessert, and I remember being amazed by how silky and smooth it was. It's definitely richer than a regular crème caramel, because it uses both condensed milk and evaporated milk, along with all the egg yolks. The ingredients are simple, but the technique makes all the difference here. You have to be quite gentle when you're mixing everything together, because you don't want to create bubbles. The caramel on top is absolutely glorious - it has this beautiful golden colour, and when you flip the flan over, it just flows down the sides. It looks so elegant, and is perfect for when you want to impress your guests with something a bit different. A word of warning: Filipino desserts do tend to be very sweet!

Preheat the oven to 160°C fan (325°F/gas mark 2-3). Mix the sugar with 2 tablespoons water in a small saucepan and place over a medium heat. Let the sugar melt and caramelise without stirring; this should take about 8 minutes. After the sugar has dissolved fully, stir occasionally and cook for a further 4-5 minutes until the caramel turns a deep amber colour. Quickly divide between the flan dishes, tilting to coat the bottoms evenly. Set aside to cool and harden while you make the custard.

In a large bowl, gently whisk the egg yolks until combined - try not to beat too hard to avoid getting too much air into the mixture. You want a silky-smooth custard mix, not an aerated one.

Add the condensed milk, evaporated milk and vanilla, and stir gently until smooth and well combined.

Strain the custard through a fine sieve, then pour over the set caramel in the flan dishes. Cover tightly with foil.

Arrange the flan dishes in a large baking tray, then pour hot water into the tray so that it comes halfway up the outsides of the flan dishes. Carefully place in the oven and bake for 50-55 minutes, or until set.

Once cooked, let the flans cool to room temperature, then place into the fridge for at least 4 hours, or overnight, to set fully.

To remove the flans from the dishes, run a knife around the edge of each flan and invert on to a serving plate to release the caramel topping before serving.

TIPS

- ✱ If your caramel hardens before you've had a chance to pour it into the flan dishes, you can place the whole saucepan into a large bowl of just-boiled water until the caramel turns to liquid again.
- ✱ A more traditional way to cook the leche flan is by using a steamer. To do this, cover the moulds with foil and place them in a steamer set over a pan of gently simmering water. Steam for 30-40 minutes, or until a toothpick inserted in the centre comes out clean. Keep an eye on the temperature - you want to keep the heat low to avoid bubbles forming or the flans overcooking.

Matcha Basque Cheesecake

Serves: 8–10

Prep time: 10 minutes **Cook time:** 1 hour, plus chilling time

butter, for greasing
150g (5½oz) white chocolate
3 tablespoons matcha powder, sieved
425g (15oz) cream cheese
125g (4½oz) caster (superfine) sugar
3 large eggs
200ml (7fl oz) double (heavy) cream
1 teaspoon vanilla bean paste
pinch of salt
1½ tablespoons plain (all-purpose) flour

Matcha fans, this cheesecake is for you! This recipe is just heavenly. It has just the right balance of sweetness from the white chocolate and bitterness from the matcha, with a wonderful toasted top. I know matcha can be a bit of a controversial flavour, but trust me, this cheesecake is a real crowd-pleaser. Even my non-matcha-loving friends have devoured this.

Preheat the oven to 220°C fan/425°F/gas mark 7. Butter a deep 20cm (8in) springform cake tin and line the base and sides with baking paper (make sure the paper is taller than the tin as the cake will rise above the tin).

Melt the white chocolate in a heatproof bowl set over a pan of barely simmering water. Once melted and smooth, take it off the heat and whisk in the matcha powder to turn it a vivid green. Set aside to cool.

Combine the cream cheese and caster sugar in the bowl of a stand mixer and beat for 2 minutes until the mixture is silky and no longer grainy. Add the eggs one at a time, beating really well in between each addition. Scrape down the bowl, then add the cooled white chocolate, along with the cream, vanilla and pinch of salt. Beat once more to combine.

Sift the flour over the top then mix in, beating for 2 more minutes. Strain the mixture through a sieve into the prepared tin, and give the tin a sharp bang on the work surface to release any bubbles.

Bake in the middle of the oven for 40 minutes until the cheesecake is deep brown on top but still has a slight wobble. It will puff up above the level of the tin, but will fall back after cooking.

Remove from the oven and leave the cheesecake to cool completely in the tin; it will fall and crack as it cools. Carefully remove from the tin and refrigerate for an hour before slicing and serving.

Brown Sugar Bubble Tea Ice Cream

Serves: 4–6

Prep time: 15 minutes **Cook time:** 30 minutes, plus chilling time

600ml (scant 2½ cups) double (heavy) cream
5 English Breakfast tea bags
397g (14oz) tin condensed milk
1 teaspoon vanilla bean paste
pinch of salt

FOR THE BROWN-SUGAR SYRUP

200g (7oz) soft dark brown sugar
50g (1¾oz) salted butter
2 tablespoons maple syrup

FOR THE TAPIOCA PEARLS

100g (3½oz) quick-cook brown-sugar tapioca pearls
1 tablespoon soft light brown sugar

I love bubble tea. I got a taste for it when I was living and working in Hong Kong. There's something about the mix of strong milk tea with chewy, brown-sugar tapioca pearls that I find hard to resist. I first made this ice cream to celebrate my daughter Camilla's third birthday. Of all the things I served that day, this ice cream stole the show!

Add 250ml (1 cup) of the cream to a saucepan and add the tea bags. Place over a medium heat and bring to a gentle simmer, then remove from the heat and leave to steep for 30 minutes.

Remove the tea bags, squeezing them to extract as much flavour as possible, then let the mixture cool completely. It should have quite a strong flavour at this point, as it will get diluted when combined with the other ingredients. When cool, strain the mixture through a sieve into a large bowl and set aside.

To make the sugar syrup, place a saucepan over a medium heat and add the brown sugar and 3 tablespoons water. Simmer for 3-4 minutes until the sugar has melted, then stir in the butter and allow to melt before adding the maple syrup and 1 tablespoon of the remaining double cream. Stir to combine, then pour into a small bowl to cool completely.

Add the remaining cream to the large bowl of infused tea cream and whisk with an electric hand whisk until medium peaks form. Add the condensed milk, vanilla and salt, and whisk again until the mixture has thickened and forms soft peaks. This is your ice-cream base.

Now, whisk the cooled syrup for 2 minutes until it turns lighter and slightly thicker.

Pour half of the ice-cream base into a freezer-proof container, then drizzle with a quarter of the brown-sugar syrup. Top with the remaining half of the ice-cream base and a further quarter of the brown-sugar syrup. Pour the rest of the syrup into a jar and set aside in the fridge. Freeze the ice cream for at least 6 hours, or until firm.

Remove the brown sugar syrup from the fridge so it can come to room temperature. Prepare the tapioca pearls according to the packet instructions, then rinse under cold water. Toss in a bowl with the brown sugar, then set aside to cool.

To serve, spoon a few tapioca pearls into the bottom of each bowl, then add a few scoops of ice cream. Drizzle over a little of the remaining brown-sugar syrup, and garnish with a few extra tapioca pearls.

Halo-Halo Ice-Cream Sundae

Serves: 8–10

Prep time: 20 minutes **Cook time:** 40 minutes, plus chilling

This sundae is inspired by halo-halo, a famous Filipino shaved-ice dessert that's loaded with all sorts of colourful toppings. I love how you can make your own combination with the jackfruit, mango and nata de coco. The colours are just stunning when you layer everything together. It's such a fun dessert to make with friends or family. This recipe does call for a few specialised ingredients, but if you can source them, it is so worth it. The ube gives it a beautiful purple colour, and the pandan adds a really lovely aromatic flavour that's quite different from anything else.

FOR THE UBE ICE CREAM

500ml (2 cups) double (heavy) cream
200g (7oz) condensed milk
1 teaspoon ube extract (see page 27)
1 teaspoon vanilla bean paste
pinch of salt

FOR THE PANDAN ICE CREAM

500ml (2 cups) double cream
200g (7oz) condensed milk
½ teaspoon pandan extract (see page 17)
1 teaspoon pandan emulco (see tip)

TO SERVE

handful of strawberries, sliced
1 mango, peeled and cut into cubes
125g (4½oz) tinned or fresh ripe jackfruit, chopped into cubes
150g (5½oz) nata de coco (coconut gel)
100g (3½oz) munggo (red mung beans) in syrup
100g (3½oz) ube macapuno (purple yam and shredded coconut; see page 27)
100g (3½oz) kaong (green candied fruit in syrup)
shaved ice

To make the ube ice cream, pour the double cream into a large bowl and beat with an electric hand whisk, or by hand, until soft peaks form.

In a separate bowl, mix together the condensed milk, ube extract and vanilla bean paste. Add a pinch of salt and stir. You want a smooth mixture here, so keep mixing until everything is well combined.

Gently fold the whipped cream into the ube mixture with a spatula, then pour into a loaf tin lined with clingfilm or a large, freezer-proof container. Cover tightly and freeze for at least 6 hours, preferably overnight.

To make the pandan ice cream, pour the double cream into a large bowl and beat with an electric hand whisk, or by hand, until soft peaks form.

In a separate bowl, mix together the condensed milk, pandan extract and pandan emulco.

Gently fold the whipped cream into the condensed milk mixture with a spatula, then pour into a loaf tin lined with clingfilm or a large freezer-proof container. Cover tightly and freeze for at least 6 hours, preferably overnight.

When you're ready to assemble, set out all your topping ingredients and let people create their own 'halo-halo' inspired sundaes!

TIP

✱ Pandan emulco is a concentrated, sweet, thick green liquid colouring with pandan flavour. If you can't get hold of it, add an extra ½ teaspoon of pandan extract.

Thai Mango Sticky Rice

Serves: 2

Prep time: 15 minutes **Cook time:** 40 minutes

- 200g (7oz) glutinous rice (see page 11)
- 250ml (1 cup) coconut milk
- 3 tablespoons caster (superfine) sugar
- ½ teaspoon salt
- 50g (1¾oz) mung beans (moong dal)
- 1 tablespoon neutral oil
- 2 fresh yellow mangoes, peeled and sliced

Every time I land in Bangkok, a portion of mango sticky rice from one of the many street vendors is always first on my hit list! It is such an addictive treat. The fresh mango is sweet and juicy, and the glutinous rice has a chewy texture that is just so satisfying. In this recipe, I steam the rice, which is the best way to achieve that wonderfully chewy texture. It requires a bit more effort, because you need to soak the rice beforehand, but it's well worth it. I've also included a crispy little garnish made with mung beans; this is optional, but always included in Thailand, and it adds a nice crunchy texture.

Rinse and wash the glutinous rice a few times, until the water runs clear. Tip into a bowl and cover with clean water. The water should cover the rice by at least 5cm (2in). Leave the rice to soak for at least 3 hours - if you prefer, you can do this overnight in the fridge.

Strain the soaked rice through a sieve and place in a bamboo steamer lined with some baking paper. Steam for 30 minutes over a medium heat, or until the rice is cooked and soft.

Meanwhile, combine the coconut milk, sugar and salt in a small saucepan over a low heat. Gently heat until the sugar and salt dissolve, but the mixture is still runny.

Rinse the mung beans and add them to a separate small saucepan. Add enough water to cover them and bring to a gentle boil. Simmer for 5 minutes until the beans are soft, then drain. Lightly pat the mung beans dry with a paper towel.

Heat the oil in a small frying pan over a medium heat. Add the mung beans and gently toast for 4–5 minutes until they are crispy.

When the rice is soft and ready, spoon it into a bowl and pour in two-thirds of the coconut mixture. Mix well.

To serve, fill a small cup or bowl with half the rice, press down, then turn it out on to a plate in a little dome. Repeat with the rest of the rice on a second plate. Arrange the mango slices around the rice and pour the reserved coconut sauce over the top. Sprinkle with the crispy mung beans to garnish

TIPS

- ✱ A pot steamer will also work to steam the rice, but remember to line the bottom of the steamer with baking paper.
- ✱ You can make the sauce thicker by mixing 1 teaspoon cornflour (cornstarch) with 1 tablespoon water and stirring this in, but I prefer it to be more liquid because it seeps into the rice, which makes it even more glorious.

Korean Red-Bean Doughnuts

Makes: 10

Prep time: 10 minutes, plus proving time **Cook time:** 30 minutes

- 7g (¼oz) active dried yeast
- 180ml (5¾fl oz) warm milk
- 25g (1oz) caster (superfine) sugar
- 325g (11½oz) plain (all-purpose) flour
- ½ teaspoon salt
- 30g (1oz) unsalted butter, softened
- 1 egg, beaten
- neutral oil, for greasing and deep-frying
- 200g (7oz) sweetened red-bean paste (see page 27)
- 100g (3½oz) granulated sugar, for dusting

These red-bean doughnuts always bring me back to a family trip to Seoul when my son George was just 18 months old. Across the road from the hotel was the famous Myeongdong street market, with stalls selling every type of Korean street food. The two most memorable things we tried were kimchi dumplings and these fresh, hot red-bean doughnuts. It was the first time I'd tried red-bean filling in a doughnut, and wow - they were amazing! The two ladies running the stall laughed when we returned for the third time to buy yet more. These doughnuts are fluffy on the inside and crispy on the outside, while the red-bean filling isn't too sweet and has a lovely smooth texture.

In a small bowl, combine the yeast, warmed milk and caster sugar, and set aside for 5-10 minutes until foamy.

In a large bowl, combine the flour and salt, then make a well in the centre and add the yeast mixture, along with the softened butter and beaten egg. Mix until it comes together, then knead for 8-10 minutes until smooth and elastic. You can do this by hand or in a stand mixer fitted with a dough hook.

Place the dough in a lightly greased bowl and cover with a clean tea towel. Leave to rise in a warm place for 1-1 ½ hours, or until doubled in size.

Once the dough has proved, punch down the dough and divide it into 10 equal pieces. Flatten the first piece into a small disc and place about 15-20g (½-¾oz) red-bean paste in the centre, then bring the sides up and around the filling to fully encase it, pinching to seal. Shape the dough into a ball and place, seam-side down, on a tray lined with baking paper. Repeat with the remaining dough and filling. Finally, gently flatten each ball into a disc. Cover loosely and leave to rise for another 30-45 minutes until puffy.

When you're ready to cook, pour oil into a deep-sided saucepan to a depth of about 7.5cm (3in). Place over a medium-high heat and heat the oil to 170-175°C (325-340°F). Gently lower in 2-3 of the doughnuts and fry for 2-3 minutes per side until golden. Remove from the pan and set aside to drain on a plate lined with paper towels or a wire rack. Repeat until all the doughnuts are fried.

While the doughnuts are still warm, tip the granulated sugar on to a plate and roll the doughnuts in it to coat. These are best enjoyed on the day they are made.

Acknowledgements

To have the opportunity to write my own cookbook has been an absolute dream come true. To see it on the shelf nestled amongst my cookbook collection is a real pinch-me moment. I am unbelievably thankful to everyone who has helped me to realise this dream.

To my newfound Murdoch family, Céline Hughes and Hazel O'Brien, for bringing me this opportunity and for believing in me. To Virginia Birch and Melissa Kayser, for your continued support, guidance and encouragement. Although you are both based in Australia, I think our timing has worked out perfectly. I am a bit of a night owl, but I didn't feel bad sending out emails at 1am, as I knew they would get to you during your working day. To Sarah McCoy, for designing such a beautiful book – and having the patience of a saint as I obsessed over the smallest details. I'm thrilled with it. To Tara O'Sullivan, for your editing prowess. Your attention to detail and ability to condense two pages into one is a true skill! After dreaming of it for so many years, the experience of creating this cookbook with you all has been everything I had hoped for and more.

Charlotte O'Connell – where to start?! You're amazing at everything from recipe development to styling, propping, prepping, testing and planning all the elements of the photoshoot to make sure everything runs smoothly. I feel so lucky to have had you with me on this journey. And, of course, Susan Willis, a big part of our 'go girl power' photoshoot days. You are so much fun to have on set and so hardworking. I love our banter, and can't wait for our next project together.

To Tara Fisher: it was such an honour to work together on the photoshoot. Your style, professionalism and calming nature was a joy to experience, and I miss your daily playlists!

To Jocelyn Gonzalvo and Leah Nicolas, for your help and incredible stamina in the gruelling recipe-testing phase. There were good days when we managed to finish six to eight recipes in a day, and others when we would end up making the same dish two or three times to get it just right. I would also like to thank everyone in the Asia Market offices for being my guinea pigs!

To my amazing Asia Market dream team, Karan Gupta, Valerie Lee, Val Becker, Thea Jia, Yujin Jung and Nigel Cole. Special thanks to Karan, who has been such a great support in creating this cookbook right from the start. You were there for everything from brainstorming recipe ideas to helping me start the writing process by taking my voice notes and making sense of them all! You are a true gem, and I am so grateful for your support and to have you on my team. To Valerie, my superhero assistant who arranges my schedule so efficiently and helps me with literally everything: I would be lost without you. To Nigel, my longest standing Asia Market soldier: you've been with me through thick and thin. You have worked tirelessly to build the Asia Market brand and transform our stores, for which I am forever grateful.

To Donal Skehan, food writer and TV host supremo: I've followed you for years and have always admired everything you have done. I remember when you first connected with me on Instagram, I nearly fell off my seat. You've been such a great mentor and guiding light through everything from bringing my first TV show to life to navigating the world of food writing. I treasure our friendship.

Thank you to Brian Walsh at RTÉ for having faith in me and for commissioning my first two TV series. Thank you also to Maria Chong and Thousand Hui from Lee Kum Kee, not only for their sponsorship, but also for their belief in what I'm doing and my vision. It is a partnership that I am thrilled and proud to be a part of.

To my beloved mum: you have been my rock in everything I do. You always encourage me to go for it, push harder, try new things and say yes! And Dad, thank you for the wonderful memories of Saturday mornings at the market and spending the afternoon cooking together, and – if for nothing else – for fostering my passion for cookbooks. You are both great cooks and your work ethic is truly inspiring.

A special thank you to my husband Tom, for always being by my side, both at work and at home. I knew you were a keeper when you happily ate century egg paired with pink ginger on our second date! We have been on such an amazing journey together, and always have so much fun, no matter what life throws at us. You are my forever soulmate.

Last but not least, to my beautiful little bears, Camilla and George. I love how adventurous you are with food, and I'm so excited to see my passion passing on to the next generation. You bring so much joy and happiness to my life, and I love you both to bits.

Index

A

adobo, chicken 155
anchovies, dried, about 26
apple and banana fritters 181
aromatic duck pancakes 164
Asian cooking techniques 33
Asian cucumber salad 132
Asian snacks and drinks, author's favourite 28
Asian-style coleslaw 133
avocados: salmon sushi bake 38

B

bacon and kimchi fried rice 55
bananas
- banana and apple fritters 181
- miso caramel banoffee pie 182

banana shallots, about 16
bánh mì, Vietnamese lemongrass pork chop 114
banoffee pie, miso caramel 182
bao buns, steamed, five-spiced pork belly with 116–17
basmati rice, about 11
batch-cooking 30
bay leaves, about 18
beans, green. *See* green beans
beansprouts
- about 16
- bibimbap, Korean beef 46
- curry prawn laksa 68
- pad Thai with prawns 76
- phở bò, Vietnamese 65–66
- Singapore noodles with char siu pork 61

beanthread noodles, about 12
beef
- beef and enoki mushroom rolls, Japanese 82
- beef bibimbap, Korean 46
- beef bò kho, Vietnamese 153
- beef with broccoli in oyster sauce 176
- beef rendang, Malaysian 148
- beef salad, Thai 130
- black bean beef 167
- black pepper beef with crispy noodle pancake 75
- japchae, Korean 71
- phở bò, Vietnamese 65–66
- shaking beef with red rice, Vietnamese 50

biang biang chilli oil noodles 59–60
bibimbap, Korean beef 46
bing tang, about. *See* rock sugar, Chinese, about
black bean beef 167
black fungus mushrooms, dried, about. *See* wood ear mushrooms, dried, about
black pepper, about 18
bok choy. *See* pak choi
bonito flakes, about 26
broccoli, beef with, in oyster sauce 176
brown sugar bubble tea ice cream 193

C

cabbage
- coleslaw, Asian-style 133
- gyoza, Japanese chicken 112–13
- K-toast: Korean ham-and-cheese toastie 120
- pancit bihon, Filipino 67

cake, onde onde 188–89
Cantonese sticky rice with Chinese sausage 54
capsicum. *See* peppers
caramel
- Filipino leche flan 190
- miso caramel banoffee pie 182

carrots: bibimbap, Korean beef 46
char siu pork 61
cheese: K-toast (Korean ham-and-cheese toastie) 120
cheesecake
- Hokkaido-style cheese tarts 184–85
- matcha Basque cheesecake 191

chicken
- chicken adobo 155
- chicken congee 49
- chicken curry, Chinese 159
- chicken and sweetcorn soup 137
- chicken tikka masala 158
- fried chicken, Korean 107
- gyoza, Japanese chicken 112–13
- kung pao chicken 171
- oyakodon with chicken, Japanese 44
- pancit bihon, Filipino 67
- satay chicken 172
- sesame ramen noodle salad, cold 139
- teriyaki chicken 173
- wonton soup 129

chilli bean paste, about 22
chilli oil, about 24
chilli sauce, sweet, about 24
chillies
- chilli oil 59–60
- crispy tofu in chilli garlic sauce 177
- laksa paste 68

Chinese cabbage. *See* Chinese leaf
Chinese chicken curry 159
Chinese crispy stuffed lotus root with pork and prawn 90
Chinese cumin lamb skewers 121
Chinese dumplings, classic 108–9
Chinese five-spice, about 19
Chinese leaf
- about 16
- kimchi, simple 92
- Sichuan boiled fish stew, spicy 151

Chinese sausage, Cantonese sticky rice with 54
Chinese soybean paste or sauce, about 22
Chinese spinach
- bibimbap, Korean beef 46
- japchae, Korean 71

Chinese spring onion pancakes 95

chocolate, white: matcha Basque cheesecake 191
chu hou paste, about 22
cilantro. *See* coriander, fresh
cinnamon, about 18
cloves, about 18
coconut, freshly grated, about 27
coconut milk
  about 30
  curry prawn laksa 68
  lamb massaman curry 152
  beef rendang, Malaysian 148
  green prawn curry, Thai 143
  mango sticky rice, Thai 197
  red curry dumplings, one-pot Thai 156
  tom yum soup 125
coconut whipping cream, about 27
cod: miso cod ochazuke 53
coleslaw, Asian-style 133
congee, chicken 49
cooking techniques, Asian 33
cooking utensils 31
coriander, fresh
  about 15
  Vietnamese summer rolls 85-86
coriander, ground, about 19
cornflour, about 30
crispy tofu in chilli garlic sauce 177
cucumber salad, Asian 132
cumin, about 19
curry
  chicken tikka masala 158
  Chinese chicken curry 159
  curry prawn laksa 68
  Japanese pork katsu curry 147
  lamb massaman curry 152
  Malaysian beef rendang 148
  Thai green prawn curry 143
  Thai red curry dumplings, one-pot 156

D

daikon
  about 16
  pickled daikon 96
dangmyeon, about 13
dark soy sauce, Chinese, about 21
dashi
  about 25
  dashi stock 25
doenjang, about 22
doubanjiang, about 22
doughnuts, Korean red-bean 198
drinks and snacks, Asian, author's favourite 28
duck
  aromatic duck pancakes 164
  duck in plum sauce 175
dumpling wheat flour, about 30
dumplings
  Chinese dumplings, classic 108-9
  gyoza, Japanese chicken 112-13
  Thai red curry dumplings, one-pot 156

E

edamame, about 17
egg noodles, dried, about 13
eggs
  bibimbap, Korean beef 46
  curry prawn laksa 68
  fried rice, bacon and kimchi 55
  fried rice, classic 37
  K-toast: Korean ham-and-cheese toastie 120
  leche flan, Filipino 190
  oyakodon with chicken, Japanese 44
  pad Thai with prawns 76
enoki mushrooms
  about 16
  beef and enoki mushroom rolls, Japanese 82
  Thai red curry dumplings, one-pot 156
equipment for cooking 31

F

fermented black beans, about 24
Filipino leche flan 190
Filipino pancit bihon 67
Filipino soy sauce, about 21
fish sauce, about 24
fish and shellfish
  boiled fish stew, spicy Sichuan 151
  dumplings, classic Chinese 108-9
  green prawn curry, Thai 143
  king prawns, salt-and-chilli 163
  lotus root, Chinese crispy stuffed, with pork and prawn 90
  miso cod ochazuke 53
  onigiri 42-43
  pad Thai with prawns 76
  salmon miso soup 138
  salmon sushi bake 38
  scallops, steamed beanthread noodles with 72
  sesame prawn toast 101
  tom yum soup 125
  Vietnamese summer rolls 85-86
  wonton soup 129
five-spice paste, about 22
flan, Filipino leche 190
flours, about 30
flowers, edible: Vietnamese summer rolls 85-86
fried rice, bacon and kimchi 55
fried rice, classic 37
fritters, banana and apple 181

G

galangal, about 16
ganjang, about. *See* Korean soy sauce, about
garlic
  about 15
  pak choi with garlic oil 81
ginger, about 15
glutinous rice, about 11
gochugaru, about 19
gochujang, about 24
green beans
  green beans with pork, Sichuan dry-fried 89
  pancit bihon, Filipino 67
  Thai green prawn curry 143
gula melaka, about. *See* palm sugar, about
gyoza, Japanese chicken 112-13
gyoza wrappers, about 30

H

halo-halo ice-cream sundae 194
ham-and-cheese toastie, Korean (K-toast) 120
herbs, Asian, about 15-17
herbs, storing fresh 15
hoisin sauce, about 22
Hokkaido-style cheese tarts 184-85
hongshufen, about 13
hot-and-sour soup 126

I

ice cream
- brown sugar bubble tea ice cream 193
- halo-halo ice-cream sundae 194
- pandan ice cream 194
- ube ice-cream 194

J

jackfruit: halo-halo ice-cream sundae 194
Japanese beef and enoki mushroom rolls 82
Japanese chicken gyoza 112-13
Japanese mayonnaise, about 25
Japanese oyakodon with chicken 44
Japanese pork katsu curry 147
Japanese soy sauce, about 21
jasmine rice, about 11

K

K-toast (Korean ham-and-cheese toastie) 120
katsuobushi, about. *See* bonito flakes, about
kecap manis, about 22
kimchi
- bacon and kimchi fried rice 55
- Korean kimchi tofu stew 144
- simple kimchi 92

kombu, about 26
Korean beef bibimbap 46
Korean chilli paste, about 24
Korean fried chicken 107
Korean ham-and-cheese toastie (K-toast) 120
Korean japchae 71
Korean kimchi tofu stew 144
Korean red-bean doughnuts 198
Korean red pepper flakes, about. *See* gochugaru, about
Korean soy sauce, about 21
Korean tteokbokki rice cakes 102
kung pao chicken 171

L

laksa, curry prawn 68
lamb
- Chinese cumin lamb skewers 121
- lamb massaman curry 152

lap cheong: Cantonese sticky rice with chinese sausage 54
lemongrass, about 16
lotus root
- about 16
- Chinese crispy stuffed lotus root with pork and prawn 90

low-gluten wheat flour, about 30

M

makrut lime leaves, about 17
Malaysian beef rendang 148
mangoes
- halo-halo ice-cream sundae 194
- Thai mango sticky rice 197

marinating technique 33
massaman curry, lamb 152
matcha powder
- about 27
- matcha Basque cheesecake 191

mint: Vietnamese summer rolls 85-86
mirin, about 25
miso
- about 22
- miso caramel banoffee pie 182
- miso cod ochazuke 53
- salmon miso soup 138

morning glory
- about 15
- stir-fried morning glory 81

mushroom powder, about 19

N

nam prik pao. *See* Thai chilli paste, about
neutral oil, definition of 22
noodle dough: biang biang noodles 59
noodles
- about 12-13
- beanthread noodles, steamed, with scallops 72
- biang biang chilli oil noodles 59
- black pepper beef with crispy noodle pancake 75
- curry prawn laksa 68
- japchae, Korean 71
- pad Thai with prawns 76
- pancit bihon, Filipino 67
- phở bò, Vietnamese 65-66
- sausage gochujang udon 62
- sesame ramen noodle salad, cold 139
- Singapore noodles with char siu pork 61
- Thai beef salad 130
- Vietnamese spring rolls, crispy 104-5
- Vietnamese summer rolls 85-86

nước tương, about. *See* Vietnamese soy sauce, about

O

ochazuke, miso cod 53
onde onde cake 188-89
one-pot thai red curry dumplings 156
onigiri 42-43
oyakodon with chicken, Japanese 44
oyster mushrooms: tom yum soup 125
oyster sauce, about 22

P

pad Thai with prawns 76
pak choi
  about 15
  pak choi with garlic oil 81
  Thai red curry dumplings, one-pot 156
  wonton soup 129
palm sugar, about 27
pancakes
  aromatic duck pancakes 164
  spring onion pancakes, Chinese 95
'pancakes': black pepper beef with crispy noodle pancake 75
pancit bihon, Filipino 67
pandan leaves, extract and emulco
  about pandan leaves 17
  onde onde cake 188
  pandan ice cream 194
panko breadcrumbs, about 30
pantry staples 30
peanut dipping sauce 85-86
pepper, dried black and white
  about 18
  black pepper beef with crispy noodle pancake 75
pepper, Sichuan
  about 19
  cumin lamb skewers, Chinese 121
  dumplings, classic Chinese 108
  kung pao chicken 171
  Sichuan boiled fish stew, spicy 151
  Sichuan dry-fried green beans with pork 89
peppers (capsicum)
  black bean beef 167
  black pepper beef with crispy noodle pancake 75
  satay chicken 172
  sweet-and-sour pork 168
perilla: Vietnamese summer rolls 85-86
pickled daikon 96
pie, miso caramel banoffee 182
pineapple: sweet-and-sour pork 168
plum sauce 175
pork
  bánh mì, Vietnamese lemongrass pork chop 114
  char siu pork, Singapore noodles with 61
  dumplings, classic Chinese 108-9
  green beans with pork, Sichuan dry-fried 89
  hot-and-sour soup 126
  kimchi tofu stew, Korean 144
  lotus root, Chinese crispy stuffed, with pork and prawn 90
  pork belly, five-spiced, with steamed bao buns 116-17
  pork katsu curry, Japanese 147
  pork stir-fry, Thai basil 97
  spring rolls, crispy Vietnamese 104-5
  sweet-and-sour pork 168
  wonton soup 129
pork sausages: Sausage gochujang udon 62
prawns
  curry prawn laksa 68
  dumplings, classic Chinese 108-9
  green prawn curry, Thai 143
  lotus root, Chinese crispy stuffed, with pork and prawn 90
  pad Thai with prawns 76
  salt-and-chilli king prawns 163
  sesame prawn toast 101
  Singapore noodles with char siu pork 61
  tom yum soup 125
  Vietnamese summer rolls 85-86
  wonton soup 129

R

red-bean paste, sweetened
  about 27
  doughnuts, Korean red-bean 198
rice
  about 11
  bibimbap, Korean beef 46
  congee, chicken 49
  fried rice, bacon and kimchi 55
  fried rice, classic 37
  how to cook 33
  miso cod ochazuke 53
  onigiri 42-43
  oyakodon with chicken, Japanese 44
  red rice, Vietnamese shaking beef with 50
  salmon sushi bake 38
  sticky rice, Cantonese, with Chinese sausage 54
  sticky rice, Thai mango 197
rice cakes, Korean tteokbokki 102
rice noodles, flat, about 13
rice paper wrappers, about 30
rice vermicelli, about 12
rock sugar, Chinese, about 27

S

sake, about 25
salmon
  salmon miso soup 138
  salmon sushi bake 38
salt-and-chilli king prawns 163
satay chicken 172
sausage, Cantonese sticky rice with Chinese 54
sausage gochujang udon 62
scallions. *See* spring onions
scallops, steamed beanthread noodles with 72
seasoning a wok 33
seasonings and spices, about 18-19
sesame oil, about 22
sesame prawn toast 101
sesame ramen noodle salad, cold 139
sesame seeds, about 19
Shaoxing wine, about 22
shichimi togarashi, about 19
shiitake mushrooms
  about 16, 26
  bibimbap, Korean beef 46
  hot-and-sour soup 126
  japchae, Korean 71
  lotus root, Chinese crispy stuffed, with pork and prawn 90
  salmon miso soup 138
  sticky rice, Cantonese, with Chinese sausage 54
short-grain rice, about 11
shoyu. *See* Japanese soy sauce, about
shrimp, dried, about 26

Sichuan boiled fish stew, spicy 151
Sichuan dry-fried green beans with pork 89
Sichuan pepper, about 19
Singapore noodles with char siu pork 61
skewers, Chinese cumin lamb 121
snacks and drinks, Asian, author's favourite 28
soybean pastes and sauces, about 22
soy sauces, about 21-22
spices and seasonings, about 18-19
spring onions
 about 15
 spring onion pancakes, Chinese 95
spring rolls, crispy Vietnamese 104-05
sriracha, about 24
star anise, about 18
steaming technique 33
sticky rice, Cantonese, with Chinese sausage 54
stir-frying technique 33
sushi: salmon sushi bake 38
sweet-and-sour pork 168
sweet chilli sauce
 about 24
 sweet chilli dipping sauce 85-86
sweet potato glass noodles, about 13
sweetcorn: chicken and sweetcorn soup 137

T

tamarind paste and concentrate, about 24
taochiao, about 22
tarts, Hokkaido-style cheese 184-85
teriyaki chicken 173
Thai basil
 about 15
 Thai basil pork stir-fry 97
Thai beef salad 130
Thai chilli paste, about 24
Thai curry pastes 24
Thai green prawn curry 143
Thai light soy sauce, about 21
Thai mango sticky rice 197
Thai red curry dumplings, one-pot 156
Thai sweet soy sauce, about 21
thin soy sauce, about 21
toban sauce, about 22
tofu
 about 30
 crispy tofu in chilli garlic sauce 177
 hot-and-sour soup 126
 Korean kimchi tofu stew 144
 salmon miso soup 138
tofu puffs: curry prawn laksa 68
tom yum soup 125
toyo. *See* Filipino soy sauce, about
tteokbokki rice cakes, Korean 102
tuna: onigiri 42-43
tung choi. *See* morning glory
turmeric, about 19

U

ube and ube products
 about 27
 ube ice cream 194
udon noodles, about 12
utensils 31

V

vegetables, Asian, about 15-17
Vietnamese beef bò kho 153
Vietnamese lemongrass pork chop bánh mì 114
Vietnamese phở bò 65-66
Vietnamese pork roll (ingredient) 85-86
Vietnamese rice paper
 about 30
 Vietnamese summer rolls 85-86
Vietnamese shaking beef with red rice 50
Vietnamese soy sauce, about 21
Vietnamese spring rolls, crispy 104-5
Vietnamese summer rolls 85-86
vinegars, about 24-25

W

wakame
 about 26
 wakame seaweed salad 132
water chestnuts
 lotus root, Chinese crispy stuffed, with pork and prawn 90
 wonton soup 129
white pepper, about 18
wok, how to season a 33
wontons 129
wonton soup 129
wonton wrappers, about. *See* gyoza wrappers, about
wood ear mushrooms
 about 26
 hot-and-sour soup 126
Worcestershire sauce, about 24

Published in 2026 by Murdoch Books, an imprint of Allen & Unwin

Murdoch Books UK
Ormond House
26–27 Boswell Street
London WC1N 3JZ
Phone: +44 (0) 20 8785 5995
murdochbooks.co.uk
info@murdochbooks.co.uk

Murdoch Books Australia
Cammeraygal Country
83 Alexander Street
Crows Nest NSW 2065
Phone: +61 (0)2 8425 0100
murdochbooks.com.au
info@murdochbooks.com.au

For corporate orders and custom publishing, contact our business development team at salesenquiries@murdochbooks.com.au

Publisher: Céline Hughes/Melissa Kayser
Editorial manager: Virginia Birch
Editor: Tara O'Sullivan
Designer and illustrator: Sarah McCoy
Photographer: Tara Fisher
Food and prop stylist: Charlotte O'Connell
Production manager: Natalie Crouch

Murdoch Books Australia acknowledges the Traditional Owners of the Country on which we live and work. We pay our respects to all Aboriginal and Torres Strait Islander Elders, past and present.

EU Authorised Representative: Easy Access System Europe, Mustamäe tee 50, 10621 Tallinn, Estonia, gpsr.requests@easproject.com

ISBN 978 1 76150 167 8

NATIONAL LIBRARY OF AUSTRALIA

A catalogue record for this book is available from the National Library of Australia

A catalogue record for this book is available from the British Library

Colour reproduction by Megan Ellis
Printed in China by Hang Tai Printing Company Limited

OVEN GUIDE: You may find cooking times vary depending on the oven and oven setting you are using. The recipes in this book are based on fan-assisted (convection) oven temperatures. For non-fan-assisted (convection) ovens, as a general rule, set the oven temperature to 20°C (25–50°F) higher than indicated in the recipe.

10 9 8 7 6 5 4 3 2 1

FSC www.fsc.org MIX Paper | Supporting responsible forestry FSC® C023121